# AMERICA ...

## a nation that's lost its way.

## What's Wrong With America!

by Joseph V. Kulbacki

# America ... a nation that's lost its way.
Author: Joseph V. Kulbacki

Front cover art
Photo rights for front cover purchased by:
Orffeo Printing Company
Additional cover art by:
Wendy Bus and Greg Orffeo
Back cover photo of author by:
Judi Kulbacki

ISBN: 978-1-935018-12-4

Publisher:
Five Stones Publishing
493 Republic Street
Potter, KA 66002
randy2905@gmail.com

Contact: Joe Kulbacki at either of his web sites:
America-a-nation-thats-lost-its-way.com
or
JoeKulbacki.com

The publisher does not have any control over and does not assume any responsibility for author or third-party Web sites or their content.

# Table of Contents

Acknowledgements ----- 5

Introduction ----- 6

About the Author ----- 8

Chapter 1  History of Past Civilizations ---- 11

Chapter 2  America's Historical Sequences ----- 17

Chapter 3  A Godly Nation ----- 45

Chapter 4  A Divided Nation ----- 77

Chapter 5  Education ----- 81

Chapter 6  The Media ----- 111

Chapter 7  The Judiciary System ----- 123

Chapter 8  Lawyers and Lawsuits ----- 133

Chapter 9  Immigration ----- 143

Chapter 10  The Global Warming Hoax ----- 153

Chapter 11  America's Economy and Its Heritage ----- 159

Chapter 12  Competing in Today's Global Economy ----- 179

Chapter 13  Democracy and Capitalism ----- 203

Chapter 14  Politics and Politicians ----- 209

Chapter 15  Our Enemies ----- 249

Chapter 16  Closing ----- 273

Appendix ----- 285

Notes ----- 308

# Acknowledgements

S ince this is my first attempt at writing a book, I never realized the difficulty and time such a task required. With the assistance of the following people, this book was made possible.

I want to thank my wife, Judi, for all her patience, support, encouragement and vineyard photo of me. I am grateful for her understanding of the many hours that I spent researching and writing. Also important was her timely input to the subject matter of this book.

I am thankful to other people who made this book possible. Dear friend Peggee Templeton assisted and did the first edit of the manuscript. To my new friend Mary Pratt for her continual input into the editing process. My good pal and fishing partner, Nick Mecca, generously crafted details of the life of the author. I appreciate Leo Ward's advice regarding the publishing of this book. Many thanks also to Wendy Bus and Greg Orffeo for the illustration on the front cover.

Above all, I would like to thank our Heavenly Father for His continued inspiration during the four years it took to complete the task given me. Throughout the writing of this book, I was constantly reminded that we were designed to be vessels suitable for His use.

# Introduction

**H**istory reveals that the pattern of all civilizations is that they rise, flourish, and then perish. The pages of this book review the history of America and how our government, culture and society parallel the phases of past civilizations.

Cataloging and commenting on the momentous changes occurring in American society today, this writing focuses on a changing culture which is taking America in new and dangerous directions. I reach into more than 200 years of American history to rediscover the bedrock heritage, values and principles that are the foundation of our nation's prosperity and world power.

America's increasingly suicidal mentality, disturbing internal misdirection and eroding value system is overlaid against this historical backdrop. Spiritual amnesia has set in and we have forgotten the Source of our freedom, abundance and strength as God is continually being removed from our public life. The cover of this book shows our past presidents at Mount Rushmore with tearing eyes. I believe that if they were alive today, this would be their expression as the America they envisioned is slowly falling apart. This book affirms that the United States is at an historical crossroads. America's existence as a republic is rapidly approaching critical mass and time is a key ingredient to what is now a "must win" struggle for the soul of America.

I offer insights into the causes contributing to our nation's plight. My series of indictments extend to all segments of the American experience, from our founders to the state of our nation today. A government with its inept, do-nothing, elected officials and our radical judicial system are the major reasons for the dilemma in which America finds itself.

To those who would adversely reshape America and deny its legacy to our children, I extend my most damning criticism. Our history, as a nation, is written with the blood of our ancestors. Both the will and conviction of today's citizens are questioned as a mindset of apathy and complacency is governing our way of life. If our nation is to survive the cultural war, the patriots of today must show the same sacrifice and conviction as our ancestors. What man once did, man can do again to save freedoms for future generations. It is with the collective effort of ordinary citizens that the power to quiet this gathering storm rests. President Dwight D. Eisenhower said, "There is nothing wrong with America that the faith, love of freedom, intelligence and energy of her citizens cannot cure."[1]

Regarding the major issues confronting America, I offer historic truths and prophetic insights into the evolving demise of our nation as freedoms and values are being lost due to our disobedience and misdirection. We are a nation that has lost its way. There may yet be time to recapture the glory of yesteryear. To do so, however, will require an inspired effort, rededication, and return to the Godly principles that propelled America as a world leader in education, industrial growth, and the hope for other nations.

# About The Author

Entrepreneur, farmer, vintner, outdoorsman, former professional athlete, and now author, Joseph Kulbacki is living the "American Dream". Born in 1938, the proud son of a small, rural community in Northwestern Pennsylvania, Kulbacki remembers a time of moral imperatives and defined values, of commitment to family, and a strong sense of community. His early years were idyllic. He swam in the backwood streams, fished, trapped, hunted game, and hiked through the valleys and over the mountains of his native state.

Kulbacki received his early education in public schools. He remembers, vividly and wistfully, that classes each day began with recitation of the Lord's Prayer, the Pledge of Allegiance, and a spiritual hymn. This daily regimen reinforced the values espoused by his family and his Christian faith, which today continue to be the supportive and compelling forces in his life.

Kulbacki was a star running back in high school, and his prowess on the gridiron earned him scholarship offers from several of the top universities in the nation. Enamored with the prospect of playing in the Big Ten Conference – and with a keen interest in engineering – he entered Purdue University in 1956. He graduated with a B.S. degree in Industrial Economics, combining curricula in both engineering and economics, including advanced studies in marketing.

Upon graduation, having successfully completed the ROTC program, he received his commission as a second lieutenant in the U.S. Army.

Kulbacki was a high draft choice of both the Washington Redskins of the NFL and the Boston Patriots of the newly formed AFL. However, it was the Buffalo Bills, who had obtained his draft rights from the Patriots, for whom he would play. After one year of professional football, Kulbacki interrupted his career to fulfill his service obligation to the U.S. Army. Following his two-year stint as an officer in the military, he returned to the Bills in 1963. His business career began in 1965, he later formed his own engineering consulting company, specializing in the integration of manufacturing systems for industry.

Some may call it an epiphany; those more secular might prefer another frame of reference, a moment of self-realization, perhaps. Kulbacki, however, is unequivocal when referring to his spontaneous decision to write *America, A Nation That's Lost Its Way,* calling it "divinely-inspired." Suddenly awakened from a dream state in the early morning hours, he was urged to rise, go to his desk and write. His "dream" posited 10 major crises confronting the United States, each and collectively of enormous import. Fearful that any delay would cause him to forget even one of these critical issues, he immediately began to document them.

While Kulbacki has long been concerned about the all-consuming political self-interest of America's leaders and their patent lack of courage, he was also deeply upset by the nation's economic mismanagement; a growing abandonment of America's founding principles, popular disinterest in governmental affairs, and moral malaise. He found himself called to do something, to change America's direction, and to help refocus our national energy toward solutions to these seemingly insurmountable problems. Kulbacki believes strongly that discovering and implementing those answers will determine America's continuity as we know it or more significantly our survival as a nation. To help recapture those ideals which America alone in the world once embraced is the central intent of Kulbacki's work.

## History of Past Civilizations

Most great civilizations and empires from the beginning of history have lasted about 200 years. French historian Arnold Toynbee counted 19 to 21 major civilizations that have existed since man began to form governments. He said, "America is only one of five that remain".[1] He indicated in his report that none of the former nations were overthrown by outside aggressors, but died from spiritual and moral decay – in essence, destroyed from within.

The Roman Empire had advanced transportation, communications and infrastructure. It had the world's most flourishing society and economy. Prosperity in commerce gave the Romans a robust standard of living. The Empire's military was the world's strongest, with no other nation posing any threats to the Roman way of life or its borders.

Roman technology was the most advanced the world had ever seen. The sewage system designed by the Romans 2500 years ago is still used today in Rome. The world was amazed by Roman architectural feats. The cities that the Romans built, such as Rome, London, and Paris, withstood centuries because of the concrete that they designed. The arch design gave them the ability to construct buildings to greater strength and height than any other civilization.[2]

The Romans designed the most advanced system for water distribution, being able to direct hot and cold water in and out of their recreation spas. These baths were similar to the country clubs of today, where the average citizen could relax and enjoy sporting events. They also included a library and provided other adult entertainment.[3]

The Roman Coliseum was an engineering feat, which gave the Romans a theater to fulfill their need for sensationalism and instant gratification.  The entertainment included the killing of animals, and competitions between gladiators, who fought to their death.

The Coliseum, at 160 feet high, was the tallest structure ever built by the Romans.  The Coliseum was shaded from the sun by an enclosed top structure that had a 30-foot-wide opening in the center that allowed the light to enter the Coliseum.  It was round in design, with restrooms.  The Coliseum had the capacity to seat approximately 76,000.  Does this sound very much like our modern-day sports stadiums?

## The Fall of Rome

Modern scholars and historians have declared that the fall of the Roman Empire was due to internal problems.  Economic strain, high taxation, decline of public spirit, reluctance of citizens to serve the state, and pressure from the Goths led to the fall.[4]

Rome showed itself unequal to the trials of government, as taxation became so severe it stifled free enterprise and brought about economic disaster.  Members of the old governing class chose to flee rather than pay exorbitant taxes.  They refused to serve the state as barbarians and intruders ravaged Rome, making state positions dangerous.[5]

People soon lost confidence in their government leaders.  Excessive government spending quickly exhausted the money supply.  Younger Romans became liberal, particularly in their love lives.  Augustus attempted to set moral standards as he grew older, but he failed with the young Romans.  The Romans began to believe in cults and sexual excessiveness.  Their religious dedication began to diminish as sex and pornography replaced their moral values.  The family became less important.  Abortion was commonly performed in the streets.[6]

A senator stated the following: "I fear for our nation. Nearly half of our people receive some form of government subsidies. We have grown weak from too much affluence and too little adversity. I feel that soon we will not be able to defend our country from our sure and certain enemies. We have debased our currency to the point that even the most loyal citizen no longer trusts it."[7]

Does this sound like a typical senator describing the United States of America today? YES! Prophetically, those were the words spoken by a senator of the Roman Empire in the year A.D. 63.

Does this sound familiar? If the word "America" were substituted for "Roman Empire", would we be describing our nation today? Is our nation any different from other past great civilizations in history? If you believe that what happened to the Greek, Persian and Roman empires, along with other civilizations, couldn't happen to the United States, you would be either uninformed, indifferent or both. Indeed, America is no exception.

## America Today Versus the Roman Empire

Throughout this book, I relate to the Roman Empire, because the history of America closely follows that of the Romans. The Roman Empire started out as a republic form of government, as did America. Both nations began with a government in which the balance of power was to remain in control by its people. A republic is the highest form of government depending on a higher source of authority, which is the Lord of the Universe. This type of rule, if not disciplined, will deteriorate into a lesser, out-of-control form of government. This occurred in Rome, and we are experiencing the same in America today as we distance ourselves from His Providence and our Constitution.

Our founders chose the eagle to be America's emblem. They believed that the eagle best symbolized their perception of America's greatness. The eagle, known as a bird of great vision and strength, has the ability to rise above storms and turbulence. The Romans also used the eagle as their national symbol. During their conquering of other nations, the Roman soldiers carried poles called standards. On each standard was mounted a brass eagle signifying Roman authority.[8]

Large columns on buildings were a signature of Roman architectural design. Many buildings in Washington D.C. and elsewhere in America imitate this construction design.[9]

Ancient Rome had a hill called Capitolina, where lawmakers met. We have Capitol Hill in Washington, D.C., where Congress meets.[10]

The Roman Senate directed the political affairs of the empire. The decisions by this governing group to overtax its people became so severe in Rome, that free enterprise was stifled.[11] Today our Congress directs our nation's legislation as we are threatened with economic erosion caused by overtaxation.

In Rome, Christians were despised and in many cases were put to death for political gain. The radical courts of America continue to strip Judeo-Christian beliefs and moral values out of our lives.

Entertainment in Rome consisted of barbarous, bloodthirsty battles in the Coliseum. Americans have trended toward pro-wrestling, ultimate fighting, and violent Hollywood movies as the trends for brutal, uncivilized entertainment.

Gluttony became overwhelming in Rome, as life for its residents became too easy and complacent, with fresh fruits and foods imported from all parts of the world. We, like the Romans, are a spoiled nation with excessive abundance and complacency. Adults in the United States have one of the highest obesity rates in the world. Nearly 1/3 of adults, ages 20 years and older, are obese. One-third of our children and young adults, approximately 25 million kids ages 2-19, are overweight.

The final phase of the mighty Roman Empire went from complacency to apathy, to government dependency, then to bondage. History shows that all great civilizations have experienced similar sequences or phases regarding their cultural and social changes. Throughout history, great civilizations such as the Persians, Greeks and Romans experienced similar social and cultural paths as they progressed through the following sequences.

They have gone from:

- bondage to spiritual faith;
- spiritual faith to great courage;
- great courage to liberty;
- liberty to abundance;
- abundance to selfishness;
- selfishness to complacency;
- complacency to apathy;
- apathy to dependency;
- dependency to bondage.[12]

President Richard Nixon, on civilizations, stated,

*As we read the pages of history, we find those pages strewn with the wreckage of great civilizations in the past, those who lost their leadership just at the time that they were the richest, and at the time when they had the capability of being the strongest. They lost their leadership because their leader class failed to meet the responsibilities and challenges of the times. They, in other words, turned away from greatness. They grew soft. They did not welcome the opportunity to continue to lead, which was their destiny at the time, and those civilizations are forgotten except as they are read about in the pages of history.*[13]

During our more than 230 years as a nation, we are experiencing the same cultural changes and historical sequences as the Romans.

The ensuing chapters of this book will give the reader a historic view of our nation as envisioned by our founding fathers versus where we find the state of America today. We will review the media, government, education, politics, economy, judiciary system, and value system, and how each affects America's lifestyle today. The facts presented may anger you, as they did me, to find this nation aimlessly following in the footsteps of history's failed civilizations.

The following pages will review the events that occurred over the history of our nation as we find ourselves at a crossroads, somewhere between complacency and dependency, the social sequences prior to bondage.

# America's Historical Sequences

## America's First Sequence
## From Bondage to Spiritual Faith

Bondage as defined by Webster: "is under the control of another or slavery."[1]

When the Pilgrims came to America, they escaped from the bondage of King James of England to pursue freedom of worship and to gain spiritual expression.

In 1607, William Bradford in his journal, *The History of Plymouth Plantation*, wrote that it was impossible to continue the worship of God under bondage of English rule. Bradford was a member of a religious group called the "Brownists". Robert Browne led this group of Christian believers, who, by willing covenant made with God, were under the government of God and Christ. They did not have a physical church they attended, but had their meetings in the homes of its members.

King James was disturbed by the disrespect they demonstrated for his authority. He considered them religious "fanatics" and told them to "either conform yourselves to the Anglican Church of England or leave the country."[2]

The congregation met and decided for the safety of their women and children to flee England. The Pilgrims decided to resettle in Holland, where they were told that they would have religious freedom.

Life in Holland became very difficult. They feared the corruption of their children by the nation's youth. After much contemplation and prayer, they chose to leave Holland and arranged for a vessel to pursue life in America.[3]

Prior to boarding their ship, the Pilgrims' pastor, John Robinson, told them, "He visioned that God beckoned his people to go to this new land to build a New Jerusalem." Robinson saw that as "the people of God were called out of Babylon, the place of their bondage, they were to come to Jerusalem and there, build the Lord's temple."[4]

Predicting conflict with the non-Christian travelers on the Mayflower, Robinson's particular concern was that the Pilgrims exercise patience, to be tolerant to those who did not share their views. He advised that the form of government established should be democratic. Selected leaders were to report and to serve according to the wishes of the people. Therefore, we see in Robinson's letter to the Pilgrims many characteristics that prevail in our form of government today.[5]

On August 5, 1620, the Mayflower set sail for America. They encountered several storms on their voyage that caused their ship to go off course, as the Mayflower was continually battered by the storm-driven waves that cradled the ship as if it was a wooden log in the sea. The weary Pilgrims were confined to the lower deck, huddled in semi-darkness with very little fresh air because the hatches could not be opened. The air became contaminated with the results of ocean sickness. To their surprise, they only lost two people on their journey.[6]

Having landed outside the Virginia boundary, they were no longer under the jurisdiction of the charter of the Virginia Colony issued by King James. They were not subject to any legal authority. Without the legal control over the people, rebellion started among some of the passengers. Those Pilgrims in authority had to take action to avoid a mutiny that would stifle the expedition. Bradford wrote in his journal that the Pilgrims gathered and drew up an agreement or 'covenant' that they called the Mayflower Compact.[7]

## The Compact

*In the Name of God, Amen.   We, whose names are underwritten, the loyal subjects of our dread sovereign Lord King James, by the grace of God, of Great Britain, France and Ireland King, defender of the faith, etc., having undertaken, for the glory of God, and advancement of the Christian faith, and honor of our king and country, a voyage to plant the first colony in the northern parts of Virginia, do, by these presents, solemnly and mutually, in the presence of God and one of another, covenant and combine ourselves together into a civil body politic, for our better ordering and preservation, and furtherance of the ends aforesaid; and by virtue hereof to enact, constitute and frame such just and equal laws, ordinances, acts, constitutions, and offices, from time to time, as shall be thought most meet and convenient for the general good of the colony; unto which we promise all due submission and obedience. In witness whereof we have hereunder subscribed our names at Cape Cod the 11 of November, in the year of the reign of our sovereign lord, King James of England, France, and Ireland and the eighteenth, and of Scotland the fifty-fourth, Anno Dom. 1620.*[8]

The charter the Pilgrims drew up allowed them to elect their own officers, and bound them to work together for their common good. This agreement was the first document that was the beginning of a government "of the people, by the people, for the people."[9]

It established the Pilgrims' priorities. Little did they know that this compact was the first in recorded history in which free and equal men created their own civil government.

This concept of equal laws was very much like that of the Jewish tradition in the Old Testament. They had a covenant with God. The Ten Commandments applied to the Pilgrims in the same way as they did the Hebrews. The Compact gave the Pilgrims the stability, convictions and unity they needed to face the adversities and hardships ahead of them.[10]

This foundation paved the way for our founders as they formulated the Constitution of the United States. It was more than a legal document, it was a covenant drawn up by our founding fathers as an oath or contract with God. This same kind of oath is taken by our President, as well as by all Supreme Court justices. Both promise before Almighty God to uphold our constitution.


### Our Nation's Second Challenge against Bondage


After the Pilgrims escaped the bondage of King James of England, the colonies fought through their infancy for the next 100 years. During that time, King George of England challenged our freedom.

The American Revolution against England was the outcome of a century of conflicts between England and the colonies. The disputes had two fundamental causes: economic and political. At times, both causes were simultaneously involved.

The French and Indian War, known as the Seven Years War in Britain, had just ended in 1763 in a colonial triumph for Great Britain. France was forced to surrender Canada and all lands east of the Mississippi River except the port of New Orleans. However, victory had come at a high price. The British government was almost bankrupt. The national debt had nearly doubled, and English citizens were burdened with excessive taxation. With the British treasury almost empty, King George III and leaders of the British government decided that the American colonies must produce greater income for England. The policy called the "Mercantile Theory" reflected the King's belief that the thirteen colonies existed mainly for the benefit of the mother country.[11]

Along with several unfair taxes, the British Parliament passed the Navigation Act. That basically stated that no goods from countries other than England might be brought into the colonies without first stopping in England for payment of duty, and that the colonies might not manufacture any goods that could be made in England nor export specified goods to and from ports served by England. The Sugar and Stamp Acts followed with the purpose of gaining more revenue for England from the ever-growing colonial economy. The colonists intensely protested against these economic restrictions, but their protests fell on deaf ears.[12]

In 1767, the English Parliament passed the Townshend Act, promoted by then Minister of Finance, Sir Charles Townshend. This act imposed heavy duties to the colonists on glass, tea and lead imports. The Townshend Act also provided for the issuance of general warrants that allowed the colonists' houses to be searched for smuggled goods. Once more, the colonists violently protested, but to no avail.

In 1774, at the Port of Boston, Massachusetts, when the English tried to force the colonists to buy cheap tea smuggled from India, the colonists dressed as Indians and raided the ships, dumping the cargo of tea into the water. The British wanted compensation for the loss of their tea, and threatened to close the Boston port.

This act was all the colonists could tolerate. The colonies decided to take joint action and met at Philadelphia in September 1774. This meeting, known as the First Continental Congress, consisted of representatives from all thirteen colonies. King George of England considered the Continental Congress as a gathering of a criminal group trying to overthrow his rule. On May 15, 1775, the second Continental Congress met at Philadelphia, and acting as a central government for the thirteen colonies, declared war against Great Britain.

The early settlers took this stand against England, which at this time had the world's greatest military forces. However, the colonists were willing to give up their lives to provide freedom for the colonies and their children. They knew that they would either gain their freedom from England, or go back to bondage under English rule.

The American Revolution was a defensive revolution. The radicals were the British, not the Americans. The British government, while trying to expand its empire, was attempting to take away traditions and values that America cherished. The colonists only wanted to manage their own affairs and return to their old ways.

On Thursday, July 4, 1776, the Continental Congress approved the Declaration of Independence. The delegates did not officially sign it until a month later. Thus were born the United States of America and liberty for the colonists. The official copies of the Declaration were reported in all the colonies' newspapers, posted on buildings, and in many cases, copies were delivered by horseback to extreme locations of the colonies.

Upon drawing up the Declaration of Independence, the delegates to the Second Continental Congress were potentially guilty of treason against the British Crown.  They realized if the British captured them, it would mean possible death.

The Founding Fathers, whose lives were now in grave danger, showed great courage by ending the Declaration with a bold and selfless vow – "And for the support of this Declaration, with a firm reliance on the protection of Divine Providence, we mutually pledge to each other our lives, our fortunes, and our sacred honor."[13]

Later, citizens of New York City, celebrating the Declaration and their new liberty, pulled down a large equestrian statue of the King of England, which was later cast into musket balls used against the British troops.

## America's Second Sequence
## From Spiritual Faith to Great Courage

It was during the Revolutionary War that one man stood out above all others.  He was George Washington.  Washington displayed great courage and battle instinct, when as a young officer he was commissioned to General Braddock of the British Army during the French and Indian War.  His bravery amazed the British regulars and his reputation as a soldier grew as news of the war spread throughout the colonies.  His perseverance and patience through our young nation's hardships were an example of the ideals by which he lived his life.

Because of  his accomplishments and fame, George Washington was put in charge of the Continental Army as its commander-in-chief. At Yorktown, enduring the cold winter of 1777, the Colonial Army of 15,000 men, including French land troops, was trapped with its back against the Delaware River engaging British troops.  Washington's army was starving, ill equipped, wearing rags for clothes and burlap for shoes. Many had toes and fingers amputated due to frostbite. More soldiers died from the cold and illness during the winter of 1777 than were killed by the British Army.

Three factors motivated Washington and his troops to great courage:

1) a desire for freedom;
2) a better life for their children;
3) the belief in a Creator.

Washington often showed his faith by rallying his soldiers with these words, "If God be for us, who can stand against us."[14]

General Cornwallis, in charge of the British forces during the major battle action in September and October 1781, knew the Americans were in bad shape due to the weather and lack of supplies. The British General waited for a favorable wind so that he could position his gunboats to shell the Colonial Army to defeat. This delay gave Washington time to evacuate his army by rowboat during the night. Washington's staff, against his decision to move the troops, said to the General, "If the wind shifts the fog while our men are caught in the open, they will slaughter us like fish in a barrel. The British will show no mercy. That we can be certain of."[15] General Washington replied to his staff, "I am persuaded that God would not bring us so far to let us fail. With God's providence, we will succeed."[16]

A heavy fog rolled across the river, covering the troops on all sides. Washington then selected men from every battalion who had any experience with boats, and began his evacuation. They all knew any noise created by the oars as they fought the river would alert the British. The wind continued to be calm through the night as Washington moved his army and supplies in repeated trips over the river to the opposite shore. The fog began to lift after the last boat left. The British sentries had spotted the last of the American troops as they crossed the river and sounded the alarm.  By the time the British reacted, Washington's troops, with the help of the French land forces and battleship fleet, surrounded the British.

The defeat of Cornwallis and the British was the turning point of the war.  Cornwallis surrendered his entire army on October 19, 1781.  Although peace was not officially proclaimed until September 31, 1783, hostilities virtually ceased after Washington's victory at Yorktown.  This victory over the British allowed the colonies to become a separate nation, the United States of America.

## America's Third Sequence
## From Great Courage to Liberty

As the result of winning the Revolutionary War against England, the colonists came out of bondage with faith, courage, and an understanding of freedom.  It was against great odds and much bloodshed that the colonists battled their way to achieve liberty.  They knew that their once peaceful land of America would either be drenched in blood, or inhabited by slaves to the British throne.

Who were the men who signed the Declaration of Independence?  They were lawyers, jurists, merchants, farmers, plantation owners, men of wealth and well educated.  What happened to those men of valor?

- Five were captured by the British as traitors and tortured before they died.
- Two lost their sons in the Revolutionary War; another had two sons captured.
- Twelve had their homes burned.

- Nine of the fifty-six fought and died from wounds suffered during the war.
- Thomas McKean served in the Congress without pay. His family was kept in hiding; his possessions taken from him, and he lived a life of poverty.
- Francis Lewis had his home and properties destroyed. The British jailed his wife and she died while in jail. Lewis pledged all his fortune into the war effort, and never recovered financially.
- Many signers later became legislators, governors, judges, diplomats and citizen leaders.
- Benjamin Franklin was appointed as an ambassador to France.
- John Adams became America's second president after serving as our first vice-president to George Washington.
- Thomas Jefferson became governor of Virginia. He later served as vice-president to John Adams, and was elected president in 1800.
- Both John Adams and Thomas Jefferson, who were also great friends, died on the 4th of July – Independence Day – in the same year, 1826, exactly 50 years after the Declaration of Independence was signed. Jefferson left instructions to his family prior to his death that he wanted the following inscription placed on his tombstone, "Author of the Declaration of Independence".

The American independence sent out a worldwide message for individual liberty and self-government. Throughout the ages the Declaration of Independence has provided a legacy for all Americans and an inspiration for freedom to all peoples of the world.

## America's Fourth Sequence
## From Liberty to Abundance

The Declaration of Independence of 1776 and winning the Revolutionary War gave our nation freedom from any other governing nation. The Constitution of 1787 was carefully documented, and provided the fabric that George Washington and our founders realized was missing to hold this country and our new independence together. States had acted independently in arranging their own trade agreements with foreign countries. Our founders knew that the Constitution would unite the thirteen colonies, and act as a compass to direct this nation.

From 1776 through the next 100 years, our nation's culture, society and commerce grew. Prosperity abounded as the South was blessed with natural resources and abundance in agricultural products, while the North thrived with its industrial products. As our economic base expanded, the United States would lead the world in new technology and productivity. We became a strong and creative nation based on our Constitution, Christian ethics, and the energy of our people.

Alexis de Tocqueville, the famous French statesman, historian and philosopher, visited America when our nation was in its infancy. He wanted to learn what enabled a small nation as young America to gain its independence from such a strong nation as Britain. He published his observations in his classic, two-volume work, *Democracy in America*. In an effort to find the reason for America's strength and success, he studied our natural resources, school system and our government, but realized that none of these was the answer. It was not until he attended America's churches, when he stated that the pulpits were "aflame with righteousness," that he realized the answer to his question. He reported to France with this message "America is great, because America is good, and if America ever ceases to be good, America will cease to be great."

## America's Fifth Sequence
## From Abundance to Selfishness

As we approached the years of the Civil War, our nation continued to prosper in all areas of American life. The causes of the Civil War of 1861 between the northern states and southern states are contrary to what most people believe. The Civil War was not a class war, but regional struggles having roots in political, economic and social elements that were so complex, historians do not agree on its basic causes. The United States had been moving toward a divided society for a number of years. Many historians believed that the wealth and abundance of the years prior to the Civil War led to selfishness between the northern and southern states. Cultural and economic differences among the states only brought about greater division. Many historians believe that these differences and arrogant politicians were the causes of the war.

The North had an industrial base. As northern industry expanded its products, the northern companies looked to the southern states to buy its goods. The South, however, could buy the same products manufactured by the North cheaper from European countries. Andrew Jackson, who was president at the time, believed that the federal government was the higher authority and the states must agree with that authority. To protect the northern industries, Jackson issued a tariff on any goods imported by the southern colonies that could be supplied by the northern industries.

South Carolina passed the Ordinance of Nullification in November of 1832 to Jackson's tariff. This ordinance stated that South Carolina would not collect the tariff and threatened to withdraw from the Union. Secession was avoided when Congress revised the tariff in February 1833.

Differences and selfishness between the northern and southern economies became more apparent. The South was able to prosper before and after the Panic of 1837. These were difficult times due to a depression in England creating an economic blow to America. We depended on England for much of our trade. This became a great financial burden to U.S. banks, our government and the American people. This depression ravaged the North while the South and its cotton production were little affected. The clash between the wealthy South and the poor industrial North grew, as greedy and selfish abolitionists created class struggles to advance their causes. Fighting in the political arena became common, as parties turned on each other in continued political debates. From 1837 until 1861, eight men became president of our nation, but none of them served more than a single term.

After the Civil War, the presidency was marred with scandals, assassinations and one-term presidents. Self-serving politicians created great turmoil as the position and power of the president became a non-issue for the citizens of our nation. Not much was accomplished in the political arena for the next 40 years after the war. It was not until the 1900s that we began to acknowledge the Office of the Presidency. Most notable was Theodore Roosevelt, a Republican, our 26th president, who served from 1901 to 1909. He renewed the popularity of the office as he fought for what was right for the people and not the party. Other party members could not bully him in any of his decision-making. He favored labor and not big industry. He helped settle the coal strike during that time, favoring labor over management because of the poor working conditions of the coal miners.

President Theodore Roosevelt was a president of many firsts:
- President Roosevelt named the White House.
- He was the first president who told the nation we had a global responsibility. He passed a bill that built the Panama Canal as a link to other parts of the world.

- In 1906, over eight million legal immigrants came to America under President Roosevelt's watch.
- He was the first president to own an automobile and fly in an airplane.
- In 1906, he was credited with preserving over 150,000,000 acres of timberland for game preserves and national parks.

Theodore Roosevelt was strong in foreign policy. He was committed to a policy of power through naval supremacy. An unabashed expansionist, he believed in sea power and modern technology. When foreign powers tried to infiltrate South America, he reacted quickly, saying "We have no choice as to whether or not we shall play a great part in the world ... we must play the game well ... speak softly but carry a big stick." He was referring to our United States' naval power.[17]

He was a man of great stature and energy. At the end of his second term in office, he felt he had much more to accomplish for the American people.

Listed below are 1906 statistics that represent what life was like a hundred years ago in America during the Roosevelt administration:

- The average life expectancy in the United States was 47 years.
- Only 8% of the homes in the United States had a bathtub.
- Only 8% of the homes had a telephone.
- A three-minute telephone call from Denver to New York City cost $11.
- There were only 8,000 cars in the United States and only 144 miles of paved roads.
- The maximum speed limit in most cities was 10 miles per hour.

- The average wage in the United States was 22 cents per hour.
- The average worker made $200 to $400 per year.
- An accountant could expect to earn $2,000 per year; a dentist approximately $2,500.
- 95% of all births took place at home.
- Sugar cost 4 cents a pound.
- Eggs were 14 cents a dozen.
- Coffee was 15 cents a pound.
- Most women only washed their hair once a month, using borax or egg yolks for shampoo.
- The population of Las Vegas, Nevada was only 30.
- There was no Mother's Day or Father's Day.[18]

It was during this same period that our economy experienced a great industrial revolution. Over the next 60 years after the Civil War, we became one of the most prosperous and successful nations in the world. Our free enterprise system gave birth to a world of entrepreneurs and new inventions. Most of our advanced technology took place during the early 1900s. From the Roman Empire to the 20th century, not much changed. Most transportation up until the 1900s was still by horseback.

Our nation experienced tremendous industrial growth due to the inventions of the automobile, airplane, and electronics. Innovations created a vast new infrastructure for our commerce. These new technologies and natural resources led to great developments in agricultural products as we supplied not only ourselves, but most of the world with its food supply. Abundance became unlimited as America grew into the world's most prosperous nation.

In the early 1900s, the United States then experienced the Roaring Twenties, with great wealth being made in the stock market, along with great strides occurring in our industrial progress with new products. Much speculation was put into the stock market. Quick profits were common in short periods. Speculative investors bought and sold stocks within days or weeks for profits.

## America's Sixth Sequence
## From Selfishness to Complacency

Our nation went from great personal wealth in the Roaring Twenties to the Great Depression of the 1930s. Our economy, along with the world economy, collapsed, and many Americans became completely destitute as they slept in tents and owned nothing but the clothes they wore. More and more U.S. citizens began to depend on the government for their needs.

What was different in the Depression of 1929 versus other previous economic recessions? The American people were accustomed to their economic prosperity and personal wealth, and were not willing to give them up. They were willing to give up their freedoms instead for economic and selfish personal gains.

Franklin D. Roosevelt, our 32nd president, was elected in 1933 based on his promises to restore personal and economic prosperity to America. He was the fifth cousin of President Theodore Roosevelt. He served in office from 1933 to 1945, the longest of any president in history. Franklin Roosevelt introduced big government. His administration was the start of a government that would grow into a vast bureaucracy, intruding into the lives of all Americans. He redefined the role of government as written by our founders through public works programs. He was also able to place the Federal Reserve in a position for our federal government to use its powers as a planner for our economy. He was called a defender of labor, dictator, champion of minorities, and many other things. However, he rallied the United States through the worst economic depression in our history.

During World War II, many of our constitutional rights were suspended as politicians used the war crisis as an opportunity to gain more government control. We came out of the war with government extending loans to homeowners, war veterans, colleges and business. States took a lesser role in transportation and education, as the federal government took up the slack by giving the states money for such programs through increased taxation.

During the 1930s, the government entered public life with many entitlements for its citizens. Americans became so complacent and dependent upon government that they believed they could live without working. During this phase of American history, we continued to give up our freedoms for government handouts. One of the greatest fears of our forefathers, such as Thomas Jefferson, John Adams, and Abraham Lincoln, was a possible rise of a central authority (government) that could undermine the freedoms of the United States citizens. Abraham Lincoln once said, "You cannot help men permanently by doing for them what they could and should do for themselves."[19]

## America's Seventh Sequence
## From Complacency to Apathy

After World War II and through the 1970s, the results of the Franklin D. Roosevelt programs and Lyndon Johnson's Great Society placed the federal government into the role of a great provider. Their administrations grew the size of government as more and more entitlements and handouts were given our citizens. Our federal government evolved into a provider, protector and decision-maker for America. It now determines issues concerning the economy, race, workplace, religion, education and many others. Americans have become complacent and comfortable in their lifestyles, resulting in a mindset of indifference that has become apparent in all aspects of American life due to our abundance.

Apathy takes away passion and emotion, creating insensitivity and lack of vision. As a result, people forget their meaningful purpose in life. Apathy is also shown in our moral values as we become indifferent to God. No longer do we give glory to Him for our freedom and abundance. God is gradually being removed from many facets of our lives as moral values and Christian heritage are being lost. Recent presidential elections are an example of apathy and the "whatever attitude". We have averaged a turnout of approximately 55% of eligible voters for the five presidential elections prior to 2008. This low turnout shows the apathy and passive attitude of the U.S. citizens, and is a disgrace to our ancestors who gave their lives to secure America's freedoms.

## America's Eighth Sequence
## From Apathy to Dependency

Apathy brings on dependency for a short time. Dependents are often not aware they are dependent. They have a false impression of security, and mislead themselves while enjoying their great lifestyles. They remind themselves "we never had it so good" and "we can still vote, can't we?" In time, abundance gradually diminishes, and dependency, in its true nature, becomes bondage.

Apathy and dependency have created a situation in this nation that is no different from that of other great civilizations. The Roman and Greek empires all followed the same social and cultural paths we are presently experiencing.

At one time Greece was the most advanced of pagan cultures. Secular humanism, man can do all, as is expressed in our world today, had its origin in Greece. As with many civilizations, it has been asserted that ancient Greece started with a democracy. However, the lesson learned from the Greek experience, as with the French Revolution, is that democracy without the foundation of a "Higher Law" can be just as tyrannical as other forms of government.

John Quincy Adams stated, "The experience of all former ages had shown that of all human governments democracy was the most unstable, fluctuating and short lived."[20]

## Republic vs. Democracy

Many American citizens do not understand the difference between a republic and a democracy. Our citizens are taught that we are a democracy. The intent of our founding fathers is quite clear; our form of government was to operate as a republic. The significant difference between the two is the source of authority. Founder Noah Webster said, "Our citizens should understand that the genuine source of correct republican principles is the Bible, particularly the New Testament, or the Christian religion."[21]

It is a well-known fact that the majority of the signers of the Declaration of Independence believed that Christian moral teachings would support the newly formed republic. The signers believed that all three branches of government, including the judiciary, were to be guided by God and His Word - each judge would answer to a higher authority. They realized that a creator is always above and greater than that which He creates.

Regarding our government as a republic, economist Walter Williams stated: "Does our pledge of allegiance to the flag say 'to the democracy for which it stands' or does it say 'to the republic for which it stands'? Or, do we sing 'The Battle Hymn of the Democracy' or 'The Battle Hymn of the Republic'? Plus the word democracy appears nowhere in the Declaration of Independence or the Constitution."[22]

Laws and principles that do not change, such as the Constitution and the Ten Commandments, rule a republic. They are a standard for all members of society to follow. This was to insure that the growing army of politicians, judges and lawyers would not run the country, and that the power of the republic would remain in a government controlled by the people with the blessings of the Creator. Under a republic, a government's power is limited and decentralized through a system of checks and balances.

Our founders declared this nation a republic, a state in which the base of power is to remain in the control of the people. The citizens are entitled to vote, and to select officials to represent them in government. However, this form of government is never to be controlled by a monarch or dictator. The founding fathers saw a democracy as another form of tyranny, in that a democracy would lead to the same kind of tyranny the colonies suffered under King George III of England.

A republic is the highest form of government designed by mankind, but it also requires the greatest amount of discipline and care. If neglected, it can deteriorate into a lesser form of government, such as democracy.

The founders were very careful not to call our government a democracy. They knew that a democracy could not exist as a permanent form of government. A democracy is ruled by the majority of public opinion. It can only exist until the voters discover they can vote themselves generous gifts from the public treasury. From that moment on, the majority always votes for the candidate promising the most benefits from the U.S. Treasury, as happened in the 2008 Presidential election. The result is that a democracy always collapses over loose fiscal policies, leading to deterioration within a society of its economy, courts, education and morality of a nation. This deterioration is followed by a dictatorship or bondage as experienced by the Greek and Roman empires.

Unfortunately, our nation no longer operates as a republic as radical individuals, groups and judges have changed the higher rule (our Constitution and Ten Commandments) to fit their own personal agendas.

Justice John Marshall observed, "Between a balanced republic and a democracy, the difference is like that between order and chaos ...."[23]

## Demise of Democracy

Many great nations start with a democracy. Most great empires have averaged approximately 200 years. After freedom, people become successful, spoiled and complacent. They forget the battles that were fought to save their freedoms. The very government that they fought to establish becomes a crutch upon which they depend. Instead of continued hard work, they expect the government to supply their needs.

So they, in turn, vote for the political candidates that promise them the best entitlements to ensure their lifestyles. Hence, this becomes the demise of democracy and the beginning of socialism.

Our second president of the United States, John Adams, stated, "Remember, democracy never lasts long. It soon wastes, exhausts and murders itself. There was never a democracy yet that did not commit suicide."[24]

When researching the history of past civilizations, I realized that the failure or success of a nation had to do with one variable: the belief in the Creator, and the values derived from that belief.

## America's Ninth Sequence
## From Dependency to Bondage

This is the last phase to complete the cycle of social and cultural changes as encountered by past civilizations. I have described how America has experienced all the sequences from bondage, courage, liberty, abundance, selfishness, complacency, apathy and dependency. I believe our nation today is somewhere between apathy and dependency. The last sequence after dependency is back to bondage, which only time will determine. The last phase to bondage will be the result of how the American people react to the challenges of a deteriorating society, government bureaucracy, our eroding economy, and our nation's relationship with God, which are all interrelated.

America's last confrontation with bondage was the War of Independence of 1776 against England. The American Revolution was the result of economic and political disputes. King George III believed that the thirteen colonies existed strictly to benefit the mother country. He believed the colonists, being protected by the British Army, should show their appreciation by paying taxes to help the nearly bankrupt British government. Not only were the colonists overtaxed, but

England also issued other restrictions that controlled the colonists' way of life. The British government, while trying to expand its vast empire, attempted to take away the freedoms that young America cherished. The colonists were concerned, as they felt more and more pressure from England, that the traditions and values they established would be lost.

Presently, similar circumstances parallel the condition of America during the Revolution of 1776. Today, our federal government, the ACLU (American Civil Liberties Union), and radical left extremists are attempting to change an American way of life that has been successful for over 200 years. Over the years, we have found our way back to the threats of bondage as government has become the overwhelming ruler that King George III of England was in the days of the colonists. What England demanded from the colonists prior to the War of Independence is no different from what our federal government is demanding of its citizens today. Perhaps America's next tea party will be on the banks of the Potomac River in Washington, DC. The founders would be in shock if they knew that our government now takes approximately 43% of our earned wages in the form of taxes.

Along with overtaxation by our government, the courts and the ACLU over the past 40 years are continually trying to change the Constitution, leading to more and more of our freedoms and Christian heritage being lost.

As I indicate in my chapter on lawyers and lawsuits, one reason the U.S. Constitution is so brief is that the framers never visualized a nation in which the only people capable of determining whether laws have been broken were lawyers. Our ancestors believed that common sense – as stated in the Ten Commandments, not our legal system – ought to determine guilt or innocence, which is why we are so adamant about the right of trial by jury. Law students no longer study higher law principles, the principles of God, which influenced the thinking of Jefferson and the colonists. The result is increasing ambiguity in our society over what constitutes right or wrong. This nation cannot survive under these conditions.[25]

We must resist politicians' move toward increasing government control of our society. It will take a complete reversal of attitude by the American people to tell our government to step aside, as the colonists told England, and to allow the United States citizens to manage their own affairs, as intended by our Constitution.

In the same manner, the ACLU and other radical extremists need to be rebuffed by our society, so we can return to the values, traditions and heritage that made this nation great. Again, I emphasize that our nation's present state of affairs is a replay of the circumstances prior to our War of Independence. The colonists showed tremendous courage and wisdom by denying dependency and bondage to England.

Do  Americans today have the same resolve and courage as the colonists in preventing our nation from falling under the complete control of our government? We are *A Nation That's Lost Its Way*. There is a fine line between apathy and dependency. Remember, dependency's real name is bondage.

We must resist the control of more government and radical forces over our society. Economist Walter E. Williams stated, "Congress poses the greatest threat to our liberties, the framers used negative phrases against Congress throughout the Constitution such as: shall not abridge, infringe, deny, disparage, and shall not be violated, nor be denied. In a republic form of government, there is a rule of law, all citizens, including government officials, are accountable to the same laws".[26] An out-of-control government is a greater threat to our freedoms than any foreign terrorist group.

If a nation ever returns to bondage, either it is under the control of another nation, or it goes from a democracy and capitalism to socialism, which is a government or tyrant that has complete control over all aspects of life. Individual freedoms no longer exist. Socialism controls freedom to worship and speak. It controls the economy, environment, and all walks of life. Socialism has never been successful. It is a state which the Soviet Union is presently trying to escape. Over history, tyrants have controlled most socialistic governments, such as in France, Cuba, and present-day Venezuela.

There are only two ways to avert bondage. One is through bloodshed (war), as was the choice of the colonists in the War of Independence. The other is to go back to the "Ancient Principles" as stated by Thomas Jefferson, which is to return to the use of common sense as stated in the Ten Commandments of God. There are circumstances where both are needed to avert bondage.

During my lifetime, I have experienced the following changes to our society and culture.

When I was a teenager in the 1950s, America was the world leader: spiritually, economically and in the education of its youth. The nation I remember allowed students to pray and sing a spiritual hymn in public schools. It was not necessary to lock the doors of your home. Children were safe to play in their neighborhoods. Family life was greatly valued and strong family ties kept generations together. Character and integrity counted, and laws protected the unborn child. The spiritual heritage, the belief in a Creator, was passed through generations, and was responsible for our abundance and wealth.

Since 1962, when prayer was taken out of school:

- Our once, world-leading industrial base is being transplanted to what were once called third-world countries.

- The media no longer reports the actual news, but instead develops its own news to meet political agendas.
- Our courts are overruling our nation's Constitution, which has been the foundation of America for over 200 years. More significantly, the courts have ruled that it is no longer proper to pray in public, as God is taken more and more out of public life. From the schoolhouse to the courthouse, His Word is being silenced.
- The traditional emblems that once represented our strong Godly heritage are being removed from our public buildings.
- Government and politics are out of control at all levels. Government controls more of our lives, as more people depend on entitlements.
- Character and integrity no longer count, as shown often by our public officials and corporate officers.
- Abortion has taken the lives of over 48 million unborn American children since 1973.[27]
- Our medical costs continue to explode, along with our national debt. American consumers have followed our government's footsteps by creating record personal debt.
- Our educational system has failed, as our students fall farther and farther behind students of other countries.
- Illegal drug use has reached a point where it is no longer controllable.
- Terrorism has changed our lives; we now have color-coded threat levels. We take off our shoes at airports as x-ray machines examine our bodies.

- Pornography and sexual predators engulf the Internet while same-sex marriage threatens our historical marital standards.
- In the last three decades, our nation's prison populace has exploded. More than one in every 100 American adults is behind bars. One in every nine black men, ages 20 to 34, is serving time, as is one in every 36 Hispanic men. Nationwide, the prison populace is almost 1.6 million, which surpasses all other countries. The fifty states last year spent close to $44 billion in corrections, up from $11 billion in 1987.[28]

We are following the same blueprint of other great civilizations that had their places in history. America is being reformed before our blind eyes without most citizens realizing it. Decay is slow, and after 232 years, we are at a crossroads for the future of our nation.

Remember – the great ambition that drives progress also will bring about its demise. I believe our failure as a nation, if it were to be, would be the demise of our social and cultural path due to our immoral decay and loss of values.

# A Godly Nation

Our nation and its government were established upon the principle of God's Word. In our first 175 years, those principles were reflected in all walks of American life.

In the beginning of America, the Pilgrims came to this nation on two different occasions. In 1607, the first settlers landed in Jamestown, and their first act was to erect a large wooden cross on land then owned by England. They then fell upon their knees and thanked God.

Thirteen years later in 1620, the second group of Pilgrims landed in Plymouth after being wind-swept off course by ocean storms. According to William Bradford, their elected governor who recorded the history of the Pilgrims, "Being thus arrived in good harbor and brought safe to land, they fell upon their knees and blessed the God of Heaven."[1]

The Pilgrims' goal was freedom – freedom to worship, freedom of choice in their careers, freedom of independence, and freedom to live according to God's plan. They believed freedom could only come from God. God gives man freedom.

That was the beginning of America, and our relationship with God. This reverence to the Creator continued in other charters and agreements through the early years of this nation, as shown in the New England Confederation of 1643, which was a union of all the New England communities. It stated: "Whereas we all came unto these parts of America with one and the same end aim ... that is to advance the Kingdom of our Lord Jesus Christ and to enjoy the liberties of the Gospel in the purity with peace."[2]

This heritage continued in the Declaration of Independence that says, "We hold these truths to be self-evident, that all men are created equal, that they are endowed by their Creator with certain unalienable rights." It speaks of God, creation and God-given moral rights, all of which are religious teachings.

In each of the fifty states making up our nation, the mention and reference of Almighty God is in each state's constitution. Some examples are:

New Jersey 1844, Preamble:

> *We, the people of the State of New Jersey, grateful to **Almighty God** for civil and religious liberty which He hath so long permitted us to enjoy, and looking to **Him** for a blessing on our endeavors.[3]*

Florida 1885, Preamble:

> *We, the people of the State of Florida, grateful to **Almighty God** for our constitutional liberty, establish this constitution...[4]*

California 1879, Preamble:

> *We, the people of the State of California, grateful to **Almighty God** for our freedom.[5]*

Alabama 1901, Preamble:

> *We the people of the State of Alabama, invoking the favor and guidance of **Almighty God**, do ordain and establish the following Constitution.[6]*

I have quoted only a portion of four of our fifty state constitutions. In reviewing the remaining forty-six states, they all acknowledge the belief, blessings and guidance of the Creator in their constitutions, and that our freedoms and liberties only come from God.

In the nation's earlier years, twenty-three of the first twenty-six universities in this nation were Christian-based colleges. The Supreme

Court in 1952 (Zorach) affirmed that we are a religious people whose institutions presuppose a "Supreme Being".

Our Creator's footprints are shown throughout our capitol in Washington D.C. All of the monuments show testimony to this nation's faith in God. Inside the Capitol building are numerous sculptures and paintings that show Christ and events that took place by the founders of our country. The Supreme Court building displays twenty different symbols and pictures of Moses and the Ten Commandments. In Congress, both in the House of Representatives and in the Senate, the words: "In God We Trust" are carved in the wall above the chair where the leaders sit. All sessions are opened with prayer.

John Adams was the first to inhabit the White House. Over the fireplace in the dining room, he had carved the words: "I pray Heaven to bestow the best of blessings on this House and all that shall hereafter inhabit it."

The Washington Monument, the tallest monument in Washington D.C., is dedicated to President George Washington. At the very top of the monument, six hundred feet in the air, is a metal cap that reads, "Praise be to God." Several other Christian writings are shown as you walk the stairways of the monument.[7]

The Pilgrim forefathers, our founding fathers, and the generations following them have openly and gratefully acknowledged their dependence upon God and His hand in this nation's history. We are a nation governed by law, God's law. Because His law governs us, there is liberty.

## The Bible – The Word of God

Most of the founding fathers of our nation were Christians with few exceptions. George Washington was a devoted Christian; he read the book of prayers that he wrote as a young man. He also read the Bible while on his knees for one or two hours daily.[8]  As a general in the army during the Revolutionary War, he prayed with his troops, and in private, for help and the blessings of God.

As our first president, George Washington placed his hand upon the Bible, bent over and kissed the Bible. The Bible has been part of the presidential oath ceremony ever since. Washington stated later that "It is impossible to govern ... without God and the Bible."[9]  In every inaugural address given by each president since Washington, without exception, the mention of Almighty God has been included.

Since the earliest beginning of America, God has been the most important ingredient in our nation's prosperity. The Bible, the Word of God, is our directive for life. Without it, we do not have a standard or compass to follow. It gives us guidance for all aspects of our life, for men and nations. Our forefathers realized this importance. The Bible guided them and this nation in the right path from the time of the Pilgrims.

Man feels more secure knowing his boundaries, rather than having unrestricted freedom. The Ten Commandments serve this purpose. Instead of viewing the Commandments as a list of "Thou-Shalt-Nots," we need to see them in terms of guidance and standards on how we should conduct our lives. Without God and the Bible, there are no disciplines for man to follow.

The Bible is a record of what God promises us. It is also a record of what happens when we do not trust His promises. God has always kept His end of the bargain. He is the same today as He was yesterday, and as He will be tomorrow. God and the Bible do not change. Right and wrong do not change. They are not moving things. Man is the only variable.

William Gladstone, Prime Minister of England, stated: "I have known 95 great men in my time. And of those, 87 were followers of the Bible."[10] President John Quincy Adams declared, "The Bible is the book above all others, to read at all ages, and in all conditions of human life."[11]

Suppose forty architects set out to design one building. Some know what others are doing, others are unaware anyone else is doing anything at all. When they gather to compare notes, the result is a common, magnificent blueprint. What are the odds this could happen? It did with the Bible. No publisher commissioned it. No committee outlined it. No earthly editor oversaw it. It was penned by an unlikely assortment of men, including fishermen, farmers, kings, and shepherds – from Moses to the apostle Paul. One subject is common throughout the Bible; that theme is man's salvation through Jesus Christ.

What rivals the durability of the Bible? Today we award the book that remains on top of the bestsellers list for weeks at a time. If one book claimed the lead for several years, we would bronze each page. The Bible is the most widely published and translated book in history. It is available in over 2000 different dialects. Why? Because it works! Its principles apply to all aspects of your life. Peter's prophecy in the Bible states: "The Word of the Lord will live forever."[12] The question is: does it live in your heart?

Man is made up of three components: body, mind and spirit. When we refuse to accept God into the spiritual part of our lives, we create a void that allows evil to enter. Does evil exist? The following story may or may not be true, but it relates to man and the state of our nation's spiritual direction today:

*A university professor, teaching a course in religion, challenged his class: "Did God create everything?"*

A student quickly replied, "Yes, sir. God created everything."

The professor continued, "If God created everything, then He created evil too. And, because our works define who we are, then God is evil".

The class became silent. Suddenly, another student raised his hand and asked, "Professor, does darkness exist?"

The professor responded, "Yes."

The student replied, "No, sir, darkness does not exist. Darkness is just the absence of light. Light we can study, but not darkness. In fact, we can use Newton's prism to break the white light into many colors and study the various wavelengths of each color. But, you cannot measure darkness. A simple ray of light can break into a world of darkness and illuminate it. How can you know how dark a certain space is? You measure the amount of light present. Darkness is a term used by man to describe what happens when there is no light present."

Then the young man asked the professor, "Sir, does evil exist?"

The professor responded, "Of course. I told you earlier that God created evil."

To this the student replied, "No, evil does not exist, sir, or at least it does not exist unto itself. It is simply the absence of God. It is just like darkness, a word that man has created to describe the absence of light. God did not create evil. It is the result of what happens when man does not have God's love present in his heart. Evil

*is like cold that comes when there is no heat, or the*
*darkness that comes when there is no light."*

*The professor sat down.*

*The young man's name was Albert Einstein.*[13]

As stated in the aforementioned story about Albert Einstein, evil exists when we are without the presence of God in our hearts. It results in man's sin, his iniquity to other men, in creating crime and violence. The absence of God can only result in tyranny.

### Darrell Scott Testimony

Darrell Scott, the father of Rachel Scott, a victim of the Columbine High School shootings in Littleton, Colorado, was invited to address the House Judiciary Committee's subcommittee. What he said to our national leaders during this special session of Congress was painfully truthful. They were not prepared for what he was to say, nor was it well received. What he said needs to be heard by every parent, every teacher, every politician, every sociologist, every psychologist, and all members of society. Scott's courageous words are powerful, penetrating and deeply personal.

He said,

*Since the dawn of creation there have been both good*
*and evil in the hearts of men and women. We all contain*
*the seeds of kindness or the seeds of violence. The*
*death of my wonderful daughter, Rachel Joy Scott, and*
*the deaths of that heroic teacher, and the other eleven*
*children who died must not be in vain. Their blood cries*
*out for answers.*

*In the days that followed the Columbine tragedy, I was amazed at how quickly fingers began to be pointed at groups such as the NRA. I am not a member of the NRA. I am not a hunter. I do not even own a gun. I am not here to represent or defend the NRA – because I don't believe that they are responsible for my daughter's death. Therefore, I do not believe that they need to be defended. If I believed they had anything to do with Rachel's murder, I would be their strongest opponent.*

*I am here today to declare that Columbine was not just a tragedy – it was a spiritual event that should be forcing us to look at where the real blame lies! Much of the blame lies here in this room. Much of the blame lies behind the pointing fingers of the accusers themselves. I wrote a poem just four nights ago that expresses my feelings best. This was written way before I knew I would be speaking here today:*

*Your laws ignore our deepest needs,*
*Your words are empty air.*
*You've stripped away our heritage,*
*You've outlawed simple prayer.*
*Now gunshots fill our classrooms,*
*And precious children die.*
*You seek for answers everywhere,*
*And ask the question "Why?"*
*You regulate restrictive laws,*
*Through legislative creed,*
*And yet you fail to understand,*
*That God is what we need!*

*What has happened to us as a nation? We have refused to honor God, and in so doing, we open the doors to hatred and violence. And when something as terrible as Columbine's tragedy occurs – politicians immediately look for a scapegoat such as the NRA. They immediately seek to pass more restrictive laws that contribute to erode away our personal and private liberties. We do not need more restrictive laws. Eric and Dylan would not have been stopped by metal detectors. No amount of gun laws can stop someone who spends months planning this type of massacre. The real villain lies within our hearts.*

*As my son Craig lay under that table in the school library and saw his two friends murdered before his very eyes – he did not hesitate to pray in school. I defy any law or politician to deny him that right! I challenge every young person in America, and around the world, to realize that on April 20, 1999, at Columbine High School prayer was brought back to our schools. Do not let the many prayers offered by those students be in vain. Dare to move into the new millennium with a sacred disregard for legislation that violates your God-given right to communicate with Him. To those of you who would point your finger at the NRA – I give to you a sincere challenge. Dare to examine your own heart before casting the first stone!*[14]

When God is taken from a culture, evil can only grow. That growth is like a slow-moving cancer that magnifies and creates weakness in all parts of a society. It destroys the foundation of a nation without the people being aware that it is happening. As evil increases, the contrast between good and bad becomes more evident.

## Separation of Church and State

In history, the king or ruler of a nation often had some form of religion or spiritual worship he personally followed. He then demanded that all of his subjects, or people of that country, worship as the ruler did.

Great Britain had an established religion, the Anglican Church. The colonists rebelled against Great Britain because our founding fathers did not want the government to force anyone to worship in a particular way as Great Britain did. The Puritans came to this nation risking their lives in the search of freedom of religion.

Our First Amendment to the Constitution of the United States says the following about religion: "Congress shall make no law respecting an establishment of religion, or prohibiting the free exercise thereof." The First Amendment does not separate God and government, but actually encourages religion. The first clause declares that the federal government cannot establish one religion for all the people. They meant that there would not be any official American religion. It says nothing about "separation of church and state." The second clause insists that the government should do nothing to discourage religion.

In 1962, the Supreme Court made a misconceived decision that the Constitution mandated a separation of church and state. History indicates that the Constitution intended only that the federal government not be allowed to establish an official 'State" religion, as was established in England, or what should not occur was the establishment of, say the Catholic or Baptist Church, as the official faith of the nation. Our nation is based on the faith of Jesus Christ. In the first 175 years, Judeo-Christian beliefs were reflected in all facets of American life.

This decision by the Supreme Court led to an assault on Christianity in this country. It opened an opportunity for secular leftist groups such as the ACLU (American Civil Liberties Union), the extreme liberals and radical court judges to take God out of our nation. Due to the lawsuits by the ACLU and liberal court decisions, traditional Christian values have been challenged, and several removed from our culture and memorials over the past thirty to forty years.

From the days of our founding fathers, religious education was part of our educational system. As mentioned earlier, twenty-three of the first twenty-six colleges in this nation were established as Christian colleges. These included Yale and Harvard.

Public schools had prayer for over 200 years before the Supreme Court ruled that state-mandated school prayers were unconstitutional (Engle 1962). Almost every poll taken in 1962 when the Supreme Court made this ruling, i.e. The Gallup, Associated Press and other major polls, showed that 80% of Americans supported school prayers. This decision radically went against an overwhelming majority. The Supreme Court sided with opponents of prayer such as the ACLU and a few leftist radicals.

Opposition to school-sponsored prayer or any reference to God is a basic issue of the American Civil Liberties Union. The ACLU believes that any program of religious instruction – direct or indirect – in public schools or by use of public resources is a violation of the constitutional principle of separation of church and state, and must be opposed. This is a complete contradiction to what our signers had set forth in our Constitution.

When court decisions such as this are handed down to the public changing our way of life, something is very wrong! What was good for this nation for over 200 years no longer prevails. The basic fiber that made this nation so different and so prosperous from others was changed overnight. A government "of the people" ought to reflect the values of the people it is to govern. Why should 80% of the citizens of a nation dramatically change their culture for a few extremists who want to change the face of this nation to accommodate their political and godless agendas?

Taking God from our lives is a complaint of the Christian right. We do not expect to force our beliefs on others, but why should our religious freedoms be taken away from our lives when we have had them since the beginning of this nation?

Likewise, in a recent poll by NBC about taking out the words, "In God We Trust" and "God" in the Pledge of Allegiance, 86% of Americans wanted to keep the words and 14% were against it. Why should our nation cater to the minority? [15]

Jay Leno stated recently in his quote of the month, "With hurricanes, earthquakes, fires out of control, tornadoes, flooding and severe thunderstorms tearing up our country from one end to another, with the threat of bird flu and terrorist attacks, are we sure this is a good time to take God out of the Pledge of Allegiance?"[16]

Our modern courts have interpreted the subject of "separation between church and state" not on the words of the Constitution, but on a letter written by Thomas Jefferson, which was addressed to the Danbury, Connecticut Baptist Association on January 11, 1802. Jefferson stated:

> *Believing with you that religion is a matter which lies solely between man and God, that he owes account to none other for his faith or his worship, that the legislative powers of government reaches actions only, and not opinions, I contemplate with sovereign reverence that an act of the whole American people which declared that their legislature should make no law respecting an establishment of religion or prohibiting the free expression thereof; thus building a wall of separation between church and state.[17]*

Jefferson was specifically referring to the "whole American people," meaning the federal government could not impose a national church. As Jefferson explained later in a letter to a Presbyterian minister, "Certainly no power to prescribe any religious exercise or to assume authority and religious discipline has been delegated to the general government. It must then rest with the states as far as it can be in any human authority."[18]

What the federal government was prohibited from doing, in Jefferson's view, was prescribing a particular set of religious rites or promoting a particular religious sect at the expense of others.

Since the decision by the courts to take prayer out of school, our nation has been in a steady moral decline between 1962 and now. Studies show that during this period, divorces have doubled, teen suicide has increased over 300%, teenage pregnancy went up over 200%, and violent crime increased more than 500% and abortion over 1000%. Since the Roe vs. Wade decision on January 22, 1973, over 48 million babies have been killed by abortion (up to the year 2005).[19] This number is greater than the population of the cities of New York, London, Moscow, and Paris combined. If a cemetery were required for these 48 million aborted babies, it would measure approximately 100 miles long x 100 miles wide. A whole generation of citizens has been eliminated due to abortion. These statistics confirm the effect this court decision had on the decline of morality in this nation.

Values and morality must be taught, but cannot be taught without religion. There cannot be moral law without a belief in the Divine Creator, which was proven by France when the French government was in the middle of its revolution. After the Revolutionary War, our founders felt that they owed the French a favor for their assistance in the war, helping to defeat the British fleets at Chesapeake Bay in 1781. Thomas Jefferson went to Paris to assist Lafayette and his associates to draft the French Declaration of Rights. Jefferson wrote a letter to Madison stating, "That the draft of the French Declaration contained the basic principles of our Declaration of Independence. In many respects the French Declaration appeared superior to our Declaration of Independence."[20] Whereas the American Revolution ended in the establishment of a constitutional republic, a government under law, the French Revolution ended in tyranny and government by the guillotine, followed by the rise to power by Napoleon. So, what went wrong in France?

The French Declaration of Rights did not acknowledge that the source of man's rights is man's Creator, as Jefferson had declared in this nation's Declaration of Independence. The French Declaration did not state that rights are inherent, inalienable or derived from any supreme authority. An 'enlightened' government granted rights given to the French in their Declaration. French historian Alexis de Tocqueville noted the difference when he addressed his compatriots a half century later – that America's experiment in liberty was firmly rooted in the fact that "in the United States the sovereign authority is religious."[21]

The French Revolution was anti-religious, with secular humanist beliefs and thus could not duplicate the American Declaration. One of the goals of the French Revolution was to destroy established heritage and religious institutions, which its leader, Rousseau, saw as responsible for corrupting their lifestyles. His society rejected all forms of Christianity. Rousseau believed that the protection of individual rights was in opposition to a Supreme Authority. This is the same philosophy being used by the ACLU today regarding our nation. France eventually broke all relationships with the past and Christianity. The revolution eventually turned against itself and began to self-destruct. Over 20,000 people were executed along with their leader, Robespierre, who was guillotined.[22] The revolution was an example of how people react when they are unchecked and do not have a Godly blueprint to follow.

A British diplomat, Edmond Burke, in addressing the British Parliament in 1773 after making a trip to France, concluded that the French political direction could only produce tyranny. "The most horrid and cruel blow that can be offered to civil society is through atheism."[23] Burke placed the blame for France's failure on the philosophy that denied God.

## Our Creator is the God of Nations and of Man

God sanctions nations. George Washington stated on October 3, 1789, "It is the duty of all nations to acknowledge the providence of Almighty God. To obey His will, to be grateful for His benefits, and to humbly implore His protection and favor".[24]

The Creator is the God of nations as He is the God of man. He chooses nations He blesses, and ordains key men and events at times when those nations can accomplish great things.

God is very much involved in human history. In the Old Testament, He chose and anointed men who knew God's heart, and those who were a friend of the Creator. They were righteous men from the prophets to Noah, Abraham and Moses. Throughout history, God called those who were sometimes the least qualified to do great tasks. I believe He wants to prove the worth of all. God has a divine purpose for everyone, but we must listen to Him to determine that purpose.

He wants us to be a fruitful vessel to accomplish great things for humankind. He knew us before we were born. He knows our capacities and capabilities beyond what we can visualize or realize is possible. He chooses those not necessarily because of their abilities or intelligence, but because He knows the given task will be completed no matter what the obstacles. He expects the best of our talents. God always calls us for a specific purpose, never in generalities.

However, God has always been disappointed in man and nations that He has blessed. Right and wrong never change, and God never changes. Only man and his desires and aspirations change.

The Creator is very intolerant when man or a nation becomes disobedient. When God disciplines us, He is showing us His love. Discipline is a way of sharing God's holiness, and He requires our obedience. If we avoid obedience, we will eventually face the consequences of sin, whether as an individual or nation. God will curse an entire nation because we are robbing Him of our dedication and obedience.

When the Lord is neglected, great catastrophes can happen. This has happened throughout the history of the world:

- God warned Adam and Eve of the forbidden fruit in the Garden of Eden.
- Through the testimony of Noah, God warned the generation of Noah's day of the coming judgment of the flood.
- Through the testimony of Lot and the angels, He warned the citizens of Sodom of the coming judgment.
- The nation of Israel disobeyed the Lord fourteen times in the Old Testament, but He took His nation back out of bondage each time.
- Other civilizations failed due to disobedience, such as the Persian, Greek and Roman empires.
- France during the French Revolution vs. the American Revolution. The outcomes of such revolutions have been determined based on belief or disbelief, and the obedience or disobedience to the Creator.

Did the Lord of the universe have a plan for America? Did He ordain specific men by placing them into positions at the "right" time so this nation would become the most prosperous civilization in history? As happened with other nations in history, God sanctioned America. Many men in our nation's history have been responsible for America's survival, success and prosperity. I believe that He placed the following men into prominent positions to advance the freedoms and blessings of this great nation.

### Christopher Columbus

History books teach us that Columbus discovered the new world "by accident" while on his journey to find a trade route to the Indies. Nothing is taught about his faith, or that he believed God gave his mission to him, nor that his journey was to evangelize the Word of God. Of ten modern biographies by major publishers, none makes mention of Columbus' faith, or his motivation to spread the gospel.

Throughout the ages of history, many great men in all walks of life have acknowledged the Bible and Holy Spirit as the foundation for their accomplishments. Christopher Columbus was no exception. Columbus wrote the *Book of Prophecies* which described his motivation for his voyage to the new world. He said in his journal that he simply had to fulfill Isaiah's prophecy in the Old Testament. Columbus believed the world was round, as stated in the Book of Isaiah, Chapter 40; Verse 22, which reads: "He sits enthroned above the circle of the earth." Transcribed from Columbus's *Book of Prophecies* are the following excerpts, confirming his faith and commitment to the Bible as his source of inspiration:

> *It was the Lord who put into my mind (I could feel*
> *His hand upon me) the fact that it would be possible*

*to sail from here to the Indies.  All who heard of my project rejected it with laughter, ridiculing me.  There is no question that the inspiration was from the Holy Spirit, because He comforted me with rays of marvelous inspiration from the Holy Scriptures ... I am a most unworthy sinner, but I have cried out to the Lord for grace and mercy, and they have covered me completely. I have found the sweetest consolation since I made it my whole purpose to enjoy His marvelous presence.  For the execution*

*of the journey to the Indies, I did not make use of intelligence, mathematics or maps.  It was simply the fulfillment of what Isaiah had prophesied.  No one should fear to undertake any task in the name of our Savior, if it is just and if the intention is purely for His holy service.  Our Lord has assigned the working out of all things to each person, but it all happens according to His sovereign will, even though He gives advice. He lacks nothing that is in the power of men to give Him.  Oh, what a gracious Lord, who desires that people should perform for Him those things for which He holds Himself responsible.  Day and night, moment by moment, everyone should express their most devoted gratitude to Him.*

## William Bradford

William Bradford kept a journal of the Pilgrims' journey to America.  He called it *The History of Plymouth Plantation*.  In his journal was a copy of the Mayflower Compact, an agreement drawn up by the Pilgrims that was a covenant with God, and a charter that allowed the Pilgrims to set up their own government. Little did they know that the Compact was the first record in history from which free and equal men created their own civil government. The Ten Commandments and the Bible guided the Pilgrims, giving them the stability, convictions and unity they needed to face the adversities and hardships ahead of them.

The Pilgrims elected William Bradford as the first governor in 1623. He had the foresight to understand that the people of the young colony would need to be self-sustaining if they were to survive the hard, New England winters. He understood that every person must carry his or her own weight, do his or her share of work and be disciplined for the coming winter. The principles he incorporated were taken from the Bible and utilized in their daily lives. The governor also recommended a proposal that each family be given a parcel of land. He believed that the Pilgrims owning their own land would make them more responsible, productive, and better citizens for the colony.

The Mayflower Compact was the first document in America that was the beginning of a government "of the people, by the people and for the people." The principles in the Mayflower Compact were the foundation that paved the way for our founding fathers, as they formulated the Constitution of the United States of America.

## George Washington

George Washington stood out above all others in the years prior to and during the Revolutionary War. He was a self-educated man who grew up in the Blue Ridge Mountains of Virginia as a surveyor. He loved his native land, and always wanted to be a farmer. However, his service to our nation was his priority in life. He was a man of great physical stature at 6'3", weighing 230 pounds, with a size 13 shoe. He was a towering figure in the front lines, as he displayed great courage and battle instinct as a military officer.

When he joined forces with General Braddock of the British Army during the French and Indian War, he had two horses shot out from under him and left the battlefield with four bullet holes in his clothing, but no blood. In a letter he later wrote to his brother, he indicated that it was the providence of God, which kept him safe during the battle. Stories of his heroic acts and military leadership became part of our nation's history. Later, as the Continental Army's commander-in-chief, Washington inspired great loyalty in his troops, and through the sheer force of his personality kept the Continental Army together for eight tough years of combat. His perseverance and patience as a leader proved to be the motivation our colonial troops needed as they defeated Cornwallis and the British at the Battle of Yorktown, which proved to be the turning point of the war.[26]

If we had lost the Revolutionary War, we might still be living under the bondage of English rule. I believe it was the hand of God that protected and ordained George Washington to accomplish great things for this nation. Washington shared his faith by rallying his soldiers with these words, "If God be for us, who can stand against us." Washington believed that a man's religious expression should be private, and a relationship between the individual and our Creator. There is little doubt about his Christian belief, which was revealed in his prayer book of 24 pages, handwritten by him and entitled *Daily Sacrifice*. The first entry, called "Sunday Morning," reads as follows:

> *Almighty God, and most merciful father, who didst*
> *command the children of Israel to offer a daily sacrifice*

*to Thee, that thereby they might glorify and praise Thee*
*for Thy protection both night and day ... I beseech Thee,*
*my sins, remove them from Thy presence, as far as the*
*east is from the west, and accept of me for the merits of*
*Thy Son Jesus Christ ... Let my heart, therefore, gracious*
*God, be so affected with the glory and majesty of (Thine*
*honor) that I may not do mine own works, but wait on*
*Thee ... As Thou wouldst hear me calling upon Thee in*
*my prayers, so give me grace to hear Thee calling on*
*me in Thy word, that it may be wisdom, righteousness,*
*reconciliation and peace to the saving of my soul in the*
*day of the Lord Jesus.*[27]

When he was elected as our first president of the United States, he took the oath of office by placing his hand on the Bible, which has been a presidential tradition of all presidents since. He also stated during his term in office that, "It is impossible to govern rightly without God and the Bible."[28]

## Abraham Lincoln

Abraham Lincoln was not an educated man; his formal education did not go beyond the first grade. Throughout his young life, he continued to read to obtain knowledge. He received his law degree in the state of Illinois due to his own ability to learn. He grew up in a rural area with humble beginnings. Lincoln learned much through adversity – with the death of his mother when he was age 9, followed by his sister, and later, his father.

When Lincoln took the oath of office in 1860, he had inherited a war. The Confederates had already seized all federal forts and navy yards in the states under their control, except Fort Pickens in Florida, and Fort Sumter in Charleston, South Carolina. Upon becoming our 16th president, Lincoln had four difficult years during the war that aged him quickly.

The mental pressure on Lincoln during the war was overwhelming. He experienced more deaths during the Civil War than any president ever experienced in any war. This war was the bloodiest in human history, as over 600,000 Americans died. Lincoln's son, Willie, died during the war of typhoid fever in 1862 at age 12. Neither he nor his wife, Mary Todd, truly recovered from Willie's death. The loss of his son, along with the earlier deaths of his mother and sister, prepared him for what he was to face in lost lives as president during the Civil War.

In his early years, Lincoln did not mention much of God, but in his later years, Divine Providence and his past gave him wisdom and insight beyond the ordinary man. Lincoln came onto the American scene at a time when our nation was divided both economically and politically. We were a divided society that, without proper leadership, could self-destruct. Lincoln rose above politics to greatness as he did what he believed was best for our nation. John Hay described Lincoln as "the greatest character since Christ." The nation's people throughout the annals of our history have admired him. He remains an American messiah, murdered on Good Friday, a man of truth, reverence, honesty and strong moral fiber.

God guided Lincoln as he protected and led our nation through grave times. He relied on the power of the Creator to hold this nation together. He depended on the Power of Divine Providence. Lincoln expressed his relationship with God several times during the Gettysburg Address and in his second inaugural address.

During the Civil War, Lincoln overheard someone remark that he hoped "the Lord was on the Union's side." Lincoln responded sharply, "I am not at all concerned about that, for I know that the Lord is always on the side of the right. But it is my constant anxiety and prayer that I and this nation be on the Lord's side."[29]

During his second inaugural address, Lincoln spoke about the Creator having His own purpose, and that we must carry out His purpose; even when both sides pray to the same God, we do not know what God's intent is.

Through the years of our nation's history since Lincoln, there has been none to equal him. As one historian noted, "Lincoln was the mold and the clay."

## Ronald Reagan

Ronald Reagan, a Republican, was our 40th president who served two terms from 1981 to 1989. Reagan entered politics for two reasons. He believed that government was growing too big, and that United States citizens were being overtaxed.

Ronald Reagan solved our nation's and the world's problems by speaking in a language not understood by the left-wing media and university professors, that is, the language that Thomas Jefferson reminded us to return to – the language of common sense and patriotism. They still do not understand it today as they continue to dismiss the achievements of Ronald Reagan who was one of the greatest liberators and presidents of the 20th century.

He became president, inheriting the economic disaster of the Jimmy Carter administration of the late 1970s, and the nuclear threat of Russia in the mid-1980s. Reagan initiated sweeping economic programs called "Reaganomics," including major tax cuts, budget reductions, and increased defense spending to build up our military. His economic package is what sparked the United States into one of the greatest economic expansions in the history of our nation. His programs promoted the Internet expansion of the 1990s, and carried us into economic prosperity in the 2000s.

He shocked the world in his 1981 speech when he called the Soviet Union an "Evil Empire." His peace through strong military policy caused the Communists to both fear and respect Ronald Reagan. Reagan made history when his three summit meetings with Russia's Mikhail Gorbachev resulted in a crucial nuclear arms treaty.

With Ronald Reagan, we not only received great leadership, but he also inspired the nation to put aside any negative thoughts about our future, and to embrace hope, patriotism and providence of God. In his farewell address to the United Nations in 1988, Reagan stated, "My mother gave me many things in life, but her most important gift was knowledge of the happiness and solace to be gained in prayer. It's the greatest help I have had in my presidency ... " The Bible that Ronald Reagan placed his hand upon at his inaugural belonged to his mother. A special scripture was marked in that Bible which read, "If my people, who are called by my name, will humble themselves and pray and seek my face and turn from their wicked ways, then will I hear from heaven and will forgive their sin and will heal their land" (2 Chronicles 7:14. NIV Topical Study Bible).

Ronald Reagan spoke of George Washington several times while serving as president. In 1981: "We come filled with pride and gratitude to honor George Washington, Father of our Country, knowing that because of what he did, we're free and we're Americans ... He did more than live up to the standards of the time; he set them. George

Washington and his generation of Americans met their challenges. We can, we must, and we will meet ours."[30] In 1983: "The image of George Washington kneeling in prayer in the snow is one of the most famous in American history. He personified a people who knew it was not enough to depend on their own courage and goodness, they must also seek help from God, their Father and Preserver."[31]

These men were champions chosen by God to steer our nation to greatness. These Godly men of integrity and perseverance were inspired by His Spirit to accomplish great things, when this nation needed leadership through wars, depressions, political and economic chaos. They were Godly men of integrity, perseverance and passion. Great men are disciplined, and they follow the rules, whether the rules are those of the Bible, the Ten Commandments, the Mayflower Compact, or our U.S. Constitution. These leaders never deviated from those directives to keep the people of this nation in personal freedom and prosperity.

## Christianity vs. Humanism

America is a divided nation in the midst of a movement that the United States has never seen before. We are moving from the principles of God's Word to a belief of each man doing what is right in his own eyes – namely humanism. Secular humanism or atheism is a philosophy that rejects all forms of religious faith and worship.

## Some positions taken by Christianity vs. Humanism:

| Biblical Beliefs | Humanistic Beliefs |
|---|---|
| Believes God gave us our freedoms and is the Supreme Authority | Believes in man as supreme authority and freedoms are man-made |
| Man exists for God | Man exists for himself |
| Man is the product of Creation (God) | Man is a product of evolution (atheism) |
| Morality is based on God's law | Morality is based on man's logic |

Humanism has always failed and has never been successful in man or his nations. Humanism has only led to disappointment or morbid decay. This has been proven throughout history – from Adam and Eve, through all failed civilizations that followed. One belief, Christianity, is absolute, the standards set forth by the Bible. Humanism is subjective, where every man becomes the law unto himself. One brings about freedom and prosperity; the other creates total chaos and tyranny.

William Penn stated, "If man is not governed by God, then he must be governed by tyrants."[32]

The leader or leaders of a godless government control the direction of that nation. Instead of having God and personal freedom, it has a tyrant and few freedoms.

"For only the upright will live in the land, and those who have integrity will remain in it. But the wicked will be removed from the land, and the treacherous will be destroyed" (Proverbs 2:21-22, NLT). This happened at the end days of the Greek and Roman empires, as their godless societies went from apathy to government dependency to bondage. Hitler took Nazi Germany on the same destructive path during his reign as a tyrant.

Present-day nations such as North Korea, Cuba, Iran and Venezuela, which are controlled by tyrant leaders, believe in humanism, not God. History proves that countries like these destruct from within because of their lack of religious convictions and moral values.

A nation's transition from one philosophy, God's Law, to humanism is called pluralism, which is tolerant of all views. Most disciplinary principles are omitted as a nation moves from one form of culture to another. America's Civil War of moral values started when God was removed from the nation's schools. We have gone through the pluralistic transition of teaching evolution along with creation to outlawing the teachings of creation altogether. Creation, or today's new expression called design theory, is no longer accepted in most schools. It has been replaced by secular humanism.

Law, God's Law, has successfully governed our founding fathers and all generations since. It is God's Law, acknowledged for over 200 years, that has given us our abundance and freedom. The freedom is to become what our Lord intended us to be, not the freedom to do whatever one wants to do without the discipline of the Bible and our Constitution. The proven history that made this nation so prosperous and the envy of the world is rapidly being lost. As we continue to take the Creator out of our culture, we are moving from one God, the Lord of the Bible, to a worldview of a nation controlled by the will of the people instead of His will.

## Crisis Christians

This nation and our way of life are under the greatest moral, social and economic tests we have experienced in history. The greatest problem that we are facing is a spiritual one. It relates to our turning away from God as a nation. After World War II, we experienced in our nation's churches a growth of Christianity as church attendance increased. This spiritual growth then began to fade as our moral and Christian values were taken over by humanism. During the Reagan administration, we experienced a brief gain in our moral values, but this was a temporary reaction and one that has since faded.

This trend has continued as we have turned into a nation of temporary or crisis Christians. The hand of God has protected us for such a long time that we assume we will always be under His protection no matter what we do as a nation. A perfect example is when the 9/11 tragedy occurred. The citizens of America filled their churches with attendance for a short period after 9/11, and then apathy set in again. The period of being thankful to God was short-lived, as we went back to our complacent ways.

Across the television screens, we repeatedly heard the song "God Bless America." What the nation failed to realize is that the Divine Creator has blessed America for over 200 years. Due to 9/11, we were asking for more of His blessings. Instead of asking for further blessings, we should be on our knees thanking Him for all the abundance and prosperity He has bestowed on us.

We seem to honor His Providence in time of despair. Religion for many people is like being a spectator at a sports event. They sit back, watch and do not participate. A relationship with the Creator is not a temporary thing, nor is it about what we want in time of calamity. It is a relationship showing thankfulness, obedience and reverence to a Supreme Authority during good times as well as bad. A true relationship with the Lord is doing His will at all times. Our ancestors realized this and used the Living God and His Word as a foundation for their lives.

We have become an apathetic nation. We are losing our Christian identity without being aware it is happening. Our value system is being lost for the same reason; the two parallel each other. Apathy is taking the middle road, the "whatever" attitude. It creeps up on us without realization, much like the ways the changing seasons are quietly upon us.

One of the reasons we are spiritually indifferent is because we are a spoiled nation. A nation of tremendous wealth and prosperity. Wealth and prosperity are some of the substances that create indifference and complacency. As in the days of Rome, worldly success as a nation does not assure spiritual or moral success. What good if we gain the world, but lose our nation's soul?

The moral values of our nation have changed; no longer do we give glory to God. We are indifferent to God. Most people will change when they feel the pressure, such as when a 9/11 incident occurs. When apathy sets in, people forget their meaningful purpose in life, and only adversity will change their ways. Indifference is never creative; it is always an end. Apathy has no vision. Similarly, some people will trade their rights and freedoms for handouts or entitlements rather than leave their comfort zone.

This description of our nation today is exactly what happened to other great civilizations. The Greek and Roman empires lost their moral compasses and were without spiritual direction. Each gave away the values that once guided them to greatness.

## Passing on a Legacy

We paid for our history as a nation with the blood of our ancestors, men and women who believed and sacrificed for the freedoms we have today. If our country is to survive its future, the patriots of today must show the same willingness to sacrifice as our ancestors. What man once did, man can do again. A national awareness is needed to know what is threatening our liberties and those of our children.

Since 1962, decisions by our liberal courts created an erosion of our nation's religious life and moral values. In this civil war of values, evil never surrenders its hold on man or nations without a fight. If we lose the culture war, it is because we have given up our convictions, not because our opponent is stronger. We will have compromised with evil in exchange for our freedoms and future, instead of reclaiming what is rightfully ours. The preservation of liberty involves personal sacrifices. We never gain spiritual inheritance without the conflict of battle. Our freedoms were legacies given to us by our ancestors so that future generations might prosper, ancestors who believed that there are certain values more precious than life itself.

Parents and grandparents, what are you leaving your children? Will you be able to look back and say, "I left them a good legacy that improved their lives and that of my nation." Or, have you left your children vulnerable to evil and a nation in default? What picture do they have of you … that of a Godly person concerned about their future … or have you left them only with material things in life? Material things and money are meaningless. What you leave in their hearts is what is most important. Remember, as stated earlier in this chapter, "Without God in your heart, you have evil."

The greatest asset we can pass on to a generation is our faith. There is no way to learn of faith except through trials. Trials are God's school of faith; once the lesson of faith is learned; it is an everlasting possession and an eternal fortune gained. Our forefathers reminded us not only of the necessity of faith, but also of the patience required to let faith do its work. We should never remove ourselves from the hands of our Heavenly Counsel, or miss one lesson of His gracious discipline due to our lack of faith.

The only people who will defend the rights of the people of this nation as stated by our founders are those people who believe in God. Where the Lord is a stranger, so is liberty.  President Ronald Reagan stated on August 23, 1984,

> *Without God, there is no virtue because there is no prompting of the conscience.  Without God, there is a coarsening of the society; without God, democracy will not and cannot endure ... If we ever forget that we are One Nation under God, then we will be a nation gone under.[33]*

## A Divided Nation

In the past several years, we have become a nation divided, departing from the foundation and values given us by our founding fathers. For the first 190 years, those principles laid out in the Constitution were reflected in all facets of American life. The spiritual heritage, the belief in a Creator, passed through generations was responsible for our abundance and wealth. America continued to amaze the rest of the world with its morality, freedoms and prosperity as other nations turned to us for guidance. We were known as a Christian nation whose moral compass was taken from the Bible, and showed in all walks of our lives.

Something happened to America! Our Constitution, the record of freedoms and liberties set forth by our founders, is but a shadow of the original document. This once-solid foundation has systematically eroded along with the rights of the citizens of this great nation. The very fiber that once made this nation strong is gradually disappearing.

Thomas Jefferson said, "Can the liberties of a nation be thought secure when we have removed their only firm basis, a conviction in the minds of people that these liberties are a gift of God".[1]

As I look over my shoulder at the last fifty years, I become saddened as I examine the following changes in our nation.

The radical extremists and well-funded special interest groups have convinced the government and court systems to modify the Constitution to meet their own agendas, contrary to what the founders intended. Many of these changes are opposite of what the majority of Americans want, and without the average citizen being aware of such changes.

Thomas Jefferson was concerned that the courts would overstep their authority and instead of interpreting the law, would begin making law, resulting in rule being placed in the hands of a few over the majority. These rulings have created a divided nation, drastically changing our way of life, economy, and affecting the values, freedoms, families, and future of our nation.

Webster's dictionary defines a civil war as a war between two factions in the same country. Today, there is a civil war raging in America. We have become a nation divided spiritually, politically, and by court decisions. No longer are we fighting together to attain a common purpose or goal.

Differences are evident in many aspects of our lives. We are divided between red and blue states regarding our political preferences. There is no bipartisanship shown by our public officials in Washington. A great majority of all decisions have to do with power, egos and the good of one's party. The abortion issue is ongoing – a line drawn in the sand, with opponents continually arguing this moral dilemma. Homosexuality and family are defined in different ways depending on moral and social outlooks. While at war in Iraq, there is a great political division regarding its funding, how to fight it, when to end it. We cannot even agree how our children should be educated as government, teachers, and parents differ as to what programs are best for our kids.

The courts are rewriting the Constitution, which is dividing America such as in the days of our Civil War of 1861. However, today's civil war is an assault on traditional America and our moral values. Radical secularist and liberal judges have taken God and the Ten Commandments out of America's way of life. From the schoolhouse to the courthouse, His Word is being silenced. This anti-religious movement is against the God-given traditions we inherited from our founders. A nation has no division and there is no separation when we are under Him; then, we are one.

We must address this crisis as we have all wars, with full public and national aggressiveness, using all the resources and rights our Constitution allows us in order to salvage our freedoms and unite this nation. It could mean the life or death of America.

# Education

W ake up, America!  We are losing our world position in
education.  Our once-proud status as a world leader in
educating our children is falling apart.

When the nation's governors gathered recently for a national
education summit, their partnering organization, Achieve Inc, presented
data showing that the high school dropout rate has worsened since
1983.  Of children who now reach ninth grade, 32% disappear before
high school graduation, another one-third finish high school but are
not ready for college or work.  Thus, about two-thirds of our students
are being left behind, many of them low income and minority kids.
Currently, only the upper third leave high school ready for college,
work and citizenship.[1]

In the early 1980s, the National Education Commission concluded
that our schools faced a "rising tide of mediocrity."[2]  Educators,
governors and CEOs joined together to try to improve our education
system, from kindergarten through high school, but after a quarter
century of effort, other nations are still moving ahead of us.

Recent reports indicate that students in the fourth grade lead
all nations in math and science.  However, we lose our standing by
the time children reach the twelfth grade – we then rank 25th in the
world.  The nation's fifteen-year-olds made a poor showing on a newly
released international test of practical math applications, ranking 24th
out of 29 industrialized nations, behind South Korea, Japan, and most
of Europe.  Our students were comparable only to those in Poland,
Hungary and Spain.[3]  The United States Secretary of Education called
the results "a blinking warning light" that show the need to reform U.S.
high schools.

After the collapse of the Soviet Union, the United States emerged as a sole super power.  Paul Kennedy, a historian from Yale, said, "America had more economic, political, military and cultural power than any nation since ancient Rome some 2000 years ago."[4]  Not only are this nation's government, courts and value system being mismanaged, we are also mismanaging our educational system.

Along with the downfall of our educational system, we are also showing a decline in adult literacy in America.  A recent Federal literacy survey reported that about eleven million U.S. adults, or one in twenty adults, have such poor English skills that they cannot read a newspaper, understand the directions on a bottle of pills, or carry on a basic conversation.[5]  Recent reports indicate that there are more English-speaking people in India today than in the United States.[6]  Mark S. Schneider, Commissioner of Education Statistics, said, "The declining impact of education on our adult population was the biggest surprise to us, and we just don't have a good explanation."[7]

An additional study shows that the reading proficiency of college graduates has declined in the past decade.[8]

Michael Gorman, president of the American Library Association, stated, "Only 31% of college graduates can read a complete book and extrapolate from it.  That is not saying much for the remaining 69% of graduates.  These statistics show a 10% drop compared to a test taken in 1992."[9]

William J. Molony, Colorado's Commissioner of Education, in a recent report in *USA Today* indicates that nearly one-third of all U.S. school children have a serious literacy deficit.  Former U.S. Education Secretary Rod Paige points out those most impoverished English-speaking nations in the Caribbean have higher literacy rates than that of the United States.  Similarly, studies among poor children in Africa show levels of English literacy that would be the envy of any U.S. city.

How can a nation where education spending is nearly twice the average of those in European Union countries produce such poor results? A recently released report of the National Council on Teacher Quality and further statistics from the National Institute of Child Health and Human Development state that 85% of U.S. reading teachers were never properly trained.[10]

When those who teach our teachers are clueless or even outright hostile toward reading research, is it any wonder that our children have become the victims of literacy deficit traceable not to lack of funding or poverty, but to an unwillingness to grasp methods of teaching that have been clear to professional education in every other industrial nation?[11]

Who is to blame for the demise of our world dominance in education? What has happened in America over the past 40 years that has created such a downfall? Many fingers point in different directions. Are the parents, students, schools, teachers, government or value system at fault? I believe all have a part in our decline, but many of the answers go beyond these factors. By taking a deeper look at America's past and comparing it to what is happening today, perhaps we can unveil the events that explain the deterioration of our current educational system.

## Education:  Our Past, Our Founding Fathers

The trend in today's public schools is to teach students history occurring in the 20th century. Our history such as the Constitution, Revolutionary War, Civil War and our past up to the 20th century, too often is not being taught. How can we expect the young people to defend our freedoms if they are not taught why they are important, or how they are connected to the sacrifices of past generations?

In our founding years, Americans were among the most literate people on earth, and that put us on an upward path to greatness. Long before public education was formally introduced on a national scale by Horace Mann and others in the 19th century, Thomas Jefferson commissioned a study, conducted by his friend Dupont de Nemours, on American education in 1800, and discovered a literacy rate of better than 99%. Jefferson's report stated, "Not more than four in a thousand are unable to write legibly, even neatly."[12]

In America at that time, a great number of people read the Bible and the newspaper. Fathers read aloud to their children while breakfast was being prepared, a task that occupied mothers three-quarters of an hour every morning. Newspapers of the United States were filled with all sorts of narratives – comments on matters political, physical, philanthropies, information on agriculture, the arts, travel, navigation, and also extracts from the best books in America and Europe – disseminating enormous amounts of information. This information was helpful to young people when they arrived at the age when the father resigned his place as reader in favor of the child who could best succeed him. Jefferson's report read, "It is because of this kind of education that Americans, without having more great men than other countries, have the advantage of having a larger proportion of moderately well-informed men."[13]

Jefferson anticipated the threat to our freedom would come from a cultural drift as in the days of the Roman Empire. To eliminate or minimize this threat, he wanted all of America's students, especially those in the secondary and post-secondary schools, to receive an education on the various forms of government, political history and foreign affairs. He saw the importance of educating the nation's youth on the value of our republic and freedoms and why these values should be protected. He knew education would train our children to recognize the threats to our liberty posed by cultural apathy as had occurred in past civilizations.[14]

Jefferson's warning of future dangers is presently coming to surface in this nation. Today, politically correct teachers and professors rarely teach about Jefferson or any of the founding fathers, and if they do, it is usually not positive.

Thomas Jefferson once said, "If a nation expects to be ignorant and free, it expects what never was, and what never will be."[15]


## Raising Today's Children

To understand the reasons for our educational system's decline, let us first look at the home environment and the part parents play in raising their children. Education starts at home. Failure in the classroom is often tied to parental responsibility. Teachers have no control over student ambition and work ethic, which come from the home and from within each child.

Studies show that the present generation of children is quite different from past generations regarding motivation, self-discipline, respect and work ethics. Why are today's children so different?

Busy parents today are guilt-ridden over the minimal time they spend with their children. They are busy pursuing their own endeavors and careers. Parents, therefore, substitute organized activity, television, computer and other electronic gadgets in lieu of parenting.

Today adults organize most outdoor activities. Our children are playing sports only if a program is set up for them. Soccer, baseball, basketball and football are all structured and overseen by adults. Parents spend hours transporting their children to and from these organized events. Are we really doing our children a favor?

Recent studies show that our children are exposed to 8½ hours of media a day, which is an hour more than five years ago. The average child spends those hours enjoying television, computer and electronic games, leaving very little time for them to be creative, either mentally or physically. In fact, the average time a child, eight to eighteen years old, spends reading a day is 43 minutes.[16] The computer and television have created a new generation of youth. Donald Roberts of Stanford University says, "We have changed our children's bedrooms into little media arcades. When I was a child, 'Go to your room' was punishment. Now it's 'Go to your room and have a ball'."[17]

Children with TVs in their rooms watch about 90 minutes more a day and do less reading and homework than those without their own TVs. About half of our nation's families have no television rules. "It's alarming, because parents should be setting clear rules and monitoring media use," says Bridget Maher of the Family Research Council.[18]

The survey came amid concern about the soaring rate of childhood obesity. The more kids watch television, the more likely they are to be overweight. A recent study shows that by the year 2010, 50% of our children will be overweight.[19] Another study shows that one-third of American teenagers cannot pass a normal treadmill test because of excessive weight. For years, health experts have been concerned about kids eating more and exercising less than previous generations. This unfit condition leads to diabetes, high cholesterol and heart disease as this generation gets older, according to the Journal of the American Medical Association.[20]

Americans are living longer than ever, but not as long as people of 41 other countries. "Something is wrong when one of the richest countries in the world, the one that spends the most on health care, is not able to keep up with other countries," said Christopher Murray, Head of the Institute of Health Metrics & Evaluation at the University of Washington.

Another factor affecting children's fitness is that two-thirds of American elementary schools either have eliminated school recess, or are considering doing so. The carefree half-hour for children to play tag and other games is being removed. The alleged motive for this is safety, avoiding litigation, and protecting the feelings of children.

An even more serious concern could be changes in young developing brains from constant multitasking, says psychologist Jane Healy, author of *Endangered Minds*. "When you divide attention like this, it becomes harder to focus deeply on any one thing. They may develop habits of mind that make it hard to do in-depth thinking."[21] Kids watch about the same amount of television, nearly four hours a day, as they did five years ago, but they have added newer technology to their viewing pleasure, such as downloading music and instant messaging. When multitasking is added, the average child is exposed to 8½ hours of media a day.[22]

We have become an impatient nation. We want immediate service and gratification, whether it is in the fast-food industry, or in the learning process. Computers retrieve information that allows us to have immediate answers. Between the computer and calculators, our children can retrieve answers rapidly without really thinking how they arrived at the solution. Is knowledge really being developed without one reading and researching for answers to problems? The ready, quick answer does not develop the ability for a child or student to be creative. It does not develop a thinking process. Parents are proud that their young children can operate a computer at a very young age, but are they doing their children a favor?

The computer and television, along with other electronic gadgets, have created a different childhood for our children. They grow up looking at monitors. Hours are spent daily, both at school and at home, staring into an electronic screen. It becomes a convenience and habit, rather than a learning process. We are developing a generation of stereotyped children. The television, computer, cell phone and other electronic gadgets have created another problem, the inability of today's youth to communicate verbally with parents and friends. So much communication is done electronically, that face-to-face verbalization is lacking in the growth and development into adulthood.

Parents today have tried to create the perfect childhood for our youth, but the fact remains that we do not live in a perfect world. Today's parents have created an overprotective society for children. Parents and educators today are boosting the self-esteem of children when it is not deserved. Eventually, children need to face the "real" world where stressful situations, disappointments, and threats to one's self-esteem are a part of life. Adversity creates perseverance and opportunities if viewed in a positive way. Kids need to fail to be successful in life. Most times, more is learned from failures than from successes. It appears that many adults today are so overprotective that even the remote possibility of failure and disappointment is taken out of their children's lives.[23]

Purple is replacing red as the color of choice for teachers. Why? Educators worry that emphatic red corrections on a homework assignment or test can be stressful and demeaning or frightful to a young child. The principal of Thaddeus Stevens Elementary in Pittsburgh advises teachers to use only pleasant-feeling colors and tones.[24]

Many schools now discourage or prohibit competitive games such as tag or dodge ball to avoid hurt feelings. The principal of Franklin Elementary School in Santa Monica, California, recently sent a letter to parents informing them that children could no longer play tag during lunchtime. She explained, "In this game, there is a 'victim' or 'it' which creates a self-esteem issue."[25]

The National PTA recommends an alternative to the competitive game "Tug of War," that it should be called "Tug of Peace." Too many educators, parents and camp counselors today are obsessed with boosting the self-esteem of children. These adults not only refrain from criticizing kids when they perform badly, they also go out of their way to praise them when they have done nothing to deserve it.[26]

Children need challenges and competition. They require criticism and discipline. Most kids feel more secure in knowing their boundaries than having unrestricted freedom. Children crave discipline if started when they are young. If not, it is ineffective later. It then becomes an unacceptable act in one's life.

Parents have an opportunity to either accelerate or stifle their child's direction in life. Proverbs 22:6 NIV reads, "Train a child in the way he should go, and when he is old he will not turn from it." Childhood tendencies forecast adult abilities. God pre-programmed your child's strengths. Read them, recognize them and direct them. You hold the bow, your child is the arrow, aim him or her in the way he or she should go.[27]

Children who are being overprotected in life are being short-changed. In the global economy that awaits them, young Americans will be competing with other young people from all parts of the world, young people whose parents and teachers do not hesitate to use red pens, and who are not handled with kid gloves, as if they were fragile flowers.

In an article found in the January 20, 2005 issue of *Scientific American*, the authors, four prominent psychologists, conclude: "We have found little to indicate that indiscriminately promoting self-esteem in today's children or adults, just for being themselves, offers society any compensating benefits beyond the seductive pleasure it brings to those engaged in the exercise."[28]

Children can cope with Tug of War, dodge ball, discipline and constructive criticism. After all, my generation grew up without childproof lids on medicine bottles, and without helmets while riding bicycles. We ate cupcakes, bread and butter, and drank soda pop with sugar in it, but we were not overweight because we were always outside playing.

Many studies have concluded that we are taking creativity away from our children today. They need to go outdoors and create their own games without parents deciding their programs. Pick-up basketball and baseball games are a big part of a child's mental development. They need to be creative to compete in today's world. This lack of creativeness is evident in a recent study by Michael Cohen, president of Achieve. "Our kids know as much math as the students of other countries, but they don't know how to apply it in practical situations. Knowing mathematics and applying mathematical knowledge to real world problems is an increasingly important set of skills to have in order to get access to good jobs."[29] This loss of creativity is the result of how our children are being raised at home, and how electronic habits have produced a mental and physical imbalance in our youth.

Organized sports can be effective, but at an age when a child is more mature and requires competition. Do not cheat them of their youth. Not all children are going to be pro athletes. Parents today see the high salaries paid to professional athletes and believe that their child will become successful enough to become a professional. This attitude is okay, however, most parents go overboard and are making sports so specialized and organized that they are removing the enjoyment of the game. Remember, more than 70% of those kids who begin playing sports in elementary school will have quit by high school. According to NCAA statistics, in men's basketball 3% of athletes make the jump from high school to the college level, 6% in football. For most sports, the odds of a college athlete playing professionally are less than 2 in 100. Only one out of every 16,000 kids qualifies for some kind of professional sports team.[30]

Many times if children are exposed to too many organized activities, they do not know how to react when they have spare time. They go to Mom and Dad, advising them they are bored, "I have nothing to do," simply because they are used to having a daily agenda or schedule made up for them. Allow them to be creative.

Children at a mature age who participate in competitive sports learn lessons from these sports that stay with them through adulthood. All parents must recognize that there is a fine line between being supportive of a child, and looking the other way when undisciplined play and immature conduct occur. If a parent or coach does not demand more out of a child, especially regarding discipline, motivation and sportsmanship, the child will rarely push him or herself to excel on their own. Too many children grow up believing that anything they do on the playing field is okay. In protecting them, parents make children vulnerable to their own misguided actions.

As an example, an athlete does not perfect his/her potential without constant training and proper diet. The athlete does not show up at game time expecting to perfect their performance without the hours of proper training and preparation. Many children watching pro-sports on television believe these athletes perform and excel without paying the price of proper training to develop their high performance level. Whether it is college, pro, or youth sports, too often coaches are forced to tread too lightly. Today's athletes, regardless of their level and age, are different from yesteryear.

## Children of the 1930s through 1970s

We were fortunate to grow up during those years before lawyers, government and schools regulated our lives. Parents were not concerned about the perfect childhood. We started our day in public schools by reciting the Lord's Prayer, pledging allegiance to the flag, and singing a spiritual hymn.

Little League had tryouts, and not everyone made the team. Those who did not had to learn to deal with the disappointment. When we were disciplined in school, our parents actually sided with the teacher.

We drank water from the garden hose or stream and did not carry a bottle of processed water with us all day. We spent hours constructing go-carts, riding them down hills without brakes or wearing helmets on our heads. We fell out of trees, got cut, broke bones and yet we survived to play another day.

We played ice hockey with a cut tree limb and used a tin can for a puck, had bumps and bruises, and yet survived to play another day. We swam in streams and rivers (none of our friends had swimming pools), and yet we survived to play another day.

We had team snowball fights during the winter months with some cuts and black eyes, and enjoyed the camaraderie. We took three-mile bobsled rides down icy roads without helmets or seat belts, and it was the joy of winter. Yet we survived to play another day.

We did not have video games, cable TV with 200 channels, no VCRs, cell phones, personal computers, or Internet chat rooms. We had friends, and went outside to find them.

As kids, we had freedom, failure, success, and responsibility, and learned how to adapt to each.

My generation of children produced some of the most innovative engineers and inventors ever. Economic growth in the past fifty years was the result of this generation. As a group, middle-aged Americans, those born in the 1930s – 1950s have the highest college completion rates. Those Americans ages 25-34 have slipped from 1$^{st}$ to 10$^{th}$ place in college completion rates, not because fewer Americans are graduating from college, but because more students from other countries far surpass us in graduating from colleges.

A story relating to the generation gap … A teenager was telling a senior citizen why the older generation does not understand the younger. "You grew up in a primitive world," the teenager said. "We've got space travel, nuclear energy, cell phones and computers." Smiling, the old man replied, "You're right, we didn't have those things, that's why we invented them! So, what are you doing to bless and improve future generations?"

## Teenagers and High Schools

The decline in our educational system shows up more in high school years than grade school. A recent study indicates that a typical 9-year-old reads more each day than a 17-year-old does. The results come from the National Assessment of Educational Progress, a congressionally mandated standardized test. This shows that 17-year-olds' skills actually declined in both math and reading since 1999.[31]

Michael Cohen, president of Achieve, a group of governors and business leaders that helps states set up real world standards for schools, says, "We don't expect as much of our students as other nations. Even U.S. high school exit exams required in about half of all states rely on math that is less challenging.". Cohen states, "Mathematics and ways of thinking mathematically, and applying mathematical knowledge is an increasingly important set of skills to have in order to get access to good jobs." He says, "It's not enough for just our best kids to get access to good jobs. We need everybody."[32]

The academic skills of the typical U.S. 15-year-old are average compared with most of the industrialized world, but a larger proportion of American teens see themselves holding top-paying jobs in the future. When asked what kind of job they expect to hold by the time they are 30, 80.5% of U.S. students said they would have a 'white-collar, high skilled job' far exceeding the present national average of 62.2%. These expectations are likely the result of several factors:

1) At an early age, are our children's egos over-inflated from having done nothing to deserve it? Does this create an attitude of great expectations without their ability to accomplish much?

2) Are these studies revealing the results of children exposed to the age of electronic gadgets, television and computers?

3) Are our schools and teachers prepared to teach our students today?

4) Are our high school students the result of perfect childhoods created by their parents and, thus are not prepared to face the world?[33]

## High Expectations

We appreciate a gift when sacrifice is involved. If sacrifice is not part of that gift it is assumed a part of life and not appreciated. Many of our youth today do not realize what our past generations sacrificed so that they might have their freedoms today. They are not taught history at home or school, and assume that all our freedoms and conveniences have always been a part of American life. The perfect world philosophy to which our kids are exposed creates expectancy that America owes them their present lifestyles. This is one reason for their high expectations without sacrifice. This attitude is brought on by parents, and is continued when they go to college by the liberal left teachers who convince them that the government will take care of them.

Bill Gates, Microsoft's chairman, told a summit of state governors, "Our high schools, even when they are working exactly as designed, cannot teach our kids what they need to know today."[34]

In a speech given at a high school, Gates indicated how feel-good, politically correct teachings created a generation of kids with no concept of reality, and how this concept set them up for failure in the real world. He mentioned eleven rules that students did not, and will not learn in school.

**Rule #1:** Life is not fair – get used to it!

**Rule #2:** The world will not care about your self-esteem. The world will expect you to accomplish something BEFORE you feel good about yourself.

**Rule #3:** You will not make $40,000 a year right out of high school. You won't be a vice-president with a car phone until you earn both.

**Rule #4:** If you think your teacher is tough, wait till you get a boss!

**Rule #5:** Flipping burgers is not beneath your dignity. Your grandparents had a different word for burger flipping; they called it opportunity.

**Rule #6**:   If you mess up, it's not your parents' fault, so don't whine about your mistakes, learn from them.

**Rule #7**:   Before you were born, your parents weren't as boring as they are now. They got that way from paying all your bills, cleaning your clothes and listening to you talk about how cool you thought you were. So before you save the rain forest from the parasites of your parents' generation, try delousing the closet in your own room.

**Rule #8**:   Your school may have done away with winners and losers, but life HAS NOT. In some schools, they have abolished failing grades and they'll give you as MANY TIMES as you want to get the right answer. This doesn't bear the slightest resemblance of anything in real life.

**Rule #9**:   Life is not divided into semesters. You don't get summer off and very few employers are interested in helping you FIND YOURSELF. Do that on your own time.

**Rule #10**:  Television is NOT real life. In real life, people actually have to leave the coffee shop and go to jobs.

**Rule #11**:  Be nice to nerds. Chances are you'll end up working for one.[35]

## Colleges and College Students

Every country in the world is competing for a position in the global economy, only Americans are not aware of it. Psychologists report that human beings tend to put off necessary changes until the moment they begin to feel the pain. It is evident the pain created by our inability to educate our youth has not reached us yet. Like many aspects of our life in America, due to apathy and complacency we assume we will always be the world leader, much like the attitude of the citizens of the Roman Empire. While more Americans are graduating from college and more than ever are applying for admission, far fewer are gaining a higher education that prepares them for the competitive world.[36] Michael Gorman, President of the American Library Association said, "They're told to go to college in order to get a better job – and that's OK. But the real task is to produce educated people."[37]

World competition for jobs and industrial corporations becomes stronger every day. On a list of twenty developed nations, America ranks 16th in high school graduation rates and 14th in college graduation rates. This list of twenty nations does not include India and China, which are considered "developing" countries. However, everyone in education and industry knows that India and China are becoming America's most serious competitors.

Last year, the United States graduated 70,000 engineers, down 20% from 1985. China, by contrast, graduated 600,000 and India, 350,000. It is anticipated that in the next twenty years, 90% of the world's source of engineers will live in Asian countries.

China and India are expanding their university-level math, science and engineering programs at a pace comparable to the United States after World War II. Asian colleges now produce six times the number of engineering degrees produced in America. Despite being one-sixth the

U.S. population, South Korea graduates just as many engineers as we do. The top students in America's engineering schools are comprised of more than half foreign-born students.[38] The number of U.S. college undergraduates signing up for computer degrees is falling fast, causing concern to IBM, Intel and other tech companies that there soon will not be enough skilled U.S. workers to meet job demands. New enrollment in computer science and engineering programs has dropped for the last four years.[39]

Many low-level programming jobs have already been sent to such countries as India and China. However, high-level jobs combining technical and business skills are still in the U.S. That could change if there are not enough workers to fill them. Jack Rochart, Massachusetts Institute of Technology computer professor, says, "If we don't do anything, there are hundreds of thousands of Chinese and Indians who would love to have these jobs."[40]

Bill Gates, Microsoft's CEO, recently told the nation's governors, "I am terrified for our workforce of tomorrow." Gates pointed out that in 2001 India graduated a million more students from college than the United States did, while China has six times as many university students majoring in engineering. Many of those students are now staying in their own countries to work, saying "no" to U.S. jobs. As a result, U.S.-based companies are finding it increasingly attractive to build not only their manufacturing plants abroad, but their R&D operations as well.[41]

## Facts About College That Parents Should Know

Today's parents have tried to give their children the perfect childhood. It is important that parents are prepared and know what their children face as they enter college and the real world.

Thousands of freshmen entering college need to know the simple fact that they are not prepared to succeed. High school and college students are incapable of clearly written communications, with nearly half of all freshmen entering college requiring remedial English and math. This is the conclusion of a study released in 2004 by ACT, which administers the ACT College Admission test. Among 1.2 million high school seniors who took the test, most are not ready to tackle the math, science and literature courses they have signed up to take. Students are not taking the college preparation courses they need.

Even high school teachers and college professors differ on what courses are important for college entry. State learning standards may help high school teachers focus their coursework, but college faculty indicate they are focusing on the wrong things, creating a tremendous gap between what high school instructors teach, and what college faculty think entering freshmen ought to know.

Cyndie Schmeiser of the non-profit ACT of Iowa City states that aligning state standards is especially important, as more U.S. jobs demand a college education. Regarding what was most important for students to learn, the study found the following:

**Math**: 55% of college faculty stated that an understanding of fundamentals was more important as compared to 40% of high school teachers.

**English and Writing**: 35% of college instructors placed high importance on basic grammar and usage, such as sentence structure and punctuation, as compared with 18% of high school teachers.[42]

America, are we missing something? Even in our educational system, we are a divided nation, as different teaching philosophies direct our youth and our nation's future. The blame appears to be divided among students, parents, our educational system and government.  Students cannot be blamed for the watered-down courses, but they and their parents are responsible for not taking college preparation courses.

The annual High School Survey of Student Engagement found that most students skimp on homework, and spend far too much time socializing.  Although 80% of those surveyed expected to attend college, only 40% reported taking the college prep curriculum.[43]


## Information That Parents and High School Students Need to Know about College


Information on dining plans and intramural sports is everywhere, but data about graduation rates or instructional quality is hard to find.  Currently, parents and students have considerably more facts about what students know entering college (SAT scores, grade point average, etc.) than what they know upon completion.[44]

Parents cannot easily acquire this information.  Instead, they rely on data supplied by the school that often is self-serving.  Parents should know what their children are getting for the cost of tuition being paid to attend.  Because college costs have nearly doubled in the past twenty years, parents should know whether a college is better at graduating a student in four years rather than five.  Education should prepare our kids to be contributing members of our society.  The facts that I have previously listed, however, prove that this is not happening.  As our children go to higher levels of education, the circumstances worsen.[45]

In recent years, American universities have made an effort to overturn our culture and value system.  Through the efforts of the ACLU and leftist liberal extremists, young American students are being stripped of our traditional beliefs and values, and are being indoctrinated with atheistic views and socialism by colleges and universities. Universities have been successful through faculty members who teach socialism, and indoctrinate our students with their anti-Christian, anti-American philosophies. This movement has been one of the major reasons for the collapse of our educational standards and moral values today.

I personally know of college educators who have transferred colleges because of the socialistic, anti-Christian philosophy exposed by the administration of one college versus another.

David Horowicz, professor of philosophy at the University of Virginia, states that in a recent poll taken of Ivy League colleges to determine faculty political and civic affiliations on campus, "only 3% of the faculty in all the Ivy League identify themselves as Republicans. Forty-four percent (44%) named an organization that best represents their views as the ACLU. Zero percent (0%) identify with the Christian Coalition; one percent (1%) with the N.R.A."[46] So, to whose values are our students being exposed today?

This anti-Christian view and the decline in educational standards are far from what our forefathers intended. As mentioned previously, in the early years of college education, twenty-three of our first twenty-six universities and colleges were Christian schools.

Another poll shows that 57% of all university faculty members are Democrats, compared to 3% reported as Republicans. Sixty-four percent (64%) declared themselves as liberals, with six percent (6%) as Conservatives. Sixty-one percent (61%) of those teaching at universities want the federal government to solve more of the country's problems rather than individuals, communities or private enterprise.[47]

This is the anti-Christian philosophy being taught to our children, along with indoctrination toward socialism. This attitude created by college instructors describes where we are as a nation when we start depending on our government for our needs. This was the attitude of the Romans before the fall of their civilization.

## Students Are Suffocating from Debt and Loans

A new study indicates that rising college costs have increased the average debt burden of college students as more students from all income groups borrow more to finance their undergraduate studies. Undergraduate students borrow on average $19,000 from all sources, up $12,000 from ten years ago. Many undergraduates have debt exceeding $40,000.[48] These debts have huge implications for this generation of college graduates. The result of the debt is forcing many graduates to put off getting married, buying homes and saving for retirement, which affects our economy in many ways. Because of the high levels of student debt, more and more college graduates are moving back with their parents to save on their cost of living and to reduce their debt load.

## College Drinking Habits
## and the Consequences of Alcohol on Campus

Parents of students starting college are now getting a letter warning that high-risk drinking is the main reason students flunk out of college. According to 2002 research of college students between ages 18 and 24, the effects of alcohol go far beyond a hangover. Some alcohol-related statistics are:

- 1,400 students die each year from alcohol-related, unintentional injuries, including motor vehicle crashes. This figure is much greater per year than our military deaths in the war in Iraq.
- 500,000 college students are unintentionally injured while under the influence.
- More than 70,000 are victims of alcohol-related sexual assault or date rape.
- 400,000 students had unprotected sex, and more than 100,000 report having been too intoxicated to know whether they consented to having sex.
- About 25% of college students report academic consequences of their drinking, including missing class, falling behind, and performing poorly on exams.
- An estimated 110,000 are arrested for alcohol-related violations such as public drunkenness, or driving drunk.
- More than 600,000 students are assaulted annually by other students who have been drinking.[49]

### Teachers and Teachers' Unions

Trying to understand the reasons for the decline of our educational system, we have looked at historical facts regarding our founding fathers and our past. We have reviewed the present generation and how parents are raising children, and what is influencing today's students. Now, let us look at the teachers, the teachers' unions, the government, and how each contributes to the deficiencies in our nation's schools.

At the turn of the century, Americans did well without the National Education Association and the U.S. Department of Education, and were, in fact, better educated. Education at the time of Jefferson was provided in the home or in community schools under parental guidance.

Literary experts and educators say they are stunned by the results of a recent adult literary assessment, which shows that the reading proficiency of college graduates has declined in the past decade with no obvious explanation. The test measures how well adults comprehend basic instructions and tasks through reading. Only 31% of college graduates were proficient. This does not speak well for the other 69% of graduates. Mark S. Schneider, Commissioner of Education Statistics, said, "It may be that institutions have not yet figured out how to teach a whole generation of students who learned to read on the computer and who watch more TV. It's a different kind of literacy."[50]

Americans were among the most literate people on earth. Education of our young has always been a key factor to our greatness. Bill Gates, CEO of Microsoft, recently commented at the nation's governors meeting, "I am terrified for our workforce of tomorrow." Gates indicated that what is needed is public recognition that "America's high schools are obsolete compared to other countries. We should not only be alarmed but ashamed."[51]

## Low Expectations

A recent report released by Achieve Inc., a group created by the nation's governors and corporate leaders to help states raise educational standards, revealed a more troubling reason we are falling behind. We have institutional low performance because of low expectations. High schools expect only a small number of students to take the advanced math and science courses that young people need. All signs suggest that future requirements for high school completion may be even less challenging. Several states concerned about achievement rates are considering easing their graduation standards, even though their exit exams are now below the tenth-grade level.[52]

Albert Shanker, head of the nation's second largest teachers' union, the American Federation of Teachers, admitted, "that 95% of the kids who go to college in the United States would not be admitted to college anywhere else in the world".[53]

## School Budgets and Teachers' Unions

Do not blame school budgets. We shell out more than $440 billion each year on public education, and spend more per capita than any [other] nation. The problem is that too many of our high school science and math teachers are just not qualified. A survey in 2000 revealed 38% of math teachers and 28% of science teachers in grades 7 through 12 lacked a college major or minor in their subject matter. In schools with high poverty rates, the figures jumped to 52% of math teachers and 32% of science teachers, and in recent studies, things continued to get worse. Gerald Wheeler, executive director of the National Science Teachers Association says, "The highest predictor of student performance boils down to teacher knowledge. How can you pass on a passion to your students if you don't know the subject?"[54]

## Education (Teachers' Unions)

The teachers' unions continually send the message that not all of the millions of dollars spent and going almost exclusively to Democratic political candidates are part of some power grab.  It is all for the kids, they say, but the evidence clearly indicates that the teachers' unions and their Democratic allies are not serving the cause of education.  Their famous response is "we just need to keep doing what we're doing, but spend more money doing it."  The teachers' unions have one goal, and it is not to improve education.  They are dedicated to maintaining the status quo at any cost, even if it means sacrificing the next generation.[55]  They achieve their goal by buying off the Democratic Party.

The National Education Association's interest is to represent the Democratic Party's view on policy matters instead of representing the interests of its own teacher members.  The teachers' unions can get away with ignoring their members' real interests, not to mention what is good for education, because their funding source cannot be touched.  As long as teachers' unions can collect hundreds of millions of dollars from teachers, whether teachers want to pay or not, and use whatever portion of that money the unions choose to elect candidates and influence legislation at every level of government, genuine education reform has little chance of succeeding.

In the 1961-62 school years, the beginning of the teachers' union, the U.S. per pupil expenditure for public schools was $3,066.00.  In 2002, this figure rose to $9,354.00.  Recent figures are $12,000.00 per pupil.  Unions have also succeeded in getting school districts to hire more teachers.  In 1960, public schools had, on average, one teacher for every 25.5 students.  By 2001, the ratio had dropped to one teacher for every 15.9 pupils.[56]  If teachers' unions were so successful at getting more money for education, reducing class size and hiring more teachers, shouldn't there have been significant gains in academic achievement?

Our school educators and administrators have claimed that the problem is lack of funds, but three major studies from the Alexis de Tocqueville Institution show that these claims are false. Analyst John Berthoud observes, "No country or civilization in the history of the planet has spent more money educating its children." Yet with all the dollars flowing into our educational system, our children are being cheated of knowledge because the concern of the unions is not our kids but to secure benefits for themselves. "The net results," says John Berthoud, "is devastation for America's children."[57]

More spending is not the answer to education, especially at the federal level. In fact, federal spending has exploded over the past decades while education has declined. This nation spends a greater percentage of its gross national product on education than any other country except Israel, and yet, it is outperformed in math and science by more than ten nations, including the former Soviet Union. Less than half of federal education dollars go to pay for classroom instruction. Bureaucrats, instead of helping the kids, devour the funds.

The federal government has proposed new inroads into education by offering scholarships to college students if they complete a course of study in high school that has been approved by the U.S. Department of Education. Three political acts created by our government have failed in education: (1) in 1958, the National Defense Education Act, (2) the federal government came back with the Elementary and Secondary Education Act, which was passed to help struggling students, (3) other programs, including No Child Left Behind, were designed to 'solve' the educational crisis of that time. All that these programs accomplished was to expand the federal education bureaucracy and its power. These programs solved no real problems, but created new ones.[58]

Joe Williams, author of *Cheating Our Kids and How Politics and Greed Ruin Education,* states, "The unions are at their best fighting for teachers, not kids ... When you look at decisions we make regarding our schools, we often spend more time debating how they impact the adults than how they impact the kids. School system employees become conditioned to the idea that they will get their due, regardless of whether children get theirs."[59]

Public education is about politics; politics is about money and power. If parents want control over their children and their children's education, they need to be more demanding, and take the control from teachers and our government.

## Education Summary

Education was such a simple task in the early days of our nation. Today it has become so complex. The conventional wisdom today is that education is a responsibility of the federal government. We are caught up in a huge bureaucracy, with teachers' unions that serve many purposes except education. Education, as proven by our founding fathers, depends on responsive and loving parents. A study released by the Department of Education, "Strong Families, Strong Schools", indicates that the common-sense approach with parental involvement in education brings high student performance. Parents should be the ones most concerned about their children's education.[60]

Education should be the responsibility of the family and the states. Parents know the importance of moral values for their children. Those values were reinforced in this nation's homes and schools until 1962, when prayer was taken out of schools. Since that time, this country has experienced its most significant decline in moral values and education. Education was always a local tradition at home, church, and school where parents could and were allowed to participate.[61]

Today, it is nearly impossible for parents to determine what is being taught to their children. Recent polls indicate that a great majority of the people want states to have greater responsibility over education than our federal government. What Americans need is not a new federal education program, but the absence of all federal education programs. Our Constitution gives states and local government the right to set their own education policies, not the federal government. If Americans are to take the Constitution and the education of our children seriously, we need to wake up, reclaim our power and rights, and 'Just Say No' to federal control of education. If the Department of Education was abolished, and the millions of dollars supporting that department redirected to the states and American families, the monies would be used more wisely, and education better controlled.

Now we are putting America's future into the hands of people who we have entrusted to educate and prepare future generations for the leadership required in a global world. The collapse of the educational system and the moral decay of our value system will not only take away America's competitive position in the world, but will place us into a position similar to the last days of the Roman Empire.

We have already lost one generation through abortion. If we do not make the changes necessary to educate children properly and continue to ignore our educational system, we will have lost another generation of youth. Can America afford to lose two generations in a row and still expect to be a world leader? These two generations would be supporting and contributing to our economy, education, social security and the world today.

President Ronald Reagan said the following about education: "For a democracy to function, its people must understand not only reading, writing, and arithmetic, but literature, history and values. Someone once said that if you think education is expensive, you should try ignorance".[62] That sums up the situation pretty well. To be American means to understand that education is the key that opens the golden door of opportunity. No civilization can survive and grow if it does not learn the lessons of its own history.

# The Media

Americans' love affair with the media is growing more ardent each year. The U.S. Census Bureau predicts that Americans in 2009 will spend nearly half of their waking hours watching television, listening to the radio and reading various publications. They will invest 3,518 hours (146 days or 5 months) consuming media-generated "news". These numbers are the result of people multitasking as we go from television, computer, radio and reading the newspaper. We interact with the media more than any other activity in our lives.

Members of the media have subscribed to a code of conduct. Therefore, they have acknowledged to the American public that they have a special responsibility and a commitment to certain ethical standards. Truthfulness is the fulcrum of journalistic integrity. Without a guarantee of honesty in reporting, journalists and media outlets not only violate their own creed but risk loss of credibility in subsequent news stories. To some in the business, these seem to be risks worth taking.

Of all the institutions in America, only the media wields unbridled power. Not even our elected officials have access to such an exceedingly vast network of worldwide communications. The power to inform has become the power to alter, to interrupt, to abuse, to hinder, hide and confuse. Over time, the media exerts overwhelming influence on public opinion as wars are fought, budgets grow or shrink, taxes rise, governments topple, and society teeters. The American people – or any nation denying truthful reporting – are grossly disadvantaged and condemned to make uninformed or misinformed decisions. That is not conducive to the proper functioning of a free and democratic society.

Freedom of the press is guaranteed by our Constitution, and it is vital in America. However, the majority of American people have identified that the press has become too powerful, too irresponsible, and too biased. As a result, people are refusing to believe what they are being told by mainstream journalists.

There are a great number of Americans brainwashed by the media. This effect is known as the law of exposure. The media knows that what repeatedly enters a person's mind occupies it, shapes it, and in the end, expresses itself in what that person does and who he or she becomes. The mind will absorb and reflect whatever it is exposed to. The material that is read, the music that is listened to, the images that are seen, the thoughts that a person entertains all shape one's mind, and eventually, one's character and destiny.[1] Brainwashing is accomplished by exposing someone to repeated messages that are often twisted, or even evil. The media uses this method to convince individuals to accept the agenda they want to accomplish.

In one of the most comprehensive recent studies of its kind, the John S. and James L. Knight Foundation attempted to measure high school students' understanding of the First Amendment and free press.

The results:

- More than one-third (35%) said the First Amendment goes "too far" in the rights that it guarantees.
- 49% said newspapers should not be allowed to publish stories without prior government approval.[2]

These students, reflecting the results of our ill-managed educational system, will soon be of voting age and supporting the older generation. Our teachers should at least be teaching our children that freedom of speech is about empowering people, not government. Our First Amendment gives people the freedom of expression, and our democracy is a government of the people, for the people, and by the people.

We now live in times in which we have been brainwashed by the media and government; that our only hope is what the government can do for us. We have been led down a disturbing path that can only lead to socialistic chaos. Both the media and government believe that federal control is the answer to problem solving in America.

The results of two surveys conducted by Lichter, Rothman, and Lichtner, professors at George Washington University and Smith College, among 344 top media professionals polled indicate the following:

- 75% consider themselves politically liberal while 19% place themselves ideologically right up the center.
- 80% agree that homosexuality is an acceptable lifestyle, and an even larger proportion, 85%, uphold the right of homosexuals to teach children in public schools. (Only 9% felt strongly that homosexuality was wrong.)
- 97% believe women have the right to choose abortion.
- 86% of those polled seldom or never attend religious services, while 8% go to church or synagogue weekly.[3]

Those leading journalists surveyed supported women's rights, homosexual rights and sexual freedom.[4] This liberal press (out of touch with the public opinion) is the same group responsible for sharing the minds of the American population. The final item of the survey indicated that 66% of journalists believe that television and all media should be a major force for social reform.

## Politics & the Media

For many years, conservative ideas were not accepted by the three major television networks; CBS, NBC and ABC. They followed the liberal direction on foreign policy, national defense, economics and social issues. A recent poll shows that the media donates nine (9) times more money to the liberal Democratic Party than to conservative Republicans. With donations so partial toward one party, how can the media be fair and unbiased? This explains why conservatives, such as George W. Bush, are always the victims of the most unfavorable headlines. Our presidential election of 2004 was a great example how the media tried to engineer and manipulate the outcome of an election.

The film *Fahrenheit 911* was made for political reasons. This movie was purposely produced to mislead the public and sway the presidential election. The media changes many of our citizens' opinions whether the message content is correct or not. There seems no end to Hollywood's extreme liberal agenda. They must come to realize that it is not a political party.

Competent journalism is falling apart, as new corruption has taken place in the media over the past couple of years. *The New York Times, USA Today,* and CBS faltered in providing good supervision over proper reporting. In the case of the *New York Times* and *USA Today,* writers deliberately made up stories. CBS carelessly accepted bogus documents alleging that George W. Bush dodged his duties in the Texas Air National Guard. CBS was warned that the documents were suspicious and could be a problem, but its producers ignored the warning. This incident was identified by Internet bloggers who have access to endless information in which they can inform the public. This false reporting damages all journalism, and only confirms that the news media cannot be trusted. The job of the media is to report factual news, not fabricate the news. Personal opinions should not enter into news reports.

In the 2008 presidential election, the mainstream media finally accomplished the objective they have been trying to attain for several years. They greatly influenced the outcome of a presidential election. A double standard was obvious in the news media including television, magazines and newspapers.

The media showed partiality as they promoted the Democratic Party. They did what was necessary to influence, misinform and confuse the public, by promoting their own liberal agenda in an attempt to sway the election.

Negative stories about McCain were three to one versus Obama. This ratio persisted throughout the entire campaign as the media portrayed a negative picture of the Republican Party. There was no limit in their attempts to assassinate the characters of Sarah Palin and "Joe the plumber".

Truth was camouflaged as the media attempted to ridicule and destroy anyone who stood in the way of their own agenda.

The media in all forms is out-of-step with the public, much like our politicians, with both having big egos and focusing on power. The Annenberg Public Center at the University of Pennsylvania conducted a national survey of 673 journalists and 1500 adults. The survey revealed a great difference between how well journalists ant the public think news organizations do in admitting mistakes: 74% of journalists said their outlets quickly report serious errors, while only 30% of the public thinks so. The study also highlights a social divide on same-sex marriages, with 59% of journalists favoring them, compared to 28% of the public. Nine percent (9%) of journalists claim to be conservative, compared with 38% of the public.[5]

Several once-popular newspapers and magazines have become so radical with irresponsible reporting that the American public has refused to read their publications. Some proof lies in their financial reports, which have shown a significant loss of revenue over the past several years.[6]

## The Media and Sensationalism

The media know that sensationalism and negative messages sell newspapers and television. If the messages they sell are negative, such as crimes, accidents, and national catastrophes, then the mindset of our citizens becomes a reflection of the news. This may be one of the reasons that 69% of Americans are discontented with their lives. At the same time, good, pro-American stories and other positive newsworthy reports are placed in the back sections of newspapers because of bias.

An example of this relates to the war in Iraq. We always hear of the negative results of the war instead of promoting the positive results to the public, such as democratic elections now held in Iraq, an improved economy, or the building of an organized military. The media report the negative side of every story to sell their products. As of this writing, there has been an average of 160,000 troops in the Iraq Theater of Operation over the past 22 months, with 2,112 deaths. This results in a firearm death rate of 60 per 100,000 soldiers. The firearm death rate in Washington, DC, was 80.6 per 100,000 for the same period. That means you are 25% more likely to be shot and killed in the U.S. capital than you are in Iraq. Maybe we should pull out of Washington, DC, instead of Iraq.

Unfortunately, by stressing the negative news, the media accomplish the following:

1) They undermine the world's perception of the United States, therefore minimizing support for the war effort.

2) They intend to discourage American citizens and their support of the war.

3) They intend to help the Democratic Party gain more power in the next elections.

The media realize that sensationalism sells newspapers, movies and television. They are not concerned about the aftereffects that their news stories and movie content have on our moral standards and culture. The media tear into the lives of personalities in the name of sensationalism.

A prime example of how starved the media are for news and their use of sensationalism is obvious when the television networks flood the airways with stories about Brittany Spears, Anna Nicole Smith, and Rosie O'Donnell, as well as Brad Pitt (and his girlfriend), or whether Paris Hilton should be kept or released from jail. They use the "law of exposure" by repeating these stories nightly to dominate the viewers' minds with personality hype stories that should not even be newsworthy.

Due to their relentless efforts to create sensationalism, the media have created a "copycat behavior" in this nation because of how they present the news. Continued overexposure of non-stop coverage of crimes and evil is brainwashing the minds of individuals. This repeated exposure will eventually shape a person's mind, character and destiny. Those who are vulnerable to such messages will then commit the same type of crime for publicity or a thrill.

Similarities between the Virginia Tech and Columbine High School massacres are reflected in the videos, photos and angry writings of the assailants. The words and behavior of Virginia Tech gunman, Cho Seung Hue, parallel the words and behavior of Eric Harris and Dylan Klebold of Columbine. Both showed their weapons on the videotapes, and used profanity while condemning their schoolmates. Because of continued overexposure by our media with non-stop detailed coverage of the Virginia Tech massacre, "copycat behavior" occurred that same week in our nation's schools:

- A 12,000-student school district in Yuba City, California, was locked down as authorities searched for a man they say threatened to make the Virginia Tech massacre look "mild by comparison."
- In Kalamazoo, Michigan, a threat posted on an online blog concerned Kalamazoo Valley Community College officials enough that they shut down the campus for a week.
- Classes were cancelled at a Catholic high school near Ann Arbor, Michigan, after police discovered the words "Virginia Tech Today" written on a bathroom wall.
- In St. Augustine, Florida, a 14-year-old high school student was charged with a felony for an email between friends that said, "I will top the Virginia Tech massacre by killing 100 people."
- Eight buildings at the University of Minnesota were evacuated after a professor discovered a bomb threat.

This 'copycat behavior' cannot be coincidental when all the afore-mentioned incidents occurred within a week at various locations in our nation. I believe this is proof of the irresponsibility shown by the media, and their craving of sensationalism in the news.

Female schoolteachers who have had sexual relationships with their students have shown the same "imitating behavior" over the past several years. The news media, through their methods of exploiting such incidents, have created a damaging effect on the moral standards of America.

Sensationalism shows to the extreme when most of the major television networks broadcast gruesome footage of crimes committed in Iraq by terrorists. News of the war needs to be reported to the public, but common sense also has to be a priority in reporting the war. The beheading of U.S. hostage Paul Johnson flooded the networks. This video was actually provided by the terrorists and sent to U.S. media sources. The terrorists realized how vulnerable the U.S. media are, and they were correct. Our TV networks gave the terrorists free airtime with the display of this crime over the networks.[7]

## Hollywood

A group of extreme liberal elite, with a negative opinion of our value system, currently represents Hollywood. This group of Hollywood producers and actors wants the nation to know that it has all the correct answers to our society.

Why do the Hollywood award shows become less popular every year? The Oscars and the Golden Globe awards have continued to decline in popularity due to movie content and Hollywood's finished product. The majority of Americans believe that Hollywood is out of touch with America.

In the early days of Hollywood, movie producers turned out films that made Americans feel good. We enjoyed films that represented our nation and the American Dream. The movies supported the wars, American history and God. After the 1960s, Hollywood started to rebel, as films no longer represented the morality and value system of our nation. The filmmakers began to flood movie theaters with sex and violent films. There is no reason why gay characters should be featured more often than religious people in today's movies other than to promote their anti-Christian agenda. Mel Gibson's film, "Passion of the Christ" earned the third largest amount in revenues in 2004 – $370 million dollars. This film was essentially blackballed in Hollywood and was not nominated for any major awards, because of its religious and moral content, which was against Hollywood's liberal anti-Christian way of life.

## Morality and the Media

In the early years of our nation, most newspapers were owned and published by Christians. The Bible and newspaper were both read daily by well-informed public. Today, the media are hourly selling to the U.S. citizen that evil is good, and good is evil. The anti-Christian philosophy continues to corrupt the minds of Americans. God has been removed from our daily lives by the media and big government is promoted as our source of hope.

A new survey examining America's values and the influence of the media finds that 68%, including majorities of virtually every demographic group, believe the media, entertainment and news alike, are having a detrimental effect on moral values in America. The Culture and Media Institute, based in Alexandria, Virginia, says its aim is to "preserve and help restore America's culture, character, traditional values, and morals against the assault of the liberal media elite."[8]

News programs, such as the majority of shows on television today, are anti-Christian in their views. Producers, editors and even news anchors have an agenda against Biblical values, and show liberal bias.

Benjamin Franklin, one of America's most influential and famous founding fathers who was also a scientist, author and printer, said, "A Bible and a newspaper in every house, a good school in every district – all studied and appreciated as they merit – are the principal support of virtue, morality, and civil liberty."[9]

Since the 1960s, our increasingly secular nation and the media, has openly attack our nation's conservative leaders and advocate disobedience to God. These narrow-minded groups are dragging down America. They want to reshape our nation to fit their agendas.

You have a choice! You can continue to expose yourselves to agendas of the secular media, which continue to abandon the traditions of our founding fathers and nation. On the other hand, you can stop listening, reading and watching the messages of the newspapers, magazines, movies and television. The bottom line has the greatest effect on these groups. It is all about money, and without the profits, they can no longer continue their assault on America.

The media keep us informed of the news, but misinformed of the truth. We live in times in which we have been brainwashed by the media and our government, (that our only hope is in what the government can do for us). Both have led us down a disturbing path, that can only lead to chaos. Both believe that federal control is the answer to problem solving in America. Remember – government dependency only creates more problems, as seen in the days of the once great Roman Empire.

# The Judiciary System

## What Our Founders Intended

W hen setting up our government, the founders were very familiar with England's system, where justice for the people was difficult, and sometimes unjust due to the monarchy. Therefore, a fair judiciary system was important to the founding fathers. They divided government into three branches: executive, legislative and judicial. They designed into our government a system of checks and balances so no one branch would have control over the other. The founders made it clear that the purpose of the courts were to insure that justice prevails for everyone. When writing the United States Constitution, they stressed justice second only to forming a perfect union.

Our Constitution reads as follows:

> *We the people of the United States, in order to form*
> *a more perfect union, establish justice, insure domestic*
> *tranquility, provide for the common defense, promote*
> *the general welfare and secure the blessings of liberty*
> *to ourselves and our posterity, do ordain and establish*
> *this Constitution of the United States of America.*

Our founding fathers realized that everything listed in the Constitution, such as common defense and domestic tranquility, could only happen successfully if justice was first established. In setting up the three branches of government, our founders' main concern was the judiciary branch.

It was the duty of Congress to establish the Supreme Court and, through the appointment and authority of the President, to see that justices were chosen to serve the people.

## Justices and Judges

Individuals chosen to serve on the bench, whether appointed or elected, whether federal or local, were to be faithful interpreters of the law. They were to be students of the law with no legislative or executive functions.

Our founders impressed that the courts were designed to administer law, not to make it. Judges at all levels were to be experienced in jurisprudence, morality and discipline. They were given the power to settle disputes and resolve matters of controversy.

Justices of the Supreme Court and judges in all the inferior courts in America would be dependent upon the executive and legislative branches, and equal to them in their constitutional responsibilities. The founders were concerned about judicial behavior that judges are under the scrutiny of the other branches, but always subject to the will of the people who have final say in our form of government. Supreme Court judges were to have a high degree of freedom, job security and a guaranteed income. Supreme Court judges were to be non elected, accountable to no one, and serve on the Court for life. They were given these liberties to insure their independence from undue influence.

Their tenure in the court was to be secure only if "good behavior" was maintained. The average age of our justices today is 70 years old. As our population lives longer, we could have justices serving who are over 100 years of age. There is no way to remove these justices except our Constitution gives authority to the people to remove justices on the grounds of impeachment.

### How Court Decisions Have Changed Our Nation

The Supreme Court today is involved in all aspects of our lives. The decisions of this group can influence the direction of America's society and culture by setting policies for our entire nation. The following landmark decisions made by the federal courts over the past 45 years have affected our way of life:

### June 17, 1962   Engle v. Vitale

The Supreme Court restricts prayer in school. This decision by the court to take prayer out of school was based on the court's interpretation of a letter written by Thomas Jefferson.

Our modern courts have interpreted the subject of "separation between church and state" not on the words of the Constitution, but on a letter written by Thomas Jefferson, which was addressed to the Danbury, Connecticut Baptist Association on January 11, 1802. Jefferson stated,

> *Believing with you that religion is a matter which lies solely between man and God, that he owes account to none other for his faith or his worship, that the legislative powers of government reaches actions only, and not opinions, I contemplate with sovereign reverence that an act of the whole American people which declared that their legislature should make no law respecting an*

*establishment of religion or prohibiting the free expression thereof; thus building a wall of separation between church and state.*

Jefferson was specifically referring to the "whole American people", meaning the federal government could not impose a national church. As Jefferson explained later in his letter to the Danbury Baptist Association, "Certainly no power to prescribe any religious exercise or to assume authority and religious discipline has been delegated to the general government. It must then rest with the states as far as it can be in any human authority."[1]

What the federal government was prohibited from doing, in Jefferson's view, was prescribing a particular set of religious rites or promoting a particular religious sect at the expense of others. Nowhere in the Constitution does it state that the federal government has any power to address issues of establishment of religion. In fact, it clearly forbids it to do so.

Did you know that every session of Congress begins with a prayer by a compensated preacher whose salary has been funded by the taxpayers since 1777? Is it not ironic that prayer is okay for our politicians in Congress, but our judiciary system has deemed it not necessary and unacceptable for the nation's youth to have prayer in school?

The very first Supreme Court justice, John Jay, said, "Americans should select and prefer Christians as their leaders." It is also interesting that of the 55 founders of the Constitution, 52 were members of the established orthodox churches of the colonies.

### January 17, 1980 - Stone v. Graham

The Supreme Court strikes down a Kentucky statute requiring display of the Ten Commandments in public schools.

### July 1, 2003 – Glassroth v. Moore

The 11th U.S. Circuit Court of Appeals rules that a monument to the Ten Commandments placed on Alabama's judiciary building must be removed.

Both of these decisions are contrary to what is represented and expressed on and in the Supreme Court building.

Did you know as you walk up the steps to the building that houses the Supreme Court, you see the following: near the top of the building is a row of the world's lawgivers; in the middle is one fully facing front; it is Moses and he is holding the Ten Commandments.

Upon entering the Supreme Courtroom, two huge oak doors have the Ten Commandments engraved on the lower portion of each door.

As you sit inside the courtroom, you can see the wall, right above where the Supreme Court judges sit, where the Ten Commandments are displayed.

Again, it makes no common sense. Our judges are saying, "Don't do what we do, but do what we tell you to do." What is an accepted environment for them is not for the public. Our government can have the exposure of prayer and the Ten Commandments, but not the common citizen.

### January 22, 1973 – Roe v. Wade

The Supreme Court finds that the right to personal privacy includes abortion. This was a devastating decision that has resulted in the killing of more than 48 million babies over the past 35 years. This is like erasing the countries of Canada and Cuba off the face of the earth.

This decision has resulted in eliminating an entire generation through abortion. Some of these babies could have been decision makers, perhaps a great inventor, physician, or scientist. We will never know!

One certain result is that these 48 million babies would have definitely been a great contribution to our society and economy as citizens, wage earners and consumers.

The deficit that we are currently running in our social security program could have been rectified by this generation of aborted babies. It is also sad that there are not enough adoptable babies in our nation available to meet the demand of parents wanting children. Therefore, many parents go to other nations in search of adoptable children.

## Where Did the Courts Get Their Authority for These Decisions?

Thomas Jefferson's greatest fear was that the courts would overstep their authority, and instead of interpreting the law, would begin making law – an oligarchy, a form of government in which a few have control over many. His fear has become a way of life for our judiciary system. The Supreme Court has taken upon itself the power to interject its authority into all aspects of our lives. The federal judiciary system has gained more influence over our lives than any other branch of government. The courts have made decisions overruling Congress and our President. Nowhere in the U.S. Constitution is this power given to the Supreme Court.

The justices are abusing their constitutional mandate by incorporating their own beliefs and biases. Judges change laws based on their personal whims, not necessarily on what is right, wrong or constitutional. In most cases, law is being made without the public going to the ballot box, or in many cases, without it even being aware of these decisions. The courts with their present authority inject a form of tyranny into our representative form of government and personal freedoms.

There are two kinds of judges: the "originalists" who abide and carry out the intent of our original framers of the Constitution; and the "activist" judges who consider the Constitution as a document of open text, using it as a directive that enables them to express and substitute their own views. They see the Constitution as a power source to use their own interpretation in order to achieve a desired outcome.[2]

Edwin Meese III, Attorney General under President Ronald Reagan, said, "The American people will never be able to regain democratic self-government – and thus shape public policy – until we curb activist judges." Not only do these activist judges consider themselves a higher law than the Constitution, but they have also circumvented the Commandments of our Creator.

The liberal media has played a significant part in changing our judicial direction. Columnist Thomas Sowell wrote: "One of the reasons judicial activists get away with ignoring the law and imposing their own pet notions instead is that much of the mainstream media treat the actions of judges as automatically legitimate and all criticism of them as undermining the rule of law."[3]

## Influence of International Law

We need to appoint judges who apply the law rather than make the law, and who follow the Constitution rather than make decisions based on their own ideals and opinions or reference foreign courts. In recent years, the Supreme Court is departing from employing the U.S. Constitution to interpret U.S. law and is relying on international law and opinion as the basis for legal decisions.[4]

In a recent quote from Justice Anthony Kennedy, he clearly stated that the Court would increasingly look abroad for guidance in interpreting our Constitution. He pointed out that the Court would be referring "to the laws of other countries and to international authorities as instructive for its interpretation" of the Constitution.[5]

Supreme Court Justice Ruth Bader Ginsburg said, "Our island or lone ranger mentality is beginning to change." She added that justices "are becoming more open to comparative and international law perspectives."[6]

Justice Stephen Breyer has cited the countries of Jamaica, India and Zimbabwe in his decisions, along with references to the European Court of Human Rights and the British Parliament.

Our Constitution is unique; it has guided America through 230 years of freedom and prosperity. Does not history give us a road map to follow along with our Constitution? Why should we depend on the rule of any other nation? Our American legal system guarantees our freedom, because it is based on Judeo-Christian beliefs.

As emphasized in the chapter on "A Godly Nation," values and morality must be taught, but cannot be taught without religion. There cannot be moral law without a belief in the Divine Creator.

William Henry Seward, member of Congress and later Secretary of State under President Lincoln, said the following about higher law:

> *There is a higher law than the Constitution, which*
> *regulates our authority over the domain, and devotes*
> *it to the noble purposes. The territory is a part,*
> *no inconsiderable part, of the common heritage of*

*mankind, bestowed upon them by the Creator of the Universe. We are His stewards, and must so discharge our trust as to secure in the highest attainable degree their happiness.*[7]

Unfortunately, this high level of reverence and ideals of the founders has been lost over the years. The Supreme Court of unelected judges over the past 50 years has taken upon themselves to be the higher law of not only our judiciary system, but also our land and all of humankind.

From the very beginning of American history, the founders declared our rights and freedoms to be given us by God, unlike other nation's laws, which are government-based. If our nation's heritage is to endure, our law cannot be replaced by the law of foreign countries that fail to acknowledge the God of the Bible, as proven by France when the French government was in the middle of its revolution.

Since the French Revolution, France has gone through 28 changes in its government's direction. Italy has endured 38 changes. History gives us a guide or roadmap to follow. Why should a nation with our constitutional success for 230 years depend on the rule of any other nation?

Wake up, America! We are in the midst of a moral crisis in America due in part to federal court decisions. Since the decision by the courts to take prayer out of school our nation has been in a steady moral decline. Since the Roe v. Wade decision on January 22, 1973, a whole generation of citizens has been eliminated due to abortion.[8] This confirms the effect that this court decision had on the decline of morality in this nation.

When judges throw prayer and the Ten Commandments out of our lives, they are interjecting their personal form of religion into our culture. If that religion is without God, then it is atheistic in its view. Our founders' vision of religious freedom is being eliminated by the government's judiciary system. The courts and politicians are denying us our inherited spiritual foundation, and the ability to express publicly a reverence to the Creator.

Religious freedoms and heritage are being squeezed out of our lives by unelected anti-Christian judges. The Constitution reads that government does not have the right to establish a religion for the people. Perhaps judges need to re-familiarize themselves with the contents of the Constitution.

The Supreme Court has virtually abolished a citizens right to exercise freedom of religion in public. Unless citizens and Congress make the courts accountable, this freedom will be forever lost.

Abraham Lincoln said, "The candid citizen must confess that if the policy of government, upon vital questions, affecting the whole people, is to be irrevocably fixed by decisions of the Supreme Court ... the people will have ceased to be their own rulers, having to that extent, practically resigned their government into the hands of that eminent tribunal."[9]

Beware, America! As in the days of the French Revolution and the end days of other civilizations, the last phase of an empire is when tyrants are in rule, and the citizens are in bondage.

## Lawyers and Lawsuits

Fifty years ago, law practice in the United States involved either criminal or contractual cases. There were very few lawsuits over defective materials or product. Liability lawsuits against companies regarding product use were a rarity.

Very few Americans sued each other. However, we have become an impatient nation; we want everything right now. We have become a society of "get rich quick" and "get even" attitudes. In 2004, there were over 300,000 lawsuits in America, as compared to 300 in Great Britain. Two hundred eighty (280) billion dollars were awarded to law firms, because of court cases. Twenty-three percent of that amount went to recipients, and 67% went to law firms and lawyers. Lawsuits in this nation have become the new "get rich quick" way of life for attorneys. It is the new "no lose" lottery that fills their pockets with money.

How did this change in our legal system evolve? It all happened through tort litigations. Tort is a legal term for non-criminal wrongs, a wrongful act resulting in injury to another person, property, or reputation for which the injured party is entitled to seek compensation. Tort lawsuits affect the tobacco, asbestos and medical fields. It practically overlaps every area of our lives. The typical U.S. citizen is unaware of how this affects our way of life and cost of living.

Today's liability insurance costs for corporations and professional people run into billions of dollars per year, all for protection against tort lawsuits. These costs are then passed onto the American consumer along with court costs incurred by lawyers to litigate these cases.

It has created a profession of lawyers and law firms who have become opportunists with the goal of creating huge bank accounts for themselves. These laws have made it possible for attorneys to become the only winners in class action lawsuits, with the original plaintiffs receiving only token amounts.[1]

The American legal system is completely out of control. Predatory trial lawyers and biased judges who allow frivolous lawsuits fleece businesses out of billions of dollars yearly. The effect tort litigations have on the economy is enormous. Many business owners, as well as private citizens, live in fear of lawsuits. Most cases start for trivial reasons, including minor accidents, side effects from foods, falling on one's property or in a recent case, spilling coffee on one's lap at a fast food restaurant. To illustrate my point, I will mention some recent cases.

A customer sued a dry cleaning company, because he claimed his pants were not properly dry-cleaned. The lawsuit was for 58 million dollars, and it cost the dry cleaner $100,000.00 to defend itself.

Another typical example is a recent personal injury case in Buffalo, NY. The plaintiff was forced to retire from her New York State job after 28 years of service because of a nasty fall she took in an icy parking lot. She thought she had protected herself by hiring a personal injury attorney. The settlement prompted by the lawyers was for $35,000.00. The case never went to trial. The amount actually received was broken down as follows:

Lawyers' Share: $10,000.00

Lawyers' Expenses: $3,600.00

NY State Workers Comp: $21,000.00 (to repay workers comp)

The client's share was a check for $6.60; just enough to buy a gallon and half of gas.[2] This is a perfect example of what is wrong with the legal profession, and why lawyers are the only winners.

Our family has a small "cut-your-own" Christmas tree farm. To protect ourselves, it takes 15-20% of our tree sales just to cover our yearly liability insurance costs. This insurance is required for the following reasons: should a customer's tree catch on fire at their own home, or if it falls off their car while transporting it home, or if a customer stumbles in our fields while looking for a tree. Americans look at lawsuits as a means of gaining wealth without cost to themselves. Little do they realize the expenses they are creating to the American public as well as for themselves. We pay dearly for court costs, more expensive consumer products, and liability insurance. The only winners are the lawyers.

The medical field is a perfect example of how the patient or consumer is paying a great price out of their pocket due to tort lawsuits. Fear of being sued leads many doctors to practice "defensive medicine", such as ordering unnecessary tests and avoiding risky procedures. Physicians often abandon their best judgment if they think a test might protect them in a malpractice lawsuit. Such defensive medicine such as unneeded CT scans, biopsies and hospitalizations cost the public dearly. These practices cost the public at least 60 billion dollars a year, as reported by the Department of Health and Human Services, all paid for by our insurance premiums.

In a survey of doctors, 93% admit to averting risks by use of defensive medicine.[3] Many vaccines and potential life-saving drugs never reach the marketplace because of potential litigation would create a situation where profits would not be enough to cover the litigation costs.

Our medical expenditures continue to grow each year due to government regulation agencies and litigation costs. Common sense and reason must be restored to our society. No product or industry can withstand a zero deficit environment. Side effects of medicines are not always known. Each of us reacts differently to various medicines. Side effects can happen to anyone. In the meantime, the medicine being used might save millions of lives. If your life is saved but you have a slight side effect, resulting from the medicine you are taking does not mean you should sue the doctor, drug company or hospital. Instead, be grateful you are alive. Common sense in law and litigation must be applied.

Today with tort litigation, the accuser does not have to prove the guilt of the accused. The burden falls on the defendant to prove he is innocent, and in the case of medication, that the drug did not cause death.

Our lack of common sense in today's lawsuits and courts is disappearing. Thousands of people may die, because the courts have favored one person who had a side effect from a drug. Remember, companies are in business to make money; that is how they finance their research. If a product is going to cost more than it can return in profits, it will not reach the consumer. The average lawsuit in the medical field is over $320,000.00 per case.

The number of obstetricians has declined in recent years. One out of seven has quit due to the cost of liability insurance. We need more people pursuing professions in medicine, industry, and science. What lawsuits have done to these occupations is devastating to the economy, as well as to those seeking careers.

If tort lawsuits had existed 100 years ago in the U.S., we would not be the leading industrialized nation we are today. The costs incurred by manufacturers for liability insurance, legal fees to prevent potential lawsuits, and government control to design, test and market consumer products would have limited our product development over the years. This cost to entrepreneurs and small business owners would have prevented many products from reaching the marketplace.

Tort control is so threatening to U.S. manufacturers that it is driving businesses from America to other countries such as China, India and Japan. This legal mentality in our culture is determined to destroy America's industrial base in its quest for wealth.

Entrepreneurship has always been, and still is our nation's greatest asset in developing new products. Small business is the greatest source of jobs today. The freedom of entrepreneurship has always been America's greatest avenue to new technology. If courts and lawsuits continue making it difficult for young entrepreneurs and businesses to expand by limiting their abilities through lawsuits and regulations, we will no longer be the world leader in new product technology.

The most successful individuals and companies become targets for litigation. Lawyers target these companies and individuals due to their success and wealth. Unscrupulous lawyers are always looking for new prey as they seek loopholes and weaknesses for potential lawsuits.

## Lawyers and Politicians

Politicians and lawyers in Washington have gained enormous power and influence through the court system. No longer is litigation about justice, but a method of gaining campaign dollars. Lawyers, unions, Hollywood, and radical leftist judges have all become part of the same team that has joined in the goals of the Democratic Party. One of the greatest sources of campaign money received by the Democratic Party comes from these sources. This influx of money to this party has made it very difficult to effect tort reform by our Congress. A majority of Congress are lawyers, turned politicians who take care of their own. It has become a game of reciprocation. Washington has more than twice as many lawyers per resident as other large cities in the U.S.[4] The practicing lawyers donate heavily to political campaign funds so that regulation of tort and class action lawsuits will remain unchanged. The lawyers do not want change in this lucrative system of litigation.

In the last several years, Congress failed to denounce frivolous lawsuits or to put a limit on tort litigation rewards. A case in point occurred in 1987 when President Ronald Reagan nominated Robert Bork to a Supreme Court vacancy. One of Bork's conservative goals was to enforce tort reform. This was to reduce frivolous lawsuits, and to set a limit on the amount lawyers could litigate. In Bork's opinion, tort litigation was strictly driven by greed, not common sense. The Democratic Congress, whose reason was to protect its fellow lawyers favoring tort litigation, denied Bork's nomination. This atmosphere in Washington for lawyers and politicians has created an injustice to the American people.

Practicing law at one time was a very prestigious profession. However, as the nation has aged, the integrity of lawyers has dropped to a new low in our society. They have lost their respectability, as lawyers have become opportunists with the goal of gaining wealth for themselves. Lawyers have become terrorists in disguise. They have been a cancer to our legal system through the love of money.

In the U.S., we have 30 more lawsuits per capita than in Japan. The Japanese spend .4% of their gross national product on litigation, compared to America's 2.6%. According to the American Tort Reform Association (ATRA), the hidden burden behind product litigation costs the average family about $3,600 per year. This does not take into account other associated costs, such as insurance premiums and medical visitations, etc. This cost to families is like an additional tax every year, with the greatest amounts being paid to lawyers. Litigation has increased the sales price of the following items:

| Car | 4% |
|---|---|
| Motorcycles | 17% |
| Football helmet | 35% |
| Oral vaccines | 135% [5] |

Webster's Dictionary defines a vulture as a bird that soars high, looking unscrupulously for its next prey. Likewise, lawyers from their once-prestigious past now outnumber the vultures as they circle this nation greedily looking for their next victims. The U.S. has 70% of the world's population of practicing lawyers. The reason is tort litigation laws. The new tort legislation has been the lawyers' best friend. Predatory trial lawyers and law firms advertise over the radio, television and on roadside billboards: "If you are injured at work or have an accident, call us." Lawyers, instead of chasing ambulances as they once did, are now using the media to create more and more lawsuits annually. This sort of advertising has only cheapened their occupation and law as a career while adding tremendous costs to our way of living.

One reason the U.S. Constitution is so brief is that the framers never visualized a nation in which the only people capable of determining whether laws have been broken were lawyers. The founding fathers believed that common sense, not our legal system, ought to determine guilt or innocence, which is why we are so adamant about the right of trial by jury. Law students no longer study higher law principles, which was the way of thinking of Jefferson and the colonists. The result is increasing ambiguity in our society over what constitutes right and wrong.[6]

The following is an excerpt from an anonymous email message that I received concerning common sense:

## *A Remarkable Obituary*

*Today we mourn the passing of a beloved old friend, Mr. Common Sense. Mr. Sense had been with us for many years. No one knows for sure how old he was, since his birth, records were lost long ago in bureaucratic red tape. He will be remembered as having cultivated such value lessons as knowing when to come in out of the rain, why the early bird gets the worm, and that life isn't always fair. Common Sense lived by simple, sound financial policies (don't spend more than you earn) and reliable parenting strategies (adults, not children, are in charge.) His health began to rapidly deteriorate when well intentioned, but overbearing regulations were set in place – reports of a six-year-old boy charged with sexual harassment for kissing a classmate; teens suspended from school for using mouthwash after lunch; and a teacher fired for reprimanding an unruly student, only worsened his condition. Mr. Sense declined even further, when schools were required to get parental consent to administer aspirin to a student, but could not inform the parents when a student became pregnant and wanted to have an abortion. Finally, Common Sense lost the will to live, as the Ten Commandments became contraband, churches became businesses, criminals received better treatment than their victims did and after a woman failed to realize that a steaming cup of coffee was hot. She spilled the coffee in her lap, and was awarded a huge financial settlement.*[7]

Again it is all about money and control in Washington. Republicans have long sought limit of tort litigation lawsuits on big business, which normally contributes to Republican political campaigns. On the other hand, the Democrats have traditionally focused more on the side of consumers to pursue lawsuits. The Democratic Party in turn received a great percentage of their campaign funds from the personal injury lawyers. The result is wealthy lawyers and Congressmen who enjoy long-term, elaborate lifestyles in Washington as our representatives, all being paid by us, the U.S. consumer.

Not only do attorneys canvass the business world for product failures, but they also search for court locations most favorable to their clients and the results they seek. In certain locations and regions of our country, small town judges have biased opinions toward small business owners and large corporations. The trial lawyers know these locations, and time after time go to these judges for favorable results for them and their clients. Such courts are unfair and act as a "radar trap" inside our country's litigation highway.

The citizens of this nation need to take a stand. We must take back control of our government. The legal system is completely out of control. If it is appropriate for plaintiffs and their attorneys to seek damages from defendants through lawsuits, then it should be equally appropriate for defendants to be compensated by plaintiffs and their attorneys in the event that the defendants are exonerated. This would be fairer, and a means of leveling the playing field.

Citizens need to: join with pro-business groups, write and telephone our political representation, and begin waging war against lawyers' abuses of class action lawsuits. We need to break up the fraternal environment of lawyers in Washington as a first step in our nation's moral and economic revival.

# Immigration

## Failures of Past Civilizations

I have described in this book the social and cultural paths that past civilizations have followed as they progressed through their rise and fall. Educators and historians are varied in their opinions of what caused the final demise of these civilizations.

Page Smith, a noted historian, has presented common factors that have been identified with the failure of past nations. Among these factors are:

- Loss of religious faith
- Increase in domestic crime and domestic violence
- Centralization of government power
- Proliferation of mystery cults[1]

Edward Gibbon, author of the book *Decline and Fall of the Roman Empire,* indicated the following factors:

- The injuries of time and nature
- Hostile attacks of barbarians
- Domestic quarrels of the Romans[2]

According to Historian Seymour Lipset:

- Bilingual and bicultural nations have never survived due to two or more competing languages and cultures, which create turmoil, tension and tragedy.
- A multicultural and multilingual society creates educational and economic problems.[3]

As I reviewed the reasons for the demise of past civilizations, I suddenly realized that the United States over the past 46 years has offended and violated all the factors historians identified with the failure of a nation.  Let us review each one.

- **Loss of religious faith:**  since 1962, from the schoolhouse to the courthouse, America has removed God from our public lives.
- **Increase in domestic crime:**  our prison population of 1.6 million surpasses all other countries at a cost to our taxpayers of 44 billion dollars a year
- **Centralization of government power:**  our government, as feared by our founding fathers, has grown into a federal bureaucratic monster.
- **Proliferation of mystery cults:**  many cults have appeared over recent years, such as the Strong City Cult, Branch Davidian, and many offspring cults favoring bigamy.
- **Injuries of time and nature:**  time has a tendency to change the complexion of a nation.  America is no different.  Over the years, particularly the past 46 years, extreme radical groups and new technology have changed our way of life and the direction of our nation.  People have become complacent and indifferent.  Well-funded groups and liberal judges have modified the Constitution and laws of the land to meet their own agendas.  New technologies have changed the ways in which we conduct our lives.
- **Domestic quarrels:** our nation is divided in many ways affecting our values, freedoms, economy and political direction.  This is seen more in Washington than anywhere else.  Our political divide is obvious, as our politicians – angrily hostile in their never-ending

debates – are unable to work in a bipartisan way to solve the nation's problems.

- **Hostile attacks**: the hostile attacks of barbaric terrorists during the '90s and 9/11 and the invasion of illegal aliens have dramatically changed our lives in America. Insurgents, such as the terrorists and street gangs created by illegal immigrants, have created chaos in our culture. The effect it has had on America's economy, education and social programs is beyond belief. It has become so complex that government does not know how to address it.

Throughout this book, I have drawn analogies of the Roman Empire and America. The final days of the Roman Empire resemble the challenges we face in this nation today. The terrorist/illegal alien problem is a perfect example. Toward the end of the Roman Empire, the Romans considered the Germans as barbarians. They did not want the Germans to infiltrate their culture because they believed it would lower their standards of living and have a negative effect on their economy, education and heritage. The Romans' solution to this problem was to build a wall around Germany. It was too late; Rome had already committed suicide from within. It was the Germans and other insurgent gangs that came into Rome, raiding and destroying much of the Roman art and heritage as they picked up the spoils of a once great civilization.[4]

Does this sound familiar as our government is presently considering, and is in the process of, building a wall to separate Mexico and the United States? History always repeats itself.

Immigration has become a major issue politically, socially and culturally. The standards set by the founders in our Constitution and laws no longer seem valid today. This nation's radical liberal extremists and their "politically correct attitude" want to make America one big happy multicultural, multilingual loving family. History has proven that this is not possible. History also proves that a multicultural and multilingual society with competing languages and cultures creates problems and turmoil in a nation's social, educational, and economic systems.

As proof that we have become a multilingual nation. Almost every product sold in the American marketplace has instructions printed in English, French and Spanish. Our nation is comprised of many ethnic and racial groups with their own cultures and identities, including languages, traditions and neighborhoods. What is good for one ethnic group may not be good for another. As with personalities or career selection, not one fits all.

Our nation consists of many peoples, each with its own customs. However, we are but one nation that is governed by one Constitution. A nation cannot adapt to all the different customs of many people. The same Constitution applies to all the people. If we try to change our standards and culture to adapt to many languages and ethnic groups, we will not succeed. If a person or group wants to enjoy our freedoms, it needs to adapt to this nation's Constitution and its laws.

Immigrants of yesteryear came to America because of the freedom and opportunities offered them. They came through Ellis Island. They wanted to learn English and to become part of America. They wanted to be Americans.

I would like to relate a family story concerning immigration and being an American. You have often heard the expression, "What's in a name?" My grandparents emigrated from Europe in the early 1900s along with many others from all over the world. They found them- selves on the shores of this new land. As they entered the port of New York, they looked up at that majestic view that has inspired the hearts

of millions of people. The Stately Lady towering over the harbor holding the torch of freedom, welcomed them to a land filled with opportunity. Most came with only their suitcases, not being able to speak
much English; they were without jobs and did not know their futures.
However, they believed in the freedom that America offered, and had
great faith in the Creator. Those ingredients allowed us to have the
lifestyles we take for granted today. My grandmother, at that time, was
with child, and was evidently so overwhelmed upon seeing the Statue
of Liberty, she stated, "If the child I am carrying is a girl, I will name
her after America." My mother was that child, and she was named
Amerika (pronounced Am-er-ē-ka), which means America in Italian.
Our family has always been honored that our grandparents exemplified
the expression, "Proud to be an American" as they overcame language
barriers, cultural differences and many other hardships while their focus
was on freedom and family.

Today, we allow illegal immigrants to come to America for the
"gifts" offered by our United States Treasury and government. Now
these immigrants come with demands. They demand to be taught their
own languages. They demand special privileges (affirmative action).
They demand ethnic studies that glorify their cultures. Immigrants
from Mexico and other non-European countries can come to America
and receive preferential treatment in jobs, education and government
contracts. This is what we call – using a term that is used too often –
"being politically correct."

Congress has helped to sell out this country with this pro-illegal
policy of free medical, free education, free food, free day care, etc.,
etc. With benefits and entitlements like these, you can understand why
illegal immigrants feel entitled to not only be in this country, but also
demand rights and privileges.

The founders originally gave Congress but four duties or responsibilities, two of which were to settle foreign issues and settle boundary disputes between states. I consider illegal immigration a foreign issue. Congress has interfered with all aspects of our lives; however, when confronted with its basic responsibilities, it has faltered. Our elite "do nothing" Congress failed to pass a balanced immigration law last year. If our federal government does not have the spine to pass laws regarding illegal immigrants, then the states must address it.

Corporate America has even agreed to these special privileges. These third-world immigrants are given special status by Exxon, Merrill Lynch, Boeing, Starbucks and many other corporations, called "affirmative action" or "racial privileges." Third-world immigrants can come here and immediately be eligible for special rights unavailable to Americans of European descent.

Below are facts and statistics proving how a multicultural and multilingual society creates turmoil, education and economic problems.

The nation's minority population is now over 100 million for the first time, and now makes up about a third of the United States population. Hispanics remain the largest minority group, at over 44 million, accounting for almost half the nation's growth of approximately 3 million from July 1, 2005 to July 1, 2006. Hispanics are moving into neighborhoods across the nation where whites are aging and fewer are being born.[5]

The non-Hispanic white school-age population dropped 4% since 2000 while the number of Hispanic school-age kids surged 21%. They are transforming classrooms, workplaces and entire communities.[6]

Immigration accounts for more than 40% of the U.S.A.'s growth since 2000.[7] How is this affecting our educational system? Imagine teachers in classrooms containing 30 to 40 students of widely varying attention spans and motivation, many of whom are not fluent in English. Educators are trying to obtain learning material and programs to satisfy all the different cultures and nationalities. The learning material may apply to a majority of the students; however, more pictures are used to meet the needs of the multicultural students.[8] The real problems in science and math are not being addressed. This is one of the major reasons our students today are some of the least educated in the world. Our students lack creativity in math and science. In addition, the least educated drag down the ones capable of greater learning.

Other facts:

- 12 million illegal immigrants presently live in America.
- $2 billion a year is spent on food assistance programs.
- $2.5 billion is spent on Medicaid per year for illegal aliens.
- 30% of all federal prison inmates are illegal aliens at a taxpayer cost of $1.5 billion per year.
- $90 billion is spent on illegal aliens per year for welfare and social services.
- In 2006, illegal aliens sent $45 billion back to their home countries.[9]
- Orange County, California is home to 215 gangs with 17,000 members, 98% of which are Mexican and Asian.
- According to the New York Times article of May 16, 1994, 20 years after the great influx of legal immigrants from Southeast Asia, 30% are still on welfare, compared to 8% of households nationwide.
- A most depressing statistic is that the federal government provides a single refugee with a monthly allow-

ance of $1,890.00, and each can get an additional $580 in social assistance for a total of $2,470.00 per month. This compares to a single retiree who after contributing to Social Security for 40 to 50 years can only receive a monthly check of $1,012.00.[10] How about that, taxpayers?

More statistics:

- Nearly 60% of all occupants of HUD properties are illegal immigrants.
- 21 radio stations in Los Angeles are Spanish speaking.
- Overall, an estimated 12 million illegal immigrants have entered and presently live in America. Our Congress, however, says that we would not be able to identity or locate them if a law should be passed to deport them. Does Congress believe with the "goodies" it gives to these immigrants that they will return to their native land voluntarily? What is more amazing is that our government can track a cow born in Canada to the stall where it was born, but it is unable to locate the 12 million illegal immigrants in our country.[11]

I honor the Hispanic immigrants who entered our country the right and legal way. These Americans have been a big contributor to this nation's growth and greatness.

The Constitution and our past heritage should be standards or compasses for all Americans to follow, whether citizens or immigrants, and no matter what their religion. America's basic guide, the Constitution, and our laws should prevail. The culture and values that took this nation to its greatness should remain intact. If a person, group or organization does not accept proven standards and abide by our value system, it should seek citizenship elsewhere. Why should we change when 87% of Americans want English to be our official language? Why should we jeopardize our nation for a few radicals only to accommodate our "politically correct" Congress?

It is OK to say "NO!" We are not European Americans, African Americans, Asian Americans or Latino Americans. We are all Americans and nothing but Americans.

Let me reiterate the words of President Theodore Roosevelt in 1907 when he said,

> *Any man who says he is an American, but something else also, isn't an American at all. We have room for but one flag, the American flag – we have room for but one language here, and that is the English language ... and we have room for but one loyalty and that is a loyalty to the American people.*[12]

# The Global Warming Hoax

I believe the global warming hysteria is nothing but a fabrication made up by a small group of extremists and the secular media. It is misleading information led by Al Gore and other liberal-organized groups that has created a crisis to gain control by placing more dependency on our government. The global warming myth is all about money and control. The cost to our government to address this issue is huge. It would cost our economy trillions of dollars to pursue the hysteria created by the viewpoint of a few.

First, let us look at the major source of the global warming hysteria. Al Gore's Oscar-winning documentary film, *An Inconvenient Truth,* and his address to Congress initiated this fabrication of global warming. Since then, the United Nations and other government leaders have joined in.

The film's message is as follows: "Humanity is sitting on a ticking time bomb. If the vast majority of the world's scientists are right, we have just 10 years to avert a major catastrophe that could send our entire planet into a tailspin of epic destruction involving extreme weather, floods, droughts, epidemics, and killer heat waves beyond anything we have ever experienced."[1]

Let us look at Al Gore, who won the Nobel Prize for his award-winning documentary film:

- This same Al Gore was the central figure in "Chinagate" when he accepted an estimated $5,000,000 in illegal contributions from Communist China for Clinton's re-election efforts.

- During this same period, the Clinton/Gore White House permitted the transfer of America's most sophisticated nuclear missile guidance system technology to Communist China. As a result, China's nuclear missiles now have the ability to reach most U.S. cities.

- This was not just about some illegal fundraising. "Chinagate" is about President Clinton and Vice-President Gore selling America's national security and missile secrets to a very dangerous foreign power for campaign money.

- This is the Al Gore, when being questioned by the FBI for his role in "Chinagate," lost his memory 85 times with answers and replies as follows:

  ◊ "I have no recollection" or "I have no independent recollection."

  ◊ "I can't recall" or "I don't recall."

  ◊ "I can't remember" or "I don't remember.

  ◊ "I have no memory", "I have no special memory or "I have no independent memory."[2]

For a person who has "no memory", he is the man who falsely claimed to have invented the internet in the '90s. Now Al Gore has created a global warming hysteria that goes against the findings of many scientists.

The majority of Americans are concerned about pollution and preserving as much of our natural resources country as possible. Too often, however, we become ignorant of the facts due to what the media announces.

Facts concerning global warning you should consider:

- Global warning has occurred before and it was

good. That is why Greenland was once green, and it produced crops.

- The earth may be warming naturally, but only by a tiny amount consistent with natural cycles.
- Most global warming predictions come from long-range computer modeling, which many times are inaccurate.
- In the 1970s, scientists predicted a new ice age and massive deaths due to overpopulation, which never happened.
- Some glaciers are melting, while others are growing.
- The sea level is not dangerously rising according to many top scientists.[3]
- Dr. Sherwood B. Idso, a research physicist with the United States Department of Agriculture, says, "Much of the world was a degree or two warmer about 6,000 and 1,000 years ago, when $CO^2$ content of the atmosphere was fully .80ppm less (22%) than it is today."
- Dr. Idso goes on to say," that increased levels of $CO^2$ will benefit the earth regarding plant life."[4]
- Dr. Fred Singer, Director of the Science and Environmental Policy Project, Washington Institute for Values in Public Policy, stated in his article, "Global Warming Changes: Fact and Fiction" that global cooling has been more of a problem than global warming. Dr. Singer states two examples of climate cooling. One was the "Little Ice Age" of 1816 causing agriculture losses and even famine. More recently, in the early autumn of 1991, we had tremendous losses to crops in the northern and western United States due to frosts.[5]

Since 1998, more than 19,700 scientists have signed the Oregon Institute of Science and Medicine's petition denying evidence for human-caused potentially disastrous global warming. However, Al Gore and many elected government officials have created their own crisis concerning global warming. These are bureaucrats who will gain more power to regulate our lives to serve their own financial gain. We know about Al Gore and his craving for wealth. "Chinagate" was about money.

Gore recently has organized an army of 1000 followers whom he has trained to go out into our nation. They represent him in all 50 states to preach his sermon on global warming.[6] These are individuals he has brainwashed with his global warming theory. In essence, they have become his personal sales team as they go out into society and expound on Gore's findings.

What is Al Gore's true purpose? In doing further research on Gore, I found that he is conveniently involved with several companies that manufacture or represent products relating to global warming. He has invested in a venture capital firm called Generation Investment Management, a London-based company with offices in Washington, DC for which he serves as chairman.[7] They have investments in the following companies:

- Amyris (biofuels)
- Altra (biofuels)
- Bloom Energy (solid oxide fuel cells)
- Mascoma (cellulosic biofuels)
- Great Point Energy (catalytic gasifications)
- Miasole (solar cells)
- Ausra (utility scale solar panels)
- GEM (battery operated cars)
- SMART (electric cars)
- Alta Rock Energy (geothermal power)[8]

Might Al Gore's purpose be a financial one? For a man who lost his memory 85 times after the "Chinagate" incident, could he be creating one of the world's greatest "sting operations" as he continues to convince the populace, our government and the world with his scare campaign on global warming? Gore has always been about money and wealth. This fabricated global warming crisis is a self-designed opportunity for him to add billions of dollars to his financial holdings. The only green he will end up protecting is the green that will line his pockets.

The American public must be aware that once this type of hysteria starts in the secular media, it takes on a life of its own. In addition, when a small radical group or individual left extremists start a movement such as this one, it is usually agenda-driven.

# America's Economy and Its Heritage

## Pilgrims

William Bradford was elected as the Pilgrims' first governor in 1623. The young governor had the foresight to understand that the Pilgrims would need to be self-sustaining if they were to survive the challenging New England winters. The first Pilgrims that arrived in America were the backbone of the new colony. They had experienced the worst of times in their journey to America; they were hard workers and knew that unity was important for survival.[1]

Many of the new Pilgrim arrivals complained about the living conditions. They expected to be given more than their share of rations while doing less work. William Bradford, in his journal, labeled them as "good for nothing sluggards." Governor Bradford anticipated that the coming winter would be difficult for the new colony. The summer was hot and dry and the crop output was minimal. He realized that every man must carry his own weight, do his own share of work and be disciplined for the coming winter.[2]

Reading the Bible was the Pilgrims' custom each day. Governor Bradford found his answer to the growing resistance from the newly arrived settlers in the Bible. He called a town meeting of all the settlers and read the following verse from 2 Thessalonians 3:10: "If any man would not work, neither should he eat. From now on, this will be the rule of our community." He reconfirmed, "Those who believe in the Holy Scriptures are bound to observe its teachings. Those who do not are to be bound by its consequences."[3] The settlers survived that winter; everyone did his share and the colony prospered.

In the following years, Governor Bradford recommended a proposal that each family be given a parcel of land. Owning their land gave the colonists a freedom they had never experienced. They became more productive than ever. They kept all the crops they could grow except one-tenth, which would be given to the trade company, and was a form of taxation in order to keep their government functioning.

The Pilgrims' beliefs were not based on personal possessions. Their dream was freedom – freedom to worship as they chose, freedom to lead their lives independent from the dictatorship of England, and freedom to live according to God's plan.

### Our Founders

The founding fathers of our nation, using the same principles of the Pilgrims, wrote in the Declaration of Independence "all men are created equal," meaning that each individual could pursue his own opportunities in life. All men could choose a career or skill, every person could choose to work hard and prosper, or not work and suffer the consequences of failure. Their desire for freedom and independence surpassed any need for materialism. The colonists were willing to jeopardize their material possessions and lives to provide freedom for themselves and future generations.

### Articles of Confederation

After the Revolutionary War, the thirteen states acted individually and functioned as little republics, all for the common purpose of protecting their individual liberties and boundaries.

The main concern of the Continental Congress was to establish a unified national government that could pay its debts, mediate trade and boundary disputes between states, and provide for common defense. Our founders did not trust government, and were reluctant to permit it to tax its citizens. So suspicious were the colonists in giving the central government too much power that it took five years for Congress to pass the Articles of Confederation. On March 1, 1781, the Articles of Confederation was passed and ratified without Congress having the power to tax the American people.[4] Its purpose was to confirm that there was a common union of states, and to acknowledge that the states were to be independent and sovereign. The Articles of Confederation alleviated the thirteen republic states' need to protect their own borders. It consolidated America, and allowed the United States to grow into a unified power.

The new nation grew and prospered as Americans were free to expand their businesses and agriculture. The economy expanded quickly as Americans had the freedom of entrepreneurship and to conduct interstate business. As the nation grew, Congress' responsibilities also expanded. Congress still had no authority to levy taxes to finance its operation. To obtain money, Congress had to rely on the states, which in turn needed to obtain their funds from their citizens.

Our Constitution stressed property and private ownership as the major factors of individual freedom. Most states required that property owners own a certain number of acres of land. It was believed that property owners were the most responsible citizens, and would be less likely to vote for radical changes. "Property," said Samuel Adams, "is admitted to have an existence even in the savage state of nature...and if property is necessary for the support of a savage life, it is by no means less so in civil society."[5]

As an avid outdoorsman, I can appreciate Samuel Adams' comments. The beaver has its own pond. Many other species of animals have their dens, or are territorial in their way of life. To have freedom of your own habitat is a God-given gift by design of the Creator. If other animals intrude upon a den or pond, the first reaction of the occupants is one of defense, to protect what is theirs. For this reason, the colonists feared a central power (government) might try to intrude or take over their property in the form of taxation.

John Adams wrote, "Property is surely a right of mankind as real as liberty. The moment the idea is admitted into society that property is not sacred as the laws of God and there is not a force of law and public justice to protect it, anarchy and tyranny commence."[6]

The general philosophy of the founders was for the right of the people to enjoy the rewards of one's own efforts; private property was considered a God-given right. Any government that violated that right as viewed by our founding fathers was a form of tyranny. Revolt against such a government would be justified.[7] This is one of the reasons for the Second Amendment of the Constitution: "It is the right of the people to keep and bear arms" if their rights should be infringed upon. The Second Amendment is in place in case the politicians of this nation ignore the other amendments. If you were to remove the people's right to bear arms, you create a state of slavery or bondage.

Over the course of 200 years, the United States has transformed itself from a nation with almost no government presence in the marketplace to one in which government is a dominant factor in all aspects of our lives, including the economy. The great problem of government has always been that man must run it, and man with his fallen nature seeks office in order to use the powers of government to further his own ambitions.[8] Up until the Franklin Roosevelt Administration (1930s), most politicians had the common sense to keep their noses out of the economy. No reasonable politician would have recommended that the government could do a better job of managing business than the American businessman.

During recent years, our government representatives, at both state and federal levels, have been trying to prove the forefathers wrong and attempting to prove that bigger government can manage all facets of our lives, including both state and federal economies.

Americans have not insisted on the same degree of excellence and wise use of expenditures in government that we have demanded from industry and ourselves. If our citizens were more demanding of politicians and government, we would not have the problems today that we experience in education, excessive entitlements and national debt. However, when government fails, all too often we reward incompetence with more money. This has led to a nation nearly bankrupt as politicians continue to spend more than can be generated in taxes. Many Americans are realizing government can give the people nothing that the government has not first taken away. What government gives back multiplies in cost.

Let us take an honest look at the economy and forget what the media and politicians are telling our citizens. Government, as our founders feared most, is out of control and has grown into a monster. Our politicians do what they do best, which is to spend the people's money. Due to the many special interest groups in Washington, it is not conceivable that any great changes to Congressional spending will occur without the demand of the American people. The programs being promoted by extremists, lobbyists, politicians and special interest groups are to fill the wants of their agendas. They do not resemble anything that will fill the needs of the American citizen. Most Americans agree that government today is far too costly and too intrusive in our lives.

Thomas Jefferson wrote, "I place economy among the first and most important virtues, and public debt as the greatest of dangers ... We must make a choice between economy and liberty, or profusion [lavish spending] and servitude [bondage]. If we can prevent the government from wasting the labors of the people under the pretense of caring for them, they will be happy."[9]

Let us look how government intervention has affected our economy, both in domestic and global marketplaces. Our economy faces more threats now than since the Great Depression. When we look at America today, it is quite evident that we have essentially bankrupted the most prosperous nation in the world. Abraham Lincoln said, "You can not keep out of trouble by spending more than your income."[10] Federal, state and local governments have added nearly $10 trillion to taxpayer liabilities in the past two years, bringing the total of government's unfunded obligations to an unprecedented $57.8 trillion, America's worst debt since the Great Depression. This amount is equivalent to $510,678 credit card debt for every American household. Like an unpaid credit card bill, the balance grows per year at about a rate of $25,000 per household.[11]

Our government's immediate obligation of $57.8 trillion is five times what the American people owe for mortgages, car loans, credit cards and other personal debt. The $57.8 trillion is what is due right now.[12] Our government is headed for a $620 billion deficit this year. That means the United States must borrow to finance its debt. Foreigners are presently lending America approximately $1.7 billion a day. We are relying on foreign lending to fund the federal government and satisfy America's lifestyles and its craving for imported goods. Treasury securities are issued, which are interest-bearing IOUs owed by our government. Japan as our greatest debtor owns $683 billion in US treasury securities, with China the second largest holder.

Right now, foreigners are happy to buy our treasury securities. However, if Japan and China decide they no longer wish to purchase the securities, government would need to raise interest rates to entice Americans to buy them. Commercial loans and mortgage rates would rise, and in turn, could be a greater burden to our economy. However, foreigners realize that if the United States' economy should come to a halt, the United States' purchase of foreign goods would also be affected. As an example: our trade deficit in 2006 was $726 billion, of which China makes up $202 billion of that amount, meaning China sold $202 billion more products to the United States than our nation sold to China. This arrangement makes it very difficult for our government to negotiate trade agreements with foreign nations when, at the same time, it is asking its trading partners for one more loan to finance the nation's debt.[13]

## Government Competes With Industry and Our Private Sector

Capital is the fuel that ignites the economy. Due to excessive taxation by government, our industrial base and individuals have less capital to spend on new technologies and business expansion. We compete over the same money. As government continues to grow, we experience greater costs to the taxpayer and less growth in industry and technology. Private sector jobs decreased 1,380,000 from October 2007 to October 2008 while local, state and federal jobs increased 199,000.[14]

Today approximately 51% of the workforce in the private sector is supporting 49% of the remaining population. The 49% are people working for government and those supported through entitlements such as FHA loans, farm subsidies, welfare, social security, Medicare and many others.

In the last ten years in New York State, where I reside, private enterprise has had minus growth while public (local, state and federal) employees grew 18%.[15]

When government employees outnumber the private sector, the balance will become lopsided and the working populace will no longer be able to support the growing government and those supported through retirement benefits and entitlements. When this imbalance happens, our government will be competing with the private sector over the same money. At that point, all money for savings, consumer spending, capital for business expansion and debt payments, will all go in one direction – to our government. Any new money printed by government becomes useless. As in the end days of the Roman Empire, the Romans lost all faith in their government and politicians, and the Roman dollar became worthless.

The United States Government employs over 20 million civilians. Today, over 2 million more Americans work for government than for manufacturers. Therefore, government competes directly with industry for employees. State and local governments have increased their retirement benefits as corporations and private enterprise have decreased theirs because of cost. Only 18% of private enterprise workers now have retirement pension plans, compared with more than 80% of government employees.[16]

Contrary to what most people believe, most government workers are paid more than private employees doing similar jobs are, and the difference continues to grow. A typical full-time government employee in 2006 who earned $78,853 in wages and benefits earned $25,771 more than a typical private sector employee doing the same job, as reported by the Bureau of Labor Statistics.

The United States government unfunded retirement obligation grew $200 billion last year to $4.7 trillion, the amount of money the government would need today in order to pay for promised retirement benefits.

Regarding retirement, government often adds value for overtime, unused leave and other benefits into the pension formula. The results can be devastating. A police chief in New Hampshire added more than $200,000 for severance, sick leave and other payouts into his three-year salary coverage when he retired. This boosted his retirement benefit to $125,000 a year, more than what he made as police chief.

**Growth of Government Payrolls**

1940 Government spent $7 billion monthly

1960 Government spent $18 billion monthly

1997 Government spent $51 billion monthly[17]

Government employees receive 30% to 40% higher compensation than do comparably skilled private sector workers.[18] In Chicago, a public school administrator retired after 35 years with the school system and had 315 unused sick days. He was paid $422 for every unused sick day and ultimately was paid $133,000. Great system! It is as if public and private sector workers are in two different worlds. Businesses battle in the competitive marketplace, while government makes promises and then gets the taxpayers to pay the bills by raising taxes to keep those promises. It is a double hit for small business owners, who must finance their own employees and then pay for the government's promises and employees through taxes.

## Taxes and Our Tax Code and
## How They Affect Our Economy

Our tax system fuels the growth of government. The bigger government becomes, the less likely it will be successful in taking care of its basic duties. Our present tax system is so complex it camouflages from voters the real burden of paying for government. Most Americans never see the total amounts taken out in withholding taxes, business taxes, consumption taxes and employer taxes. The withholding tax and corporate income tax are the two greatest forms of hidden taxes. The money is taken from the workers' paychecks without them ever seeing their earnings taken away.

As a nation, we have increased the household tax burden from 1900 through 1999 as follows:

    1900  Household taxes were $1,900

    1950  Household taxes were $11,000

    1999  Household taxes were $30,000[19]

One hundred years ago, the taxes listed below never existed and our nation was the most prosperous in the world. We had no national debt and our mothers stayed at home to raise the children.

- Accounts Receivable Tax
- Building Permit Tax
- Capital Gains Tax
- CDL License Tax
- Cigarette Tax
- Corporate Income Tax
- Court Fines (indirect taxes)
- Dog License Tax
- Federal Income Tax
- Federal Unemployment Tax (FUTA)

- Fishing License Tax
- Food License Tax
- Fuel Permit Tax
- Gasoline Tax (42 cents per gallon)
- Hunting License Tax
- Inheritance Tax Interest expense (tax on the money)
- Inventory Tax IRS interest charges (tax on top of tax)
- IRS Penalties (tax on top of tax)
- Liquor Tax
- Local Income Tax
- Luxury Taxes
- Marriage License Tax
- Medicare Tax
- Property Tax
- Real Estate Tax
- Septic Permit Tax
- Service Charge Taxes
- Social Security Tax
- Road Usage Taxes (truckers)
- Sales Taxes
- Recreation Vehicle Tax
- Road Toll Booth Taxes
- School Tax
- State Income Tax
- State Unemployment Tax (SUTA)
- Telephone Federal Excise Tax
- Telephone Federal Universal Service Fee Tax
- Telephone Federal, State and Local Surcharge Taxes
- Telephone Minimum Usage Surcharge Tax
- Telephone Recurring and Non-Recurring Charges Tax

- Telephone State and Local Tax
- Telephone Usage Charge Tax
- Toll Bridge Taxes
- Toll Tunnel Taxes
- Traffic Fines (indirect taxation)
- Trailer Registration Tax
- Utility Taxes
- Vehicle License Registration Tax
- Vehicle Sales Tax
- Watercraft Registration Tax
- Well Permit Tax
- Workers Compensation Tax

Ronald Reagan once said, "Government's view of the economy could be summed up in a few short phrases; If it moves, tax it. If it keeps moving, regulate it. And if it stops moving, subsidize it".[20] Government's passion for the taxpayer's money is endless. Since Ronald Reagan spoke these words, he could have added if it moves and moos, tax it. Our government is now considering a tax on cows. They propose that farmers pay $175.00 yearly for each dairy cow owned. The reason is that the left wing environmentalists claim that cows expel too much methane gas into the air and it is harmful to our environment. I firmly believe that all the hot air expelled by our politicians in Washington is much more harmful to our nation than America's dairy cows.

Our national debt is over $10 trillion and continues to grow daily. As the result of federal, state and local taxes, many American middle-income earners work nearly half of each workday to pay the government. It takes two wage earners in most middle-income families to pay for their lifestyles.

We pay taxes virtually from cradle to grave. Even when you are dead, the government is not finished taxing you. Using the Inheritance

Tax (the death tax), the federal government has sights on your life's savings and investments – the financial nest egg you worked a lifetime to create, the inheritance you had planned to pass on to your children. Our citizens and corporations are being held hostage as we are drowning in taxes and tax laws created by our government.

Ronald Reagan comically stated, "The taxpayer, that's someone who works for the federal government, but doesn't have to take a civil service examination".[21]

## Our Tax Codes and the Internal Revenue Service (IRS)

Today there are over 67,000 pages of tax regulations. In 1913, when the federal income tax was introduced, there were 400 pages. The current tax code has more than seven million words. The simplest form, Form 1040EZ has more than 30 pages of instructions while the standard 1040 form has more than 75 pages of instructions. These hundreds of pages of tax regulations have created a new profession of tax preparers. The average taxpayer hires a tax preparer mostly out of fear that they will incorrectly submit their tax return to the IRS and be penalized. Even former Secretary of Treasury John Snow needed a tax preparer.

In 1960, less than 20% of taxpayers used paid preparers. Today, 60% of Americans require paid tax preparers. Americans spend approximately 5.4 billion hours at an annual cost of $300 billion to the economy just completing the paperwork required for the federal taxes.[22]

There are four times more tax preparers than there are firefighters, and two times more tax preparers than police officers in America. There are about 1.2 million professional tax preparers during the tax season.

This is equal to the number of people who live in Hawaii. Comparably, there are about 836,000 doctors in the United States, which equates to approximately three tax preparers to every two doctors.[23]

## Who Polices the Tax Preparers?

If you want to sell life insurance or real estate, you need a license. If you want to be a tax preparer, you can start immediately, no license or education is required. Neither Congress nor anyone else in government has addressed the educational or ethical requirements of tax preparers.[24]

The Internal Revenue Service is larger than the FBI and the CIA combined. It has 102,000 employees. If the IRS were in the private sector, it would be among America's 50 largest companies.[25] Today, the IRS has broad – almost unlimited – powers to investigate Americans' finances and activities. Without a search warrant, the IRS can search an American's property and financial documents. Without a trial, the IRS can seize a citizens property.

Until the Sixteenth Amendment was ratified in 1913, the Supreme Court consistently ruled income tax unconstitutional. No law has contributed more to the growth and control in government than the imposition of the federal income tax.

Former Chief Justice John Marshall expressed taxation well when he wrote, "The power to tax involves the power to destroy."[26]

The damage our current antiquated tax code inflicts on the economy and to our families is devastating, not only to economic growth, but also to individual freedoms. As the founders firmly believed, more government means less freedom. Government consumes almost half of the national income. Americans now spend almost half of their working lives paying for government.

Economist Walter Williams of George Mason University stated, "If the government can lay claim to half of the fruits of our labor, then we are truly at most half free as Americans."[27]

I have given facts in the preceding pages in order to inform the readers, and to bring an awareness of government bureaucracy that controls our lives. For more information, also see the chapter, "Our Enemies."

## What Are Some of Our Solutions?

Our current tax code has become the monster feared by the founding fathers. Every minute of every day, it puts a noose around the economy, job opportunities and our families' investments and savings. As that noose tightens, it chokes America's ability to grow the economy, and to maintain our individual freedoms. If we do not change the size of government and we do not overhaul the present tax system, other nations will surpass us in this global economy. Our present tax code is moving us more and more toward socialism and tyranny. If continued, we will be under complete bondage to our government.

Contrary to what politicians tell us, the tax burden today falls on the wealthy, which leaves a majority of Americans feeling that taxes are not excessive. A statistic that confirms this; in 2004, 66% of all taxes were paid by the richest 10%. Fifty percent (50%) of lower income payers paid 3% of the tax burden. As Abraham Lincoln said, "You can not help the poor man by destroying the rich."[28] A change is necessary. I agree with many economists, such as Dale Jorgensen of Harvard

University School of Economics, and Walter Williams of George Mason University, that a form of flat rate consumption tax would be fair and equal to everyone. All Americans would face the same rate on items they choose to buy. This tax system would be visible to those who pay, and would allow the consumer to decide what they could afford to purchase. Consumers would pay the tax at the cash registers as they purchased goods.

This flat tax system would allow the following:
- Give every American a tax cut.
- Shrink the need of government, IRS and tax preparers.
- Cut government spending.
- Stimulate investments, savings and economic growth.
- Consumers would have the freedom to make their own decisions on how to spend their money.
- Take control out of the hands of politicians who use the present tax code to pit the rich against the poor.

Congress, of course, hesitates to address this issue because control, power and revenue would be taken away from it. Legislators would not have the freedom to pursue their pork projects as they do now. These changes will not take place unless the citizens of this nation demand more from our government, and are more selective in whom they elect to government offices. Remember —we are a nation "of the people, by the people and for the people."

## Government Regulations

Government regulations have become so severe that they are limiting the growth of new products. The government today has become a competitor to our industrial base. Politicians have become quite clever in attaining campaign objectives without raising taxes. They have accomplished their goals through regulations on the private economy or industrial base. Federal regulations over the past several years have required that private businesses spend money on worker training, health, consumer protection, safety, assistance to the disabled, environmental protection – the list goes on.[29] These hidden forms of taxation on the consumer and on businesses are crippling our economic growth. If these regulations had existed in the early 1900s, America would not have attained the economic growth and world power experienced during those times.

It is difficult to measure the burden regulations have on our economy. However, in 1986 under Ronald Reagan, the Federal Register, in which the government's regulations are listed, was 44,812 pages. Under Bill Clinton in 1998, the number of pages increased to 68,571, an increase of more than one-third. As an example, regulations add approximately 33% to the cost of building an airplane and as much as 95% to the price of a new vaccine.[30]

The environmental regulations are the fastest growing area:

- In 1970, the nation spent $25 billion on environmental regulations.
- In 1999, more than $280 billion was spent to regulate the environment.[31]

We now import from other nations over 65% of oil used in the U.S. We have not built a refinery in the United States in 30 years due to environmental regulations. No wonder the cost of gasoline has been almost

$5.00 per gallon and we continue to be held hostage by Venezuela and the Arab nations for our oil needs.

As most Americans would agree, government today is far too costly and too intrusive in our lives. Big government, higher taxes and excessive regulations are restraining America's economic growth. The government has become an obstacle to the advancement and growth of our nation's industries. History has proven not only in America, but also in other nations, that when government grows too large, it stifles the productive sector of the economy.

## Small Businesses and Government

When our founding fathers warned us about large government and the loss of individual freedoms, their vision was profound. Government today can trap small business owners by the use of regulations and obscure laws and, in some cases, sentence them to prison. This is particularly true for any violation of environmental laws and regulations.

Once the government has determined a law or regulation has been violated, it has three ways it can handle it:

1. Give a warning and then a time frame for the problem to be corrected.
2. Levy a fine or file a civil lawsuit.
3. If neither of the first two works, then the worst case
   – it prosecutes you and your business.

Small businesses employ the greatest percentage of workers in our nation's economy. However, statistics prove that if you are in business and have done nothing against the law, you have a 25% chance of being sued.  That, folks, is what our nation is about today: big government and lawsuits.  As an example, the estimated amount that U.S. companies spend annually for product research and development is $194 billion. However, the estimated amount U.S. companies spend annually on tort litigation and lawsuits is $205 billion.  More is spent on lawsuits than on developing new products for consumer use.  (See the chapter on Lawyers and Lawsuits.)

# Competing in Today's Global Economy

Americans have enjoyed unprecedented prosperity, and have been the envy of the rest of the world. We have led the world in war, inventions, space travel, and internet technology. American consumers have had access to an unlimited choice of products, from foods to electronics. We have more freedoms and property owners than any other nation in the world. We have had our choices in education and careers. However, we have become a spoiled and complacent nation that is slowly yielding to global competition—a nation that is losing its edge as a world power in education and manufacturing. Many American corporate executives classify the United States as a massive ship that is slowly losing steam, a nation that has pulled into the slow lane of global competitiveness.

Craig Barrett, Intel's chairman, stated, "Every one of the early warning signals is trending downwards. We're all fat, dumb and happy, which is one reason why this is so insidious."[1]

We are a complacent, unaware nation whose spoiled lifestyles are expected to be corrected by government grants and entitlements. Most Americans have no idea how we compare to other countries. The fact remains that other nations are simply surpassing us in education, leadership and job aggressiveness. Americans are often the last to know about fast-moving changes beyond our shorelines. There are changes occurring offshore that would be the envy of most Americans.

In Hong Kong, 60% of homes get television service through ultra high-speed broadband connections, which transform TVs into computers and make "video on demand," sophisticated gaming, and other futuristic services possible. Several cities in China are installing radiofrequency tracking systems, the most sophisticated in use anywhere, for cargo that arrives in their ports and air terminals. Throughout Europe and Asia, smart cards with memory chips are replacing credit cards and cash transactions, thereby simplifying shopping, reducing fraud, and putting an infrastructure in place for consumers to receive real-time data such as traffic and weather information. In Korea, many cell phones double as smart cards that, if waved in front of a vending machine, can make a purchase. These innovations do much more than what first appears. The new technologies are developed in areas where the infrastructure supports them. Including consumers who demand the product, and local governments that give companies the ability to grow and support the higher paying jobs that come with new technology.

"After World War II we had an unusually great share of the global economic power with China and Russia under Communist-controlled governments," says Robert Gates, our present Defense Secretary. However, progressive governments in India and China have helped harness the talents of millions of well-educated, industrious workers, increasing their standard of living and spending power. It has been proven throughout history that economic strength begets geopolitical and military strength. China, in particular, is aggressively competing with the United States for everything from arms deals to oil and gas fields.

"China could be a global super power within a few decades," predicts J. Stapleton Roy, former U.S. ambassador to China. "Terrorism will turn out to be far less significant than China's burgeoning economic growth."[2]

China today has 300 million children between ages one to eight years. We have 30 million in the Unites States of the same age. China graduated 600,000 of the world's total undergraduate degree of engineers. The United States graduated 70,000 this past year. This alone puts China in an advantageous competitive position in technology for many years to come. China is becoming the world's biggest market for consumer products, such as cars, electronics and others. This, in combination with China's overall population, which includes their future consumers and graduated engineering students, could jeopardize America's ability to compete in future years.[3]

If current trends continue, by 2010 more than 90% of the world's scientists and engineers will live in Asia, warns the Business Roundtable, which represents the nation's leading companies. Failing to reverse that trend will result in a "slow withering" of the United States' economic might. Math and science scores of high school students in this nation continue to fall. Sources from the National Science Foundation indicate the following percentage of undergraduate degrees awarded in engineering:

| | |
|---|---|
| China | 38.7% |
| Taiwan | 22.6% |
| Germany | 20.3% |
| Japan | 19.3% |
| USA | 4.7% [4] |

The percentage of engineering PhD degrees awarded in the United States that go to foreign-born students is 56%.[5]

There are other troubling statistics regarding education for our kids. Our eighth graders rank 9th in science proficiency and 15th in math proficiency among 45 countries. Yet we spend more per student for education than any other nation in the world. Only one-third of high school students graduate with a degree that enables them to get a good job, or go on to college.

In the future, the economic battles will be over technology, jobs and money. Without our youth getting the proper education and our engineering and science degrees falling behind China and India, we will lose the battle in technology, which will further affect job opportunities and lead to greater deficits and money problems in our economy.

American firms such as Intel and IBM are moving operations overseas to the fast growing Asian markets. Half of IBM's 190,000 engineers and technical experts now reside overseas. General Electric is doing the same. In lighting, power generators and many of its other products, improving quality of foreign-made goods has forced GE to move more work overseas where operating costs are lower and talent that is more skilled is available. Many U.S. companies are placing manufacturing facilities in China, such as General Motors and many electronic companies. These moves have handsomely added to corporate profits; however, how this is helping the U.S. economy needs to be determined.

The cost of Chinese products has kept our inflation down, but this could affect the rest of our economy in a negative manner, such as:

- Are the Chinese copying our technologies?
- The trade deficit last year was $56.5 billion, $23.8 billion being with China.
- Is it creating America's manufacturing and labor problems?
- Our dollar is being driven down as the result of this nation's growing national debt and trade deficit.

While our public officials are running up spending deficits, which we in turn are asking foreigners to fund, we then continue to pay them dollars to send us cheaper products, therefore, depreciating our dollar in lieu of our nation paying its own way.[6]

## The Generation Gap and Our Economy

The generation gap ranges from the younger twenty-somethings, those about 25 and younger, to the baby boomers, those born between 1946 and 1964. The twenty-somethings are part of the "millennials," also known as "Generation Y." The baby boomer generation, a stronghold of approximately 79 million, will be eligible for retirement starting in 2008.[7]

Our nation, already floating in debt, has no plan to cope with the overflow of new costs that will arrive as baby boomers begin to retire. Instead of contributing to social security, the boomers will be drawing from it.

In 2010, the annual social security surplus, used to camouflage the size of our already massive federal budget deficit, begins to shrink according to the Social Security Trustees Report. In 2016, the social security surplus presently at $68 billion turns to a deficit, further compounding our nation's debt problem.[8]

In order to fill this financial requirement, our government would need either to raise taxes or borrow more money. Either decision would take more money out of the pockets of U.S. taxpayers or increase interest rates, raising the cost of everything from mortgage to college loans. If social security were funded through new taxes, the government would expand in size from 20% of our economy to as much as 56% by 2050.

In conjunction with the boomers collecting from social security, they will be eligible for Medicare in 2011. Last year, Medicare cost $408 billion, up from $7.5 billion at its conception in 1970. However, by 2016, it is expected to more than double to $863 billion, creating a more troubling burden on our U.S. economy.[9]

If we retired our current national debt of $10 trillion and paid upfront for the projected social security and Medicare shortfalls, it would cost $46 trillion. This amount equals the estimated total net worth of all Americans combined. In other words, government could solve its debt problem by seizing all the assets of our nation's citizens – a sad picture!

## Who Will Pay For This Devastating Financial Burden Imposed By Our Government?

I describe the generation gap as the available working population that is educated and qualified to meet the job requirements of our knowledge-based economy.

The baby boomers are often referred to as the most highly educated generation in U.S. history, leading all present generations in education, job success and productivity. After the boomers retire, we could be looking at a total disaster for our economy due to the lack of educated, qualified workers, particularly in engineering and science. Corporations and industry in the United States are begging for good talent. However, these positions are increasingly being filled with foreign engineers and scientists.

## What Can We Expect over the Next Two Decades?

How does this nation find a way to bridge the gap of qualified professional workers who will be able to support the financial requirements of our government? A tremendous source of revenue is needed to pay for the burden created to cover social security and Medicare costs of the retiring baby boomers.  Social security alone is presently taking four working people to support one retiree.  Where will we get the working talent to support our growing government and its debt and still be able to be competitive in the global economy?  Our problem is three-fold:

1. the result of the abortion movement
2. the twenty-something generation
3. the educational levels of all racial ethnic groups

The first generation creating a gap in productive taxpayers is the result of the Supreme Court's decision in 1973 of Roe vs. Wade.  The abortion movement has eliminated more than 48 million babies from our society over the past 35 years, an average of 4,000 per day.  This generation of young people would have been in the age group of 35 years and younger.  This is devastating not only in the loss of innocent lives but how they would have contributed to our society.  We have eliminated a whole generation of youth that would have been a vital factor in our economy.  This group of potential consumers would have purchased homes, clothes, automobiles and consumable items that would need to be manufactured.  This generation would be today's taxpayers contributing toward social security, Medicare and many others of our nation's needs.  Assuming that this generation, lost to abortion, would each spend $15,000 annually to buy consumer items, our annual loss to the economy would be somewhere around $700 billion by 2010, during the retirement period for the baby boomers.  The abortion issue has taken out of our economy one full generation of productive Americans.

The second group that America is depending on to fill the generation gap in the next two decades is the twenty-somethings, those 25 years old and younger.  Labeled as "Generation Y," they are our next hope to fulfill the needs of our nation regarding professional positions, productivity, and to keep us competitive in the world marketplace. However, our educational system and rising personal debt are creating severe problems for this group. Only one-third of all students entering high school are being educated to qualify for high-level jobs or college entrance. This places the U.S. at a disadvantage regarding our competitive position in the world economy and filling high-level job requirements. Competition, whether one-on-one or in the international marketplace, begins in the classroom.

## The Cost of College Education

Has a college degree become so expensive that we are eliminating a generation of educated Americans? The average price of college has grown much faster than the rate of inflation. The average annual tuition at public four-year colleges and universities was $5,836 in 2006-07, up 268% from 1976-77. The percentage of students who borrowed for college jumped to 65% in 2000-01 from 34% in 1977, according to the U.S. Education Department and National Center of Education Statistics. Student loan balances rose 16% to an average of $14,379; credit card debt surged 24% to $5,781.[10]

The debt burden is suffocating our young people right when they are starting out in life. This debt has forced some to change their career plans. Of those surveyed, 22% said they have taken a job they otherwise would not have taken because they needed to pay off student loan debt. Twenty-nine percent said they have put off advancing their education because of debt, and 26% have put off buying a home for the same reason.[11]

Experience Inc., which provides career services to link college graduates with jobs, found that 58% of twenty-somethings surveyed moved back home to live with their parents. This Generation Y is nicknamed 'boomerang children" because after college they returned home because of tuition debt and lack of employment. More dependent on their parents, they have grown up in what some see as overprotective households. Their parents even have a nickname, "helicopter parents," for the way they hover over their children. This has created a generation of youth that tends to be quite casual about its future. They expect everything to be given to them. They have a sense of entitlement – many believe the government will take care of their needs. This generation would rather spend than save, and they are spending like crazy. They regard savings for retirement as something old people do.

### Credit Cards, Youth and Debt

Credit cards, the use of plastic, is available to teenagers for whatever they wish to buy. Today, 11% of teenagers have credit cards in their own names, according to a recent nationwide survey by Junior Achievement, a Colorado Springs-based group bringing financial literacy to kids. The group found that 6.2% of all 13- and 14-year-olds have credit cards.[12] Melissa Canaday, vice president for Junior Achievement's Rocky Mountain Division, said that kids have accrued such overwhelming debt by the age of 18 that they can't afford their own apartments.

Americans put $51 billion worth of fast food on credit and debit cards, up from $33.2 billion the year before, according to Card Data, which tracks the industry. Thirty-six (36) million Americans charge medical expenses to credit cards for an average of $11,600 per card-holder.[13]

This generation of twenty-somethings is straining under the weight of college loans and other debt, a huge load that separates this generation from previous ones. Nearly two-thirds carry some debt, and those with debt have taken on more in the past five years.[14]

An analysis of the credit references of 3 million twenty-somethings noted late payments are rising, and they are more likely to be late than other Americans. Nearly half of the twenty-somethings have stopped paying a debt, forcing lenders to "charge off" the debt and sell it to a collection agency, or have had cars repossessed, or have sought bankruptcy protection. The fastest growing age group filing bankruptcy is 20 to 24, Generation Y. More people (of all ages) filed bankruptcy in 2004 than graduated from college.[15]

The twenty-somethings are crunched from all sides with education costs increasing, housing and mortgage problems, overall debt, and job opportunities dwindling. This is the same age group that will be responsible for repayment of the $10 trillion debt created by the Bush and Obama administrations. Generation "Y" will pay up to $114,000.00 each in their lifetime toward this debt and that amount will only be payment toward the interest of the $10 trillion debt. This generation is expected to be supporting the retirement lifestyles of the baby boomers!

## Education of Minorities

The third factor in filling the gap for qualified professional workers is the educational levels of all racial ethnic groups. The baby boomer generation will be retiring at a time when Hispanics and African-Americans, traditionally our least well-educated minorities, become a bigger share of our working population. "Unless states do a better job in raising the educational levels of all racial ethnic groups," warns the National Center for Public Policy and Higher Education, "the average level of education of the U.S. workforce will continue to drop significantly, and with it average incomes and national wealth." This timing is critical, as a knowledge-based economy demands that most workers for all positions have higher education levels.[16]

In summary, America has a devastating problem, due not only to debt and education deficit, but also in our inability to fill the need for qualified, educated, professional workers to support our out-of-control government and the 79 million baby boomers ready for retirement. Where do we draw these workers from when we have aborted a generation of youth? The twenty-somethings have created massive debt and 58% return home to live with parents. The economy has fewer good paying jobs for our college graduates and the educational level of minority groups is below acceptable levels.

The fact remains that we are not prepared to address our nation's domestic needs, nor are we prepared to compete in the global economy.

## Savings Accounts and Our Economy

How long will Japan, China, India and other foreign countries continue to loan their savings to the United States so we can live in abundance with little concern about the future? It cannot go on forever; a time will come when the funds from overseas will cease.

Americans need to save much more so we are not relying on foreign lending to fund our federal government. Last year, Americans saved a minus 1% of their earnings, approximately $1 of every $100 earned. There are less individual savings now than at any time since the Great Depression. The reason is excessive individual spending and credit card charges.

Boomers tell the younger generation to start saving earlier. Many of the baby boomers planning to retire started saving late, assuming that pensions and social security would carry them through their retirement years, and that former employers would pay for their healthcare. The new reality of self-funded retirement plans and consumer-driven healthcare caught them by surprise.

A recent study by Thrivant Financial for Lutherans found 71% worry that they do not have enough money put away for their retirement years. When asked what advice they would pass on to the younger generations, their replies indicated that they wished they had started saving at an earlier age.[17]

## A Spoiled Nation of Abundance

Our United States citizens go undisturbed about the direction of our economy and government as long as they have their comforts and lifestyles. Why worry! As psychologists report: human beings tend to put off necessary changes until the moment they begin to feel the pain.[18] It is evident that "pain" has not yet reached us. When it does, it may be too late. Our lifestyles continue, even under false pretenses, as long as we have our discounted electronic gadgets and designer clothes produced in Asia.

A new study by the Pew Research Center indicates that Americans believe the more goods they have and the more available they are, the more they feel the need for them. Luxuries of the past become necessities of today.[19]

"New technologies not only give us something new we can covet and feel like we can't live without it; they also transform the way life is organized," says Robert Thompson, a professor of media and popular culture at Syracuse University.[20]

Pauline Wallin, a clinical psychologist in private practice in Camp Hill, Pennsylvania, says, "People are basically social and highly influenced by group pressure. Such feelings are also influenced by advertising and a consumer culture looking for something to make our lives easier. We have been a lot less self-sufficient about things and rely more on machines and technology to do stuff for us. The cell phone is the perfect example of how a gadget infiltrates the culture."[21]

A recent study by Aetna and the Financial Planning Association found 44% of 18- to 24-year-olds would rather give up their health insurance before their cell phones.[22]

## Generation Inheritance

Young people today are facing an economy in which their lifestyles will be lower than that of their parents for the first time in the history of our nation. Some reasons why:

- fewer good jobs
- more taxation
- government spending
- fewer people in the workplace to pay for the government

American tradition has always held that each generation should live better than the previous one. That is only possible if the previous generation has wisely invested in its children's future, instead of having consumed their inheritance as we are doing today. The inheritance laws today, determined by our government, are designed to prohibit parents from passing on the majority of their assets to their children because of the Inheritance tax (death tax).[23] Without drastic changes to our welfare, healthcare and Medicare systems, their problems become magnified.

Proverbs verse 13:22 of the Bible says that God's people are supposed to pass on an inheritance to their children's children. That inheritance is not supposed to be debt.

Any past generation could have left a legacy of debt, but it did not. Our nation has survived over 230 years because our forefathers had a strong Biblical commitment to future generations. Today's retirees are hesitant to give up their entitlements for their children. This is shown in our nation's obligation to pensions and healthcare. The general attitude is "I worked hard and have it coming to me."

Past generations had hope and believed in God, which carried them through wars, depressions, and loss of personal fortunes. Today, because of the movement to humanism, most citizens believe that government is our salvation. History shows that any civilization that followed the attitude "spend now and pay later" decayed from within, such as the Greek and Roman empires.

## Our Economic Future

Americans have lived in a faith-based economy. We believe deeply in education, innovation, risk-taking and plain hard work as a way to a better life. This philosophy was carried over from the Pilgrims and the founders, and this theme is what led us through the years to industrial superiority. Our faith and determination have sustained us time after time, through depressions, natural catastrophes and world wars. The economy has been tested over the years, and if given the chance, it will deliver as it has in the past. However, if it is to endure and grow, government must stay out of our way.[24]

Ronald Reagan made the word "entrepreneur" popular. His policies of more freedom, lower taxes and less government regulation unleashed America's genius, creativity and boundless energy. The Reagan years led to an explosion of new American products, such as computers, videos and cell phones. He stated, "We have every right to dream heroic dreams ... There are entrepreneurs with faith in themselves and faith in an idea who create new jobs, new wealth and opportunities."[25]

We should reward success, not penalize it. Entrepreneurship and freedom are what develop free enterprise. Without freedom, entrepreneurship cannot prevail. Freedom has always been our strongest asset since the start of this nation. Freedom to start small businesses and entrepreneurship is so important for a growing economy. Government control only limits our growth. It is essential that we abide by the Constitution and keep our liberties and freedoms. If those are taken away, we will no longer compete with the rest of the world.

Our economy is facing serious threats from many factors: healthcare, debt, an aging population, social security deficit, declining industry, lawsuits, government regulations, a generation gap of qualified workers and an ever-expanding big government.

We can possibly overcome one or two of these problem areas, but when all converge at once as they are presently doing, no economy in the world could be functional and survive.

Washington knows these problems prevail. Our politicians, who are supposed to be responsible for the nation's financial health, fail to address the $10 trillion debt issue. They lack the political will to make necessary changes; instead, they address trivial issues and still cannot agree to anything. Major changes in social security, our tax code, Medicare and retirement programs need solutions for America and future generations to survive. These programs need to be fixed, and quickly.

Bipartisanship does not exist. We are a divided nation where each party is about power and money – their own money. In the meantime, a time bomb continues to tick as our elected politicians spend more than they can raise in tax revenues. Since 1980, the government has spent more than one and one-half times new revenues.

Our pork barrel junkies in Washington promise our American citizens everything possible during political campaigns. However, what revenues are raised through taxes will first be used to fill the pockets of special interest groups and their constituents. By the time money is filtered down through the many levels of our bureaucracy, there is little left for those for whom it was meant, or to improve our standard of living.

Nothing in the economy indicates any significant long-term growth. In past years, industries such as automobiles, housing, agriculture or technology led to long-term expansion of our economy.

### Automotive Industry

The automotive industry has changed dramatically over recent years. Henry Ford started selling the Model T Ford in 1908 for $850, and it was available only in the color black. General Motors and Ford, which were the innovators in the automotive industry in the early 1900s, led the world in auto production throughout the first half of the century. However, in the last half of the century, their dominance gave way to foreign manufacturers such as Toyota, Nissan, and others. Not only are Ford and GM concerned about Toyota, who led the U.S. automotive market in sales last year, but in the next couple of years, Brazil, China and Russia will be introducing new vehicles to the American market while Ford and General Motors fight to find ways to cut costs and stay financially sound.

## The Housing Market

The recent housing downturn looks like it is going to be a long one for several reasons. To begin with, over the past several years 43% of the first-time homebuyers purchased their homes with no money down loans, according to a study released by the National Association of Realtors.

Many of the homebuyers are paying interest only, and are vulnerable to an increase in interest rates which we are currently experiencing. This has created several problems. As interest rates increase, so do the homeowners' monthly payments. Those who cannot continue their mortgage payments will find their homes going into foreclosure. The second problem is that an excessive number of foreclosures would create a surplus of homes in the market. Making the situation more difficult is the fact that many of these homes were purchased with no payment down so no equity has been established; therefore, due to the growing number of foreclosures, many homes will be worth less than what the buyers paid for them.

This surplus of homes only adds to a housing downturn that started in 2008 with the retirement of baby boomers. In the next two decades, millions of baby boomers will put their homes on the market. Nationwide, the ratio of seniors to working-age residents will increase by 67% in the next 20 years. As boomers continue to age, they will move into assisted-living centers, apartments, or live with relatives. Those with two homes will sell one and retire to their vacation home.[26]

Dowell Myers, professor of policy, planning and development at the University of California, said, "The math is simple: 79 million boomers have driven up the housing demand. That trend will reverse itself when boomers are ages 65 to 75, creating a surplus of homes where there will be three sellers for each buyer."

Median price for existing homes plunged by a record 5.1% in October 2007. Reports in February 2008 indicated that the value of homes had the greatest drop since the Great Depression. The present mortgage crisis and the retirement of the boomers only add to our long-range economic problems.

## How Will the Mortgage Market
## Affect the Rest of the Economy?

So far, the housing market troubles may seem remote to the average American. However, the housing market has a domino effect. The property owners, many who really could not afford a mortgage in the first place, will experience foreclosures.

The commercial banks, having moved their asset exposure on mortgages from 25% to 33% over the past ten years, will suffer losses due to the result of foreclosures. This has already placed major banks, such as J. P. Morgan, Bank of America, Wachovia and many others, into unhealthy financial positions where they are writing off huge amounts of money associated with the foreclosures.[27] As of this writing in 2008, twenty-five banks in the U.S. have closed their doors.

These sub-prime mortgage write-offs have created losses and a large dent in earnings for many banks. An example: Citigroup lost nearly $92 billion or 34% of its market value over the last six months of 2007. The federal government has stepped in to bail out and regulate the mortgage, insurance and stock markets due to huge losses of the major mortgage companies, Fannie Mae and Freddie Mac. This domino effect is the result of an undisciplined and greedy mortgage market, a market that gave mortgages to those who could not afford to buy a house in the first place. This market will continue its decline over the next several years with the retirement of 79 million boomers. Government cannot rescue all companies that fail. Any attempt of a federal government bailout will only add to our national debt and increase costs to taxpayers.

The real threat, however, will be a closer move toward socialism, tyranny and the continued loss of freedoms of our U.S. citizens. Capitalism only works when the markets of supply and demand take care of themselves. If companies should fail along the way, no matter what their size, they should be responsible for their lack of good judgment and suffer the consequences. We have become a nation that subsidizes irresponsibility and penalizes productivity and entrepreneurship. A government fix is only a temporary rescue to any problem that government faces. The housing crisis will further filter into the economy and affect all Americans. The cost to borrow money will be more expensive. The people with marginal credit ratings will find it more difficult to get loans for auto and home purchases. If loans are difficult to obtain, fewer cars, homes and large consumer items will be purchased. The greatest fear to the economy is weak consumer spending, high-energy costs and a slow job market; if all occurring at the same time would drive the economy into a recession.

Since I began writing this chapter, the government has stepped into the economic picture as our great "savior". Former Federal Reserve Chairman Ben Bernanke and Treasury Secretary Henry Paulson, along with Congress, proposed a $700 billion dollar bailout for financial institutions. In the meantime, the automotive industry has stepped into the breadline and is asking for $25 billion to pay for committed employee pensions and healthcare costs for their retirees. I see a trend as the breadline begins to grow. First, it was the financial institutions, now the automotive industry, next might be the insurance companies, then the airlines, homebuilders, etc. Where will it end?

Our government can accept the idea of bailouts for those companies in financial trouble. After all, Congress wrote the book on mismanagement, overspending and lack of accountability. It is very familiar with the bailout concept since Congress relies on foreign countries to bail out America for its mismanagement of the nation's money. Legislators believe there should be a reward for bad behavior. As U.S. voters, we approve of their actions by voting them back into office.

The U.S. government presently owes $2.7 trillion to foreign governments and the number grows daily. In 2001 China held $61.5 billion in U.S. debt, now it has grown to $541 billion. Russia in 2001 loaned us $10 billion. Now it has grown to $74.4 billion. Japan leads the list of debtors at $586 billion. This debt is sold to other countries in the form of U.S. Treasury securities. These statistics are reported by James Ludes of the American Security Project in Washington, D.C.[28]

Our government must pay interest on the amount borrowed. These loans are required due to excessive spending by Congress along with the need of the American people to maintain their present lifestyles. Congress has proven repeatedly that what it does best is spend the people's money. Government can't create wealth, it can only redistribute our hard earned money.

I have repeated many times in this book that the greatest fear of the founding fathers was too much control placed in the hands of a central authority (Congress) could be disastrous to our nation and individual freedoms. Again, Thomas Jefferson's words, "To preserve our independence, we must not let our rulers load us with perpetual debt; I place economy among the first and most important of republic virtues and public debt as the greatest of the dangers to be feared".[29]

Economic erosion is evident on every street corner in America as businesses continue to fail as a result of government overspending, excessive regulations and overtaxation. Our present economic woes are not a failure of capitalism; they are the result of interference with capitalism coupled with a craving for power and wealth by irresponsible groups. Under capitalism, markets must find their natural bottom. Government's intervention is only a temporary correction.

As taxes continue to increase, we find ourselves working for the government instead of the government working for us. Power of the U.S. citizen is disappearing. Every time our government has tried to regulate our economy, it has failed. The New Deal of Franklin D. Roosevelt's administration during the depression not only doubled the size of government, but many historians believe it also extended the length of the depression.[30]

This socialistic philosophy only stifles entrepreneurship, which is the backbone of free enterprise and capitalism. The re-distribution of our nation's wealth combined with extensive government regulations hinder economic growth. If such conditions had existed in the early 20th century, Henry Ford, George Westinghouse, Walt Disney, George

Eastman and J.C. Penney would not have been able to succeed as entrepreneurs. The American Dream would not have been possible.

## Technology

We created the technology market with the invention of the microchip by Texas Instruments in 1959. In 1968, the computer RAM (random access memory) was introduced in the marketplace.

We dominated in all technology until the 1980s when Japan began copying many of our inventions, and started to manufacture and export products to the United States. Since then, Asian nations, including South Korea, have become more advanced in educating their people in the fields of engineering and science. They have become far more aggressive in moving top U.S. corporations in their countries, and filling top-level job positions with their own people.

"What's happening now with cars is working its way up to higher technology," says David Calhoun, General Electric's vice-chairman.[31]

I have mixed feelings about our future economy. If we can scale down government, control spending, and stop politicians from trying to manage our businesses, perhaps the economy can recover and grow. The dollar's declining value is the result of our nation's growing national debt and staggering trade deficit. The U.S. dollar has long been the king of international exchange markets, but like our position in education, technology and industrial growth, it is losing its luster.

Instead of the government offering investment incentives to our industrial market, it camouflages economic problems by trying to control interest rates and offering stimulus rebates to the populace.

Barack Obama and Congress are voicing support for a new economic stimulus package to benefit consumers. A similar package issued in the spring of 2008 shows that only $12 billion of the $78 billion in rebate checks were spent on consumer products.[32] The remainder was used on savings or personal debt. Stimulus packages do not work; these band-aids are only a "feel good" gesture by politicians to gain back the confidence of the voters.

Instead of a stimulus package, a tax cut for capital gains and corporate profits would do more to stimulate economic growth. Historically over the past thirty years, every time the capital gains rates have been cut, capital revenues to the government have risen.[33] The average corporate tax rates, if state-level taxes are included, stands at around 40%. This compares with 26% for the European Union and other competitive nations. If these two taxes, capital gains and corporate taxes, were reduced, it would give an immediate boost to the economy and consumer confidence. These reductions would increase stock values, promote entrepreneurship; enhance business creativity, increase workers' wages and America's competitiveness in the global market.

Nobel Prize winning economist, Milton Friedman, once said that he was "in favor of any tax cut, under any circumstances." The reason, he said, had nothing to do with the complexities of the economy, but instead becomes a simple moral argument – that individuals have the right to keep what they earn.[34]

Economic growth is the solution to a number of our nation's problems. Where an economy is growing, incomes grow. When personal incomes grow, better jobs, healthcare and educational opportunities are available. Experience has shown that the key to economic growth is participation in markets when people have the freedom of expectation of profit and the confidence that the government will allow them to keep a considerable amount of their profits. Otherwise, markets and an economy will fail.

If government continues to spend, the need for funds will exceed its ability to tax or borrow money. Due to high taxation and job losses, our citizens will not have money to spend on consumer products. We will experience a time of declining productivity (a recession or depression). The government would need to print more money, therefore causing a period of inflation. The inflationary cycle of an economy is the one that would destroy America's economic base.

We have many difficulties facing us without an unseen crisis. The economy has survived recessions, unbalanced budgets and low employment. However, when other major forces converge at the same time, such as a major inflationary period, another 9/11, continued growing tort litigation, more government regulations, and declining morality, our economic base would be shattered.

If an economic crisis should develop into a national crisis, it is likely that the majority of Americans will vote away many of their individual freedoms and rights in order to regain social order and their individual lifestyles. This position of human reaction resulted with the people of other civilizations, such as the Roman Empire when its society became very spoiled as the result of abundance, and government entitlements squandered away its future.

Government and apathy of the American people have put this nation in great peril. It may take another shock like one we had in 1957 when the Soviet Union launched the world's first satellite. Only this time, it may be China that will create something so devastating it will give us another wakeup call. Will the call be too late?

# Democracy and Capitalism

Adam Smith, called the Father of Capitalism, published a book entitled *Wealth of Nations* in 1776. Our Continental Congress declared America's independence from England this very same year. The leaders of our young nation accepted his ideas. Smith's theory was that political freedom would emerge and persist under conditions of economic freedom, what we now call capitalism. Smith believed if our citizens were free to work without the control of government, they would create an America where inventions, creativity and entrepreneurship would flourish, that financial success would be available to everyone, allowing all people the freedom to pursue their own endeavors and paths in life.[1]

In the centuries since Smith's economic theory was introduced, our nation has been the epitome of economic prosperity to the rest of the world. Twice during the 20th century, America considered turning away from economic freedom: first, during the Depression of the 1930s, Democrat President Franklin Roosevelt attempted to take over several industries; and, secondly, late in the 1970s under Democrat President Jimmy Carter, government control was considered during bad economic growth and high inflation.[2]

In the 1980s under Republican President Ronald Reagan, we returned to an economy of free enterprise, individual entrepreneurs rather than government control. When we returned to full capitalism, allowing the private sector to use its business creativity, the economy boomed. The result of the 1980s has carried our nation to extraordinary economic growth throughout the 1990s and early 2000s. This is Adam Smith's entrepreneur capitalism at work.[3]

A fourteen-year study conducted by the Census Bureau shows small businesses of less than five years of age contributed to over 70% of new jobs to our nation's economy, while jobs created by more mature businesses showed very little growth.[4]

Our economic picture since 1776 reveals that when government tried to operate the economy through its bureaucratic controls, capitalism and the economy faltered. When citizens have the freedom to use their creativity without the controls of government and we allow free enterprise to take its own course, we prosper. When will the politicians in Washington learn to stay out of our way?

As I indicated in comparing a republic to a democracy, democracy can only exist until voters discover they can vote themselves generous gifts from the treasury. Democracy always fails, but capitalism provides greater freedoms. Democracy embraces bureaucracy and more government control. Capitalism targets individual freedoms, creativity and free enterprise. A democracy always collapses due to loose fiscal policies that lead to the deterioration of a nation's economy, education, courts and value systems.

The reasons our nation has survived longer than any other civilization in history are because of capitalism and the belief in the Creator. Freedom only comes from God. However, capitalism gives the people of a nation the freedom to use their God-given gifts to be innovative, creative, and to pursue their own paths and endeavors in life. Capitalism has always been the stabilizer that kept government intact. Without capitalism and free enterprise, our democracy would have failed years ago.

As I indicated earlier, when government or the public sector tried to control the economy over the years, our politicians and bureaucrats have always failed. It is for this reason the founders wanted the government to be a republic to insure this nation would not be run by politicians, judges and lawyers. That power of government was always to be in the hands of the people.

Ideally, a republic form of government that includes capitalism, the belief in God and the Ten Commandments is the perfect combination as designed by our brilliant founding fathers. Unfortunately, this brilliance has been lost; instead of our nation being run as a republic over the years, we have become a democracy. The government of the people has lost its freedoms and power to elected officials (Congress), acting in the name of government.

This leads us to the status of our nation today. The government and its elected politicians have taken control not only of the economy, but our freedoms. As I have indicated in other chapters, our nation, due to the misdirection of the elected politicians, is turning toward socialism. The founding fathers saw a democracy as another form of tyranny, and they were right. Our founders had an opportunity to establish a democracy and chose not to. In fact, the founders were quite clear that we were not a democracy, but a republic.

James Madison stated, "Democracies have ever been spectacles of turbulence and contention; have ever been found incompatible with personal security, or the rights of property, and have, in general, been short in their lives as they have been violent in their deaths".[5]

The economy today is experiencing a recession created by the decisions and controls of government. I believe it is a Congress caused recession to be followed by an inflationary period for the following reasons:

- The United States citizens and American industry are being overtaxed, taking away our freedom and creativity to expand and to start new businesses.
- The liberal left of Congress, representing special interest groups, has not allowed us to drill for oil in

the United States for the past 30 years, therefore, we are being held hostage by oil-producing countries and higher fuel prices are breaking new records. This will continue as India's and China's economies become stronger with more of their citizens driving vehicles. This will continue to drive the demand for global oil and increase our prices. The lack of oil exploration is far reaching, and it affects many areas of our economy and life. Over 900 trucking companies went out of business in 2008. The price of oil has increased the cost of all consumer products because it affects plastics, transportation of consumer items, and many other products. The price of oil has been one of the major factors in the downtrend of the stock market in recent months. Most U.S. citizens have experienced significant losses in their IRA and other investments. Again, this result is because of decisions made by our out-of-touch Congress.

- The decision by Congress to use corn for the alternative fuel, ethanol, has created higher food prices, since corn is the main ingredient in many of our foods, as well as feed for farm animals.

- Our Congress will not pass any legislation to limit tort and trivial lawsuits, which are costing the American consumer billions of dollars a year. The cost incurred by manufacturers and the medical field for liability insurance to protect themselves from lawsuits is a huge detriment to our economy and new product development. According to the American Tort Reform Association (ATRA), hidden costs of product litigation cost the average family about $3,600 per year. When industrial corporations spend more on tort litigation than product research per year, you know reform needs to be addressed. What is the reason Congress will not address tort litigation reform – simply because practicing lawyers donate heavily to political campaign funds so that tort and class action lawsuit regulations will remain unchanged. Lawyers do not want change in this lucrative arrangement. In fact, most congressional representatives have a law background. This country-club atmosphere in Washington for lawyers and politicians is an injustice to the American people.

- Regulations specified by our government are creating limitations and adding costs to consumer products being developed and produced. Some firms refuse to research new products due to the cost of excessive regulations and litigation threats. This has created a real obstacle to America's ability to product innovation.

- Our $10 trillion debt created by an overspending Congress places a tremendous burden on our economy and the American people. Abe Lincoln once said, "You cannot establish security on borrowed money."[6]

The reasons I have listed above are exactly why a democracy will fail. Without freedom for the American citizen to create, capitalism will also fail. A democracy needs capitalism to survive. If government continues to overtax, overspend, over-control, over-regulate, taking away our individual freedoms, if the liberal courts persist taking God from public life, we surely and quickly will go from complacency, dependency to bondage (socialism).

We cannot separate these wayward trends of a nation, determined by its spiritual, moral, political and economic direction, for all are interrelated. When one or two falter, all are affected, and therefore, the result is the demise of democracy. Without God and the Ten Commandments, a democracy with capitalism has no discipline, and complete chaos would exist. The will of the people would prevail. Without these disciplines and obedience, the basic nature of the people's will would turn to greed and evil.

President Ronald Reagan stated on August 23, 1984,

> *Without God, there is no virtue because there is no prompting of the conscience. Without God, there is a coarsening of the society; without God, democracy will not and cannot endure...If we ever forget that we are One Nation under God, then we will be a nation gone under.*

## Politics and Politicians

### Our Founding Fathers

George Washington led America's war for independence as commander-in-chief of our military. He then served two terms as our first president. President Washington finished his work once he helped establish a new nation built on liberty. Washington then returned to his greatest ambition – to be an excellent farmer and citizen. Throughout his life, he wanted to be a farmer. However, the historical events of that time required his commitment to the military and a political life, which forced him to take a stand and lead a new nation to independence and freedom. Washington was perhaps the greatest citizen leader in world history. He had proposed that the government not pay him for his work because he believed that it was his duty and honor to serve his country.[1]

Thomas Jefferson, James Madison, John Adams, Benjamin Franklin and every signer of America's Declaration of Independence and Constitution were citizen leaders. Not one of these founding fathers had any desire to be a career politician or to have political power. They wanted to establish a God-honoring nation built on the principles of liberty.

### Today's Politicians

Unlike the founding fathers, the politicians of today have changed dramatically. No longer do our elected officials go to Washington, D.C., with the purpose of improving the makeup of our nation. Instead they go with an agenda to establish whatever is best for them personally and for their party, rather than the people they represent.

Most elected politicians expect to make a career out of politics. The majority of government officials would have little success in any other occupation, so they become career politicians simply because of the financial and social rewards that come with the job. Too many of our elected representatives in Washington have abandoned the principles they promised to defend. They have ignored the needs of the average citizen, and in many cases, their self-serving decisions or lack of decisions hinder rather than improve the values and culture of our nation.

## Congress Today

Over the years, the duties of Congress have grown from a few responsibilities to a point where today they practically control all phases of our lives. The founding fathers were afraid that too much power if put in the hands of a few could jeopardize our freedoms. George Washington said, "that the government given too much power could become a monster." Thomas Jefferson stated, "The greatest fear to one's life was the eventual rise of a central authority [Congress] that could undermine the freedoms of the populace."[2] The fear of our founding fathers has come true.

## What Is a Career Politician?

In the case of Congress, a career politician (congressional representative) is paid $162,100 per year with a full staff and limousine service plus an excellent expense account. Their benefits are:

- Full health and life insurance coverage.
- If you desire more money, you give yourself a raise. Congressmen expect to give themselves a $5,000.00 pay hike in 2009.
- Your retirement plan qualifies you as a millionaire. Annual pension for this job is $124,000 per year.
- You only work 104 days per year.
- It is nearly impossible to be fired for not doing your job or not accomplishing what you promised the taxpayers you would do.
- Your income is $1,558 per working day and you control your own schedule.
- You can spend as much money as you want because you have the U.S. Treasury as your bank and the citizens of this nation as your money supply through taxation.
- To get this glorified job, all you need to do is make promises to the American people on how you can make their lives easier by promising them more government gifts and entitlements out of the U.S. Treasury. The more you promise, the more votes you will receive in order to win the job.
- If you decide to run for another government position such as president of the United States, you are paid your senatorial wage while campaigning for yourself.

An example is the past presidential election when Senators Obama, McCain, Biden and Clinton were paid by the taxpayers of this nation for not doing their jobs in Congress. They took a one- to two-year sabbatical with pay while trying to enhance their political positions and agendas. If they failed in their runs for higher political office, they still had their elite jobs as U.S. Senators. Can you imagine employees in the private sector telling their bosses that they are seeking new jobs and while doing so they are expecting payment of their yearly incomes during their absences? If they do not find the new positions they want, they expect to retain their old jobs.

What you just read is the job description of a United States Congressman, the ultimate career politician. Holding this congressional position is the easier task while in Congress. Once you become a member of Congress, you are an incumbent. Incumbency becomes a permanent entitlement, which politicians have very little fear of losing. In today's political world, it is almost impossible for a man or woman to defeat a sitting member of Congress. In the last congressional election, 98.5% of the incumbents kept their seats in the House.

Congressional representatives keep their jobs for the following reasons:

- The political process heavily favors incumbents over challengers. Four-fifths of all the Political Action Committee (PAC) money is funneled to incumbents.
- Congressional representatives ask their high-paid staffs to volunteer to work on re-election campaigns.
- They can send out taxpayer-funded publicity mailings.

- They can give out special favors in return for votes and campaign contributions.
- They can depend on the media exposure for name recognition.
- In the 2004 congressional elections, the average congressperson raised $24,000.00 per each working day for their next campaign and this amount increases each year.

I am curious – if the incumbents are raising this much money per day for their next campaigns and working only 104 days per year, how much time and effort is spent working for the U.S. citizen (taxpayer) in the job they were hired to do?

These advantages make it very difficult for voters to make political changes of an incumbent. We would all like to have a job that pays the salary and benefits paid to congressional members and not worry about being fired for being ineffective and non-productive in the performance of our job. You would work 104 days a year and spend enough time with your staff to raise $24,000 per working day for the next election campaign. You can then continue enjoying an elite life while spending the taxpayers' money without any accountability or questions asked.

California Governor Arnold Schwarzenegger described the incumbent (professional politician) this way: "They only know how to sign ... on the back of a check rather than the front of the check."[3]

Our founding fathers envisioned the House of Representatives as the most responsive branch in the government; the one branch closest to the people and the people's needs. This branch would have the highest turnover of politicians to respond to the shifting needs and opinions of the public. Instead, it has evolved into a club of repeat members who know they have only a slim chance of losing their positions. History shows that these professional members of Congress become more arrogant, spend more money, and are less responsive to the people's needs the longer they are in office.

Congress, both the House and the Senate, are out of touch with the people they represent. We have a Congress that has accomplished very little other than have partisan fights and serve on non-productive committees. These elite "pound on your chest" members of Congress have glorified their own world. They should be walking around wearing Roman togas with wreaths on their heads, as did the Roman politicians. They are placing this nation into the same social, political and economical position as Rome before the demise of its empire.

Public opinion polls show the present Congress approval rating has been at 9%, the lowest rating in many years.[4] Public opinion polls consistently show that Americans want the following:

- Social Security reform that will save the program for current recipients and future generations.
- Smaller government with less bureaucracy.

However, instead of Congress agreeing with the will of the people, it does what we do not want:

- Continues to raid Social Security funds.
- Creates budget deficits; our national debt is now over $10 trillion.
- Spends billions of tax dollars on unexplainable earmarks and entitlements.

Congressional representatives should stay at home after a recess. When they do return to their workplace, these power-thirsty career politicians only add new regulations and laws that will give more control to our federal government and take away additional freedoms from the people.

If these members of Congress were working in the private sector for one of America's industrial corporations, they would be fired or incarcerated, fired for being non-productive and deceitful, or in jail for misuse of funds. Over the past couple of years, several CEOs and corporate leaders from the private sector have been convicted and sent to jail for the same things that some members of Congress are doing. They are misusing and spending public tax money as if it were from their own bank account.

The most recent financial fraud is the Bernard Madoff Ponzi scheme. Madoff and his firm embezzled over $50 billion of his customer's invested funds. He likely will spend the rest of his life in jail for his criminal acts.

To draw an analogy, what difference is there between a Bernard Madoff misusing his client's money and our Congress inappropriately using our taxpayers' money? Both have misrepresented and shown little accountability for their actions. However, we convict one "Madoff" and reward the other "politicians" by electing them back into office.

Most members of Congress, if interviewed for a normal job in the private sector, would have difficulty being hired. More than 50% of Congress has been accused of crimes. These range from fraud, spousal abuse, bad checks, assault, shoplifting, bad credit card use, bankruptcy, arrests due to drug-related charges and drunken driving.[5] These are our career political leaders who not only are responsible for leading this nation, but also are the same irresponsible, out-of-control politicians who are making the laws for the betterment of society and future generations.

## Term Limits

One of the biggest problems we have in Washington is that Congress is made up of professional politicians who know that the bigger our government becomes, the more control and power they have over the nation's populace. The corruptive buddy system of Congress can only be controlled by term limits.

If the president of our nation is limited to two four-year terms, certainly the time that a congressional representative can serve should also be limited. Professional politicians in Congress know no other career than politics, such as Ted Kennedy from Massachusetts and Robert Byrd, from West Virginia. Both Democrats are among the longest-serving senators in U.S. history. They have been supported by taxpayers for their entire adult lives. The longer one serves in Congress, the more likely he will become corrupt. If we limit the amount of time in office, corruption would lessen.

New ideas are needed in Washington. Incumbency has given us a divided nation and a governing group that accomplishes very little. Our world is rapidly changing and we need a turnover of politicians who will respond to the shifting needs of our people.

Under term limits, those coming to Washington to serve would know that they will soon return to private life to live under the same laws that they made while in Congress. This might make them reconsider how they legislate while in office. It is time to amend the Constitution to limit the number of consecutive terms a member of Congress can serve. The life-long careers that congressional representatives enjoy would be cut short if term limits were implemented.

Thomas Jefferson believed strongly in "rotation of office." John Adams stated that "without [term limits] every man in power becomes a ravenous beast of prey."[6] George Mason wrote, "Elected representatives should be subject to periodical rotation. For nothing so strongly impels a man to regard the interest of his constituents as the certainty of returning to the general masses of people from whence he was taken and where he must participate in their burdens."[7]

For this very reason, Congress never allows the subject of term limits to be brought forward for a vote. As incumbency becomes a permanent entitlement for politicians, fewer challengers will run for office knowing they have little chance of being elected. On the other hand, fewer voters go to the voting booths, because incumbency places government legislators as a permanent fixture in Washington. Congress today is all about power and money.

This is not the way our government was meant to operate. The founders never envisioned that politicians would make a career of politics. This has evolved over the years along with the growth of a bigger government. If it continues, more of our freedoms will be taken away as a small group of professional politicians controls this nation. This control takes us toward greater dependency and a socialistic government.

Term limits need to be addressed by the voters of this nation. Our government was not meant to finance the luxurious lifestyles of these career politicians. We can change this trend in Washington at the voting booth or through a citizens group that is fighting for term limits. They can be contacted at the following addresses:

or

| | |
|---|---|
| U.S. Term Limits | U.S. Term Limits |
| 240 Waukegan Road | 9900 Main St. Suite 303 |
| Glenview, IL  6002 | Fairfax, VA 22031 |
| www.termlimits.org | info@ustl.org |
| info@termlimits.org | |

## Ethics in Politics

Career politicians are prime examples of how elected officials with the power given them in government positions think they are above the law. Their arrogance and recklessness due to humanism (that men can do no wrong) drives them to their downfalls.

No politician has shown more conceit and unexcused reckless use of his position than Elliot Spitzer as governor of New York State. Spitzer disgraced the office which he held and disregarded the duty expected of him by the people who elected him to office. Elliot Spitzer exemplified the misuse of power. Spitzer (known as the sheriff of Wall Street while Attorney General of New York State) enjoyed crusading against the corporate image of Wall Street. His relentless goal was to crush all the corporate greed on the Street. In addition, as Attorney General, he pursued and prosecuted prostitution rings and drug trafficking. In the end, the very same offenses he relentlessly prosecuted were his demise, as his arrogance and lack of moral integrity overcame him.

Recently sitting Democrat Governor Rod Blagojevich of Illinois is accused of trying to sell the Illinois Senate seat vacated by Barack Obama to the highest bidder. This again is an abuse of a political position for personal power and gain.

## Ethics in Washington

Both the House and the Senate have ethics committees composed of lawmakers who are supposed to investigate misconduct by their colleagues. This system in Washington is very ineffective, because committees in Congress get very few results. When investigating each other, these committees are slow to start and even slower to recommend any tough sanctions.

If anything were to be accomplished regarding ethics in federal government, it would need to involve an independent group or office other than Congress. However, our politicians in Congress would never vote for such an issue because of individual exposure. Senators show very little appetite for changing their present system of the "good old boy" network. Last year, they voted 71-27 to reject a proposed independent office of public integrity.[8]

Congress rarely recommends any severe sanctions for congressional representatives accused of misconduct. The House Ethics Committee has been very quiet over the past years regarding high profile lawmakers who are facing charges of misconduct. Examples are:

- Senator William Jefferson, Democrat, Louisiana – indicted last year on racketeering and money laundering.
- Senator Larry Craig, Republican, Idaho – pled guilty to disorderly conduct in a Minneapolis airport men's room.
- Representative Alan Mollohan, Democrat, West Virginia – accused of under-reporting assets and steering funds to non-profit groups he founded.
- Representative Rick Renzi, Republican, Arizona – indicted on extortion, money-laundering and conspiracy charges.[9]

These are only a few names of congressional representatives who have been accused of misconduct.

Scandals in Congress have a common cause. They are the result of what happens to politicians who seek power as their goal. They abuse those powers instead of using them as a means of achieving benefits for the citizens they represent. Self-pride shows up in many ways in Washington. This is why term limits are essential. The longer a congressional representative stays in office, the more abusive they become.

Those politicians breaking the law or performing corrupt actions become suspicious of everyone else. Their belligerence and arrogance overwhelm them as they consider themselves above those they represent, as well as the law. Politicians forget they first have a sworn duty to uphold the will of the people who elected them.

President James A. Garfield, also a Christian minister, reminded Americans,

> *Now more than ever before, the people are responsible for the character of their Congress. If that body be ignorant, reckless and corrupt, it is because the people tolerate ignorance, recklessness and corruption. If it be intelligent, brave and pure it is because the people demand these high qualities to represent them in the national legislature ... If the next centennial does not find us a great nation ... it will be because who represent the enterprise, the culture, and the morality of the nation do not aid in controlling the political forces.[10]*

## Lobbyists and Earmarks

A lobbyist is a person who seeks to influence lawmakers on behalf of a particular company, organization or institution. Lobbyists, who often work for large law firms, must register with the Secretary of the Senate and the Clerk of the House. Many large companies and institutions, such as universities or non-profit organizations, have their own lobbyists on staff.

An earmark is money that a lawmaker adds to a spending bill for a specific item or program that was either not requested by the agency receiving the money or authorized by previous legislation.

Since the ratification of the Bill of Rights 215 years ago, lobbying the federal government has grown into a $2 billion a year industry, employing over 32,000 people. Early in the 19th century, when few people were affected by actions of the federal government, lobbying was done on a small scale. However, with the growth of our federal government, lobbying in Washington has become big business.

Our founding fathers recognized that the tendency of U.S. citizens was to organize their own interests into a group activity. They believed that no one group would be strong enough to dominate over the others regarding public policy. However, with the tremendous growth of our government, wealthier groups behind lobbyists with inside connections can and do monopolize areas of national policy. This is not an illegal activity, but it does give well-funded lobbyists the inside track with politicians versus the common citizen who does not have the financial means to buy tickets to political fundraisers.

Last year, lobbyists contributed over $25 million to candidates, according to the Center for Responsive Politics, which tracks money in politics. All this is legal. Since 2000, non-profit groups with lobbyists among their directors paid for over 900 congressional trips worth about $4 million, again legal expenditures, based on government criteria. Lawmakers say that these trips merely buy "access" for the lobbyist.[11]

However, there is a lot wrong with this system, as history has proven. There is a very fine line between businesses conducted this way versus bribery. Members of Congress and their staffs are barred from using their positions for personal profit. However, members of their families, either spouses or other relatives, can and do cash in when lawmakers spend taxpayer dollars. *USA Today* reported in 2006 that lobbying groups employed 30 family members to influence spending bills that their relatives with ties to the House and Senate appropriations committees helped write. Combined, these family members generated millions of dollars in fees for themselves and their firms.[12]

In 2005, appropriation bills alone contained $750 million for projects championed by lobbyists whose relatives were involved in writing the spending bills. Hundreds of billions of taxpayer dollars are spent this way every year. No rules or laws prevent lawmakers or their staffs from being lobbied by relatives. Proposals to address and police this type of practice are continually being stalled by Congress. Neither the lawmakers nor lobbyists need to report if they are related.

*USA Today* reported they found 53 cases in which relatives of lawmakers or top aides worked as lobbyists. Of 30 projects, family members were involved in helping write the bills. Twenty-two (22) of the 30 succeeded in getting specific money written into the bill for their clients.[13]

Earmarks in appropriation bills have more than tripled over the past several years according to the Congressional Research Services. Taxpayer groups and fiscal conservatives in Congress point to earmarks as a major source of wasteful spending, and a way to extend special favors for campaign contributions or family members who are lobbying. Government needs to be more transparent. Pet earmarks are actually hidden and smuggled into legislation by congressional members.

This is a part of government which many citizens are not aware. As government has grown over the years, the "out of control" spending of our politicians continues to grow. The lawmakers, while walking the fine line between corruption and ethics, find ways to spend the taxpayers' money in order to satisfy their constituents, and keep themselves in the good graces of special interest groups.

## The Clintons

In my opinion, William "Bill" and Hillary Clinton are classic examples of professional career politicians. They have been paid by tax money most of their professional lives, their income and personal needs have been met by taxpayers. No one in the history of American politics has used the powers of political office more than Bill and Hillary Clinton, as they relentlessly seek power and wealth.

How did the Clintons use their political positions to attain their personal goals of power and wealth? Bill Clinton's political career began in Arkansas where he was elected Attorney General of the state in 1976. He was then elected Governor in 1978. Bill Clinton went from the Governorship of Arkansas to the Presidency of the United States, serving two terms from 1993 to 2001.

After eight years in the White House, Hillary was elected to the United States Senate, representing the state of New York. She lost her nomination for the Democratic 2008 primary for president and has been appointed by President-Elect Obama to Secretary of State. In the meantime, political rumor has it that Bill Clinton is quietly positioning himself as a possible candidate for Secretary General of the United Nations. The pursuit of political power and wealth is endless.

Our founding fathers truly served their country, unlike today's career politicians do. George Washington served his country as a military commander and then became our first president. He offered to serve without pay because he felt it was his duty. He was so famous and popular with the colonists that he could have declared himself president for life, but he did not.

James McPherson, a historian who teaches at Princeton University edited *To the Best of My Ability: The American Presidents,* a companion volume to the History Channel's recent series on the presidents. In

1989, he won a Pulitzer Prize for his history of the Civil War, *Battle Cry of Freedom*. He rates past presidents from best to worst. His assessment of Bill Clinton is as follows: "Bill Clinton arrived in Washington amid great expectations, but left with legacies that are among the most disappointing of all presidencies. Clinton, particularly, made a mess of it. With an unparalleled opportunity to reform the dysfunctional system of medical insurance, he fumbled away the opportunity and his moral lapses helped rob his own party of its historical majority."[14]

Let us review the Clinton presidency as the forty-second President of the United States. Bill Clinton promised much, but delivered little. During his campaign to run for President, Bill and Hillary Clinton said whatever was necessary to attain votes and based many of their decisions while in office on what was politically correct and on popular poll results.

President William Jefferson Clinton, in one of his very first acts as President, signed the following orders on January 22, 1993:

- He lifted the ban on federal funding of abortion on military bases around the world.
- He reversed the Reagan Mexico City Policy of not allowing federal funds to be used to finance abortion in foreign nations.
- He lifted the ban of the development of Mifepristone (RU486)
- He lifted the ban on fetal tissue research.[15]

In addition to these orders, he immediately undressed and weakened the military. He reduced the number of troops, closed military bases and endorsed the "Don't Tell Policy." This was a president with a 43% popular vote, who displayed his total disregard for God, our military, country and future generations.[16]

Election results showed that one of every four evangelical Christians voted for Bill Clinton, knowing that he endorsed policies supporting abortion, homosexuality and other lifestyles contrary to Christian and moral principles. He mockingly extended his gratitude to the Christians of our nation when he signed these executive orders on the very same day that thousands of Christians in the March for Life at Washington, D.C., had gathered to mourn the deaths of millions of babies slaughtered by abortion.

This was only the beginning of an administration that included acts of complete arrogance, corruption, lies, immoral behavior, and criminal wrongdoing.

This nation wants to thank the Clinton presidency for the following:

- Introducing us to Jennifer Flowers, Paula Jones, Kathleen Willey, Juanita Broderick, Dolly Browning and Monica Lewinsky.[17] These are women we would have never known. Their stories captivated the entertainment media for months with the mystery of "who did it...and with whom?"

- Clinton's involvement with Monica Lewinsky has been well documented over the past years. Bill Clinton's disgrace of the White House and the office of president is unparalleled.

- Creating a new White House sport called the "Spin Team" from which surfaced a new media "darling" called Monica "the Stalker." The "Spin Team" also fought weekly battles against their favorite opponent, the "Right Wing Conspiracy Team," who was falsely blamed for most accusations against Bill Clinton.

- Showing us that sexual harassment in the workplace is okay.
- For signing a bill during his term in office that disallowed us to drill in ANWAR, for which we are paying dearly today at the gas pumps.
- Reducing and softening our military capabilities and national security; after all, we were getting too powerful.
- Finding extra taxpayers' dollars to fly his family, friends, and political pals on many of his global expeditions.
- For treating Abe Lincoln's bedroom and White House as an elite bed and breakfast. I am sure the list of 938 guests that donated the $6 million toward his re-election campaign enjoyed their stays. I understand the room service and taxpayer paid gifts were greatly appreciated by the guests.

### President Clinton on Terrorism and National Security

The most damaging act of Bill Clinton's administration was his failure to protect our national security. Not only did his decisions in office lead to the 9/11 tragedy, but even more concerning is how his administration left this nation's future regarding Iraq, North Korea, China and Iran.

James Inhofe of The Washington Post best describes Clinton regarding China and our national security. On June 20, 1999, he wrote the following:

*... Too many commentators are missing the point about the national security significance of the Cox Report and its revelation of China's theft of U.S. nuclear secrets. It is time to face the truth. This president and this administration are singularly culpable for orchestrating a politically inspired cover-up to advance policies they knew were causing harm to U.S. national security. Let's not be distracted by the self-serving Clinton spin: everybody does it, that it all happened during previous administrations; that there is equal blame to go around on all sides, that Bill Clinton acted quickly and properly when he found out. All of this is wrong, a dishonest smokescreen to divert attention from the real issues. It is also an attempt to dissuade people from actually reading the Cox Report and discovering for themselves that the Clinton spin is a delusion...* [18]

*... Sixteen of the 17 most significant major technology breaches revealed in the Cox Report were discovered after 1994. The notion that Presidents Carter, Reagan and Bush knew the extent to which China's efforts to steal U.S. nuclear and military technology were successful is fantasy..* [19]

*... At least eight (and maybe more) of these breaches actually occurred after 1994 and after it was well-known to the Clinton administration that China had been illegally proliferating arms technology to rogue countries around the world. Among these breaches – occurring on the Clinton watch – are many of those that go the farthest in advancing China's potential as a direct nuclear threat to the United States.* [20]

The way out of the North Korea problem in 1994 was premised on a double fraud. North Korea deceived us because first we deceived ourselves. We paid North Korea hundreds of millions of dollars in aid – we even agreed to supply them with two nuclear plants if only they would relinquish their nuclear weapons and missile programs. Would Kim Jung keep his word? He signed the agreement, and then cheated. When caught cheating, he reneged. Another agreement with North Korea would end the same as in 1994. The Clinton approach was an embarrassing debacle for the U.S.[21]

Let us look at the terrorist attacks on America and how Clinton reacted to them during his eight years as president.

- 1992 – Osama bin Laden's attack against our military in Yemen
- 1993 – World Trade Center bombing
- 1996 – The Khobar Towers
- 1998 – The American Embassies in Kenya and Tanzania
- 2000 – The bombing of the U.S.S. Cole

As the result of the first World Trade Center bombing, America lost many lives, and hundreds were injured. Clinton responded with the following comments when asked how terrorism would affect America's way of life.

> *I certainly hope not. We've been very blessed in this country to have been free of the kind of terrorist activity that has gripped other countries. Even a country like Great Britain, that has a much lower general crime rate, has more of that sort of activity because of the political problems that it has been involved in.*
>
> *I don't want the American people to overact to this at this time. I can tell you, I have put – I will reiterate – I have put the full resources of the Federal Government, every conceivable law enforcement information*

*resource we could put to work on this we have. I am very concerned about it. But I think it's also important that we not overreact to it. After all sometimes when an incident like this happens, people try to claim for it who didn't do it. Sometimes if folks like that can get to stop doing what you're doing, they've won half the battle. If they get you ruffled, if they get us to change the way we live and what we do that's half the battle.*

*I would discourage the American people from overreacting to this ... But I would plead with the American people and the good people of New York to right now keep your courage up, go on about your lives. And we're working as hard as we can to get to the bottom of this.*[22]

After the 1996 Khobar Towers bombing in Saudi Arabia, which killed 19 and injured 200 U.S. military personnel, Clinton promised that those responsible would be hunted down and punished.

After the 1998 bombing of U.S. embassies in Africa, which killed 224 and injured 5000, Clinton promised that those responsible would be hunted down and punished.

After the 2000 bombing of the U.S.S. Cole, which killed 17 and injured 39 U.S. sailors, Clinton again promised that those responsible would be hunted down and punished.

Clinton had the opportunity to capture Bin Laden when the Sudanese government offered him in 1996, but he had the excuse of not having enough evidence against him to present a case in a court of law. This president's refusal to capture Osama Bin Laden when presented with the opportunity by the Sudanese, along with his lack of retaliation to the terrorist attacks, only encouraged further Al Qaeda missions against the American people.

The Clinton administration was presented with many opportunities to make a statement on terrorism, but did very little to protect our nation against these murderers. He treated each attack by terrorists as a criminal act by foreign individuals rather than a brutal attempt to change the American way of life. Clinton's reaction was to not take action. He refused to get the military or federal departments involved.

If Clinton knew the terrorists were a threat to the security of our nation and the world, why did he not initiate action to protect America? We may never know the answer to this question. One of the most likely sources was located in the National Archives Building. Original files of the National Security records regarding terrorism from the Clinton administration are supposed to be located there.

### The Sandy Berger Caper

In the fall of 2003, Sandy Berger, Clinton's National Security Advisor, was caught stealing files from the National Archives Building, which he had stuffed into his undergarments. The 9/11 Commission wanted to review all files concerning the Clinton administration up to the 9/11 attack. Berger admitted taking files and holding information from the 9/11 Commission which was detrimental to our nation's fight against terrorism.

Many questions need to be asked. Why were the records taken? Who was being protected? Did someone from the Clinton administration order Berger to do this? What important information was destroyed?

This entire caper is very mysterious. However, the penalty given Sandy Berger is even more puzzling. In 2005, Berger struck a misde-meanor, plea-bargain agreement of a $50,000 fine, and 100 hours of public service. Why was he not charged and convicted of a felony for taking national security files? Berger was also to take a lie detector test, which, to my knowledge, has never happened. These are more unanswered questions regarding the Clinton administration.

The 1990s were a decade of illusions in foreign policy. On September 11, 2001, that illusion ended. The United States, as the world's superpower, realized that we have serious rivals in other nations and evil groups. The Clinton administration leaned toward the United Nations as the body to determine when the United States would go to war, instead of our own Congress as prescribed by our founders.

Bill Clinton's hapless effort and flowery words concerning the terrorist attacks during the 1990s only strengthened and encouraged the terrorists, allowing them to see how vulnerable America really was. I believe that Clinton was so caught up with the legal matter of the Monica mess, along with concern that his legacy might be tarnished, that he felt that the terrorist threats would go away by firing a few cruise missiles in a haphazard attempt to frighten the enemy. What would a president like Clinton have done if faced with the same challenges as George Washington during the Revolutionary War, Lincoln during the Civil War, or Truman during World War II? It is frightening to think of those times in our history without having a president with commitment and courage to make decisions.

Bill Clinton's ratings as president were high because he did nothing to make himself vulnerable. We just reviewed his reaction to our terrorist threats.

Another Clinton delusion was that he created a great economic boom in the '90s, plus a budget surplus. We did have good economic times. However, it was not the result of what Bill Clinton created. During the '90s, he rode the results of the stock markets due to the introduction of the internet and high tech stock IPOs. This unanticipated surge of federal tax revenue from this boom brought about the federal government surpluses – something Clinton did not create. President Clinton happened to be at the right place at the right time as the stock market skyrocketed during the '90s. However, no administrative decisions were made to assist economic growth during his eight years in office. This left us in a recession as we entered the 2000s, and the George W. Bush administration.

Bill's Clinton's administration did nothing positive for the nation concerning terrorism, the economy and our national security. Therefore, his legacy will be identified with his immoral behavior, lies and criminal wrongdoings.

This is a president who during his entire election campaign told the nation, "I feel your pain," concerning the economy, entitlements and lifestyles. Evidently, these issues were more important to the average American than the moral issues. This does not speak well for our society as a whole. It indicates that most Americans will sacrifice their moral convictions for the sake of their comforts. History shows that nations follow the moral example of their leadership. Today, we are still paying the moral price from eight years of a depraved Clinton presidency.

## It's About Power and Money

Before the Clintons ended their eight years in the White House, they carefully planned their next political move. One of the few avenues left for political power was to put their energy into Hillary's political career. Since her college days, she always had a vision of being the first woman president of the United States. However, since she had no experience in elective office, the Clintons planned a strategy for her to obtain a top political position. After considering various options, Hillary decided to seek election in a state in which she had never lived. She chose to run for the Senate seat for New York about to be vacated by a longtime Democratic stalwart, Pat Moynihan. The Clintons knew that New York State had a strong Democratic base, and there was little competition for the Senate seat.

In order for Hillary to qualify as a candidate for public office in New York State, they needed to establish a residency in the state. They purchased a million dollar-plus house in Chappaqua, New York, which would be their first home ownership during their married life.

I indicated earlier in this chapter that the Clintons and other career politicians use their political positions to attain personal wealth. The Clintons have earned $109 million since Bill left the office of president in 2000. In the last seven years, they received the following income:

- Bill's book earned $12 million.
- Hillary's book earned $8 million
- Bill receives $50,000 for each speaking engagement.

The $109 million is an average income of $43,057 per *day* over the seven-year period. Comparatively, the average income for an American family is $48,451 per *year*.

Relating to the Clintons' retirement:

- Bill is eligible to receive his pension as Attorney General and Governor of Arkansas.
- As past President of the United States, he will receive a $400,000 per year pension.
- Hillary will receive a pension check for her Senate seat for the rest of her life, prorated on her years of service based on her present salary of $169,300 per year.
- Their health benefits are paid as long as they live.

- They have Secret Service protection for as long as they live.
- Bill Clinton's phone bill since leaving office in 2001 is $420,000, plus a $3.2 million office rent charge to taxpayers. Compare that to the totals run up by past presidents Bush, Carter, Ford and Reagan, who combined spent $484,000 on telephone service and $3.8 million on their rent for offices. The same Bill Clinton said he would use a bus for his campaign transportation and who told the American people he felt their pain. Do the voters who cast their ballots for Clinton for two presidential terms still believe that he feels their pain – as he laughs all the way to the bank? What a guy!

**President Bush on Terrorism and National Security**

We all know that 9/11 was a direct attack on America, and that an estimated 3000 people in New York, Pennsylvania and Washington, D.C. died as a result of that assault. We are reminded each day when entering an airport or boarding an airplane how the attacks of 9/11 affected the security of this country. We will never know the billions and billions of dollars it has cost the American people for extra security and the effect it has had on the economy and way of life.

From the very outset, President Bush indicated that the war was not between nations, but a conflict between good and evil. Stating excerpts in his address to Congress days later, President Bush explained:

*These terrorists kill not merely to end lives, but to disrupt and end a way of life. With every atrocity, they hope that America grows fearful, retreating from the world, forsaking our friend. They stand against us because we stand in their way.*

President Bush closed by saying,

*I will not forget this wound to our country or those who inflicted it. I will not yield. I will not rest; I will not relent in waging this struggle for freedom and security for the American people. The course of this war is not known, yet its outcome is certain. Freedom and fear, justice and cruelty have always been at war, and we know that God is not neutral between them.*[23]

In his State of the Union speech, President Bush stated,

*Steadfast in our purpose, we now press on. We have known freedom's price. We have shown freedom's power. And in this great conflict, my fellow Americans, we will see freedom's history.*

Here, he related to our ancestors as this nation fought many wars for the preservation of freedom.

Four months after his State of the Union address on June 1, 2002, at commencement exercises at West Point, President G. W. Bush stated,

*In defending the peace, we face a threat with no precedent. Enemies of the past needed great armies and great industrial capabilities to endanger the American people and our nation. The attacks of September the Eleventh required a few hundred thousand dollars in the hands of a few dozen evil and deluded men. All of the chaos and suffering they caused came at much less than the cost of a single tank ... We cannot defend America and our friends by hoping for the best. We cannot put our faith in the words of tyrants, who solemnly sign*

*non-proliferation treaties and then systematically break*
*them. If we wait for threats to fully materialize, we will*
*have waited too long.*[24]

President Bush after the 9/11 attack stated,

*War has been waged against us ... This nation is*
*peaceful, but fierce when stirred to anger. This conflict*
*was begun on the timing and terms of others. It will end*
*in a way, and at the hour, of our choosing.*[25]

President Bush referred to the terrorist countries as "Axis of Evil." In his address, President Bush touched on freedom, peace and evil. All are the result of having or lacking the presence of God in one's heart.

Albert Einstein said about evil: That evil, like darkness, does not exist in itself. It is a term used by man to describe a situation. Darkness is the result of the lack of light, and evil the result of what happens when man does not have God's love present in his heart.[26]

We cannot afford another Clinton administration with the problems facing our nation. We need integrity and discipline in the White House. A political party or president who thinks he can negotiate away terrorism will only bring chaos and destruction to this nation. We need leadership that has the bulldog demeanor of Ronald Reagan, with the goal of keeping and defending this country's freedom. George W. Bush has this same persona. He did not budge from his defense of the nation, although his popularity and poll ratings fell to a new low and the war in Iraq became a political issue. Between the misleading reports by the media and the accusations of the Democratic Party, the American people turned the 2006 congressional election and the 2008 presidential elections into an anti-war victory for the Liberals and Democrats, forgetting 9/11 and the national security that the Bush administration provided for the nation.

This offensive fight has kept America free from terrorist attacks over the past seven years.  It is better to fight the battle against terrorism abroad than here in America.  Bush fought the war on terror for the same reason that America is fighting the war on terror – because we have no choice.  The war on terror cannot be won at home, but it can be lost here.  It is in America that terrorists hope to inflict a devastating blow, which would kill thousands and destroy the American will to fight.  If another attack such as 9/11 should happen with our present economy, the cost of national security would put our nation in serious peril.

Ronald Reagan stated,

> *The dustbin of history is littered with the remains of countries which relied on diplomacy to secure their freedom.  We must never forget ... in the final analysis ... that it is our military, industrial and economic strength that offers the best guarantee of peace for America in times of danger.*[27]

## THE 2008 PRESIDENTIAL ELECTION

The 2008 Presidential Election resulted in the American voters and the media creating a $600 million dollar man by the name of Barack Hussein Obama.  The more than $600 million raised during his presidential campaign was approximately seven times greater than was raised by his Republican opponent, John McCain, and the most ever collected by any previous presidential candidate.  Obama broke his promise to accept public funds for his campaign money with no remorse or penalty.  His refusal of public funds became apparent when

he realized he could raise more money over the internet with no explanation or record of where the funds came from, contrary to the records
kept by other candidates.

The American Democratic voters, along with the help of the mainstream media, created a script that read like a movie storyline. They
produced a character they believed would best fit the role of president.
Obama auditioned for the part; he looked presidential and campaigned
well.   Voters listened to the way he spoke instead of the meaning of
the spoken words. He promised change and was selected for the role.
The media, enamored by Obama, became his running mate. They
camouflaged, misinformed and misled the American people in order to
accomplish their common liberal agendas.

Once Obama won the role as the Democratic candidate, the $600
million dollar man took advantage of our economic crisis along with
preaching the need for governmental change. He targeted the youth of
our nation. The result 66% of young people ages 18-29 voted for him.[28]
This age group taught by our educators that government would take care
of their every need. He also focused on the 47 million citizens who do
not pay their taxes by promising them more government entitlements,
handouts and a redistribution of wealth. The response to the Obama
promise gave him enough votes to become the 44th President of the
U.S.

This election only confirmed the fears of our founding fathers that
the American voters, if promised enough from the U.S. Treasury, will
sell their God-given freedoms to the highest bidder. In this election,
the highest bidder was the $600 million dollar man, Barack Hussein
Obama.

Along with the promise of redistribution of money from the U.S.
Treasury, the Obama campaign emphasized the need for "change". He
continually impressed upon the American voters that change and reform

were needed in our government. However, in promising change, he never explained what those changes would be. Change can be good or bad!

I have been a trout fisherman since I was 8 years old. Over the years, I have waded many brooks and streams in search of this colorful species. For the stream to flow freely, stay its course and be productive, it depends on a main water source. However, in many cases, over the history of the stream, it goes through unexpected storms, altering its direction and creating radical changes in its water flow. Once the waterway loses its main source, it no longer flows freely, becomes too diverse, no longer stays its course and becomes unproductive. It eventually dries up and perishes into obscurity.

Nations and civilizations are much like a flowing stream. Over time, radical changes alter their direction. They disregard the Source that created a free and productive society. The unexpected storms, such as an eroding economy, moral and political misdirection, change their historic path. They stray from their intended course, become unproductive and are a page in history.

Jedediah More (founding educator) said, "Whenever the pillars of Christianity shall be overthrown, our present republican form of government and all the blessings which flow from them, must fall with them."[29]

The rules are clear and simple. What worked for America for the first 150-plus years created the most prosperous nation in history - why change? Thomas Jefferson warned that for a nation to keep its course, it is important for its people and governing body to return to common sense as written in the 10 Commandments.

This nation is confronting some of the gravest challenges in its history. America faces record debt, government bureaucracy continues to grow, courts have become radical, we are losing our moral values, and our kids are not properly educated. At a time when our nation requires experienced management, stability and the need to go back to the basic principles that propelled America to world leadership, we have elected Barack Obama as President, a man that we know little about. His personal history, past affiliations and political intent are questionable. Obama spent only 143 working days in the U.S. Senate prior to announcing his run for President. He authored no significant legislation during that time. He has no executive experience, knows little about economic and foreign affairs. He has no military experience, yet has become Commander-In-Chief of our armed forces. This is not the time for a President to use his four-year term for on-the-job training. Obama embraces the socialistic philosophy of redistribution of wealth. He was considered the most liberal and radical member of the Senate. This President supports policies that are on a collision course with Biblical beliefs. His voting records as Illinois State Senator support abortion and infanticide for aborted babies born alive. Both are contrary to Christian and moral principles. This election was about the future of our nation, it was an election that will determine the culture that our children and grandchildren will come to know.

The storyline character of Barack Obama, created by the press and accepted by the voters, will have difficulty identifying his role as President. One morning reality will set in when the $600 million man will awaken and ask himself, what did I promise the American people? President Barack Obama must come to realize that he is no longer campaigning for himself. He represents all the people of this nation and his decisions must be based on what is right for America and future generations. In time, his past, his values and respect for American tradition will be revealed.

## Governor Sarah Palin

One of the bright spots in the 2008 Presidential campaign was Sarah Palin. She was an unknown governor from Alaska, selected by John McCain to be his vice presidential running mate. I believe her qualifications were greater than most of the U.S. senators running for the office of president. She has executive experience as governor where her accomplishments are a matter of record. Her poll approval rating is over 80% as governor vs. those three U.S. Senators, Obama, Biden and McCain, whose approval rating has been at a low of 9%. Her popularity was confirmed when the television audience who viewed the Palin-Biden debate was over 70 million. At the time of this writing, this television event recorded the second highest rating in history, second only to the highest-rated Super Bowl game. When Sarah Palin appeared on Saturday Night Live, the program received its highest rating in 14 years.

She brought a fresh new life to the Republican Party and the entire campaign of 2008. She related to the average citizen with her strong ethical background of faith and family. The mainstream media considered her a threat and could not accept her success, because she led the life according to the principles she articulated. She was an outsider in Washington, not part of the elite Senate group of Obama, Biden and McCain. The character assassination started immediately. She became a target of the media, the Democrats and some Republicans. They criticized her for everything from her words to her wardrobe. Why did this happen? The narrow-minded media and liberal left are dragging down the rest of America. They want to reshape our nation to fit their own agendas. They fear America will return to its Christian values of God and Truth. Today, the extreme left has a problem with truth; facts are misrepresented and camouflaged. Studies indicate that 75%

of journalists are politically and ideologically liberal. 86% of those polled seldom or never attend religious services. This certainly does not represent the core or majority of the American people. I believe the populace wants to return to the traditional values and heritage that made America great.

Ronald Reagan once said, "Too often, character assassination has replaced debate and principle in Washington, D.C., destroy someone's reputation and you don't have to talk about what he stands for."[30] This took place with Sarah Palin, when the Democrat Party sent 30 lawyers to Alaska to dig up whatever they could to destroy her character and reputation.

Sarah Palin will reappear on the national political scene at a future date and be a force for things to come. She is authentic and best represents the average citizen and the values our founding fathers held sacred.

## Your Vote Counts

Your vote on Election Day whether at local, state and federal levels is one of the most powerful ways for you to express your opinion and to influence the future direction of America. It is important when casting your ballot to know what each candidate and party represent. The trends of a nation are determined by its spiritual, moral, political and economic direction – all are interrelated. The decisions made by our elected officials will determine the course of our nation for generations to come.

It is our civic responsibility to vote. Americans are blessed to live under a government of the people, by the people and for the people. We are privileged to participate in a government that allows each citizen the freedom to vote for political candidates who best represent their values and beliefs. Millions of people in all parts of the world only dream about such a privilege. Still, many Americans choose not to vote. According to the U.S. Census Bureau, as many as 35% of eligible Americans are not registered to vote – that is 45 to 55 million people. Only 43% of evangelical Christians actually bothered to vote. Many believers fail to consider their biblical values when voting, often choosing candidates whose positions are at odds with their beliefs, convictions and values.

Are the American people becoming too complacent as apathy rages through our land of spoiled people? The chapters of this book describe what happened to other major civilizations as they went through the social and cultural phases of their histories. The most devastating phases of a nation are those of apathy and complacency. Apathy (the "I don't care" attitude), and complacency (why make the effort?), are two of the major reasons why nations have failed to survive.

When you vote, you determine who will lead our local, state and federal governments:

- Register to vote
- Be informed
- Vote your values
  ◊ Educate yourself on election issues.
  ◊ Pick your party – consider how each political party's views line up with your core values
  ◊ Choose a candidate using reasons that are good for you and the future of America.

An informed vote takes effort. The choice is not always easy, but it is always significant.

Since the administration of Franklin D. Roosevelt, government has continued to grow. Politicians know that the larger government becomes, the more control they have over the citizens of this nation. Remember – politicians will continue to promise America's citizens whatever they want to hear in order to obtain their votes. Candidates understand the psychology of running for office and play with the mindset of our citizens to gain their trust and votes. We are a people continually bombarded six-hours each day by the liberal media that misrepresent the real America.

If an incumbent is one of the candidates being considered, you need to know their record of accomplishment while in office versus the ideals of the new candidate. Unfortunately, incumbency takes away from the voter the opportunity to elect new candidates and ideas into office. The money factor of incumbency should be ignored and not sway your decision (see comments on incumbency earlier in this chapter).

## Washington is Broken

The United States Congress has created our present economic crisis. Nancy Pelosi is Speaker of the House. Pelosi "the parrot" seems to have one expression and solution to everything. Her answer to all questions is a repeated "Blame it on Bush, Blame it on Bush, and Blame it on Bush."

As an example, consider the following: In the first 6 years of the George Bush administration, the following statistics were realized:
- consumer confidence was at a new high
- regular gasoline prices were stable
- the unemployment rate was at 4.5%
- the stock market hit record highs
- Americans enjoyed vacations, travel and the ability to purchase their choice of consumer products

In 2006, our citizens voted in a Democratic Congress who promised "change" to the American way of life. In the past year, the following changes took place:

- consumer confidence has plummeted
- gasoline was over $4.00 per gallon
- unemployment is over 9% [31]
- The decision of Congress, to prevent new oil exploration and to promote fuel, and our record national debt, has created an inflationary period and an erosion of America's economy.

Based on the above facts, should we blame George Bush for the current state of America?

Our new Congress, which also proposed governmental "change" in the 2006 congressional election, now forms a team of Obama, Pelosi and Reid. All are of the same political party. All have shown a thirst for power and have embraced the socialist view of wealth redistribution through bailouts and stimulus packages from the U.S. Treasury. This team made up of extreme liberal left Democrats is taking America into a new radical version of the Constitution both in the courts and the way our government functions. No longer will we have the checks and balances the founders deemed necessary to run our government. These three will create an imbalance of legislative power in Congress and the presidency. The voting imbalance will bring with it a philosophy that those who do not agree with the views of these Democrat politicians will be overruled and taken out of play. This will lead to a "change" in the makeup of a nation that Obama, Pelosi and Reid want to create, certainly not the America intended by our founding fathers.

It is our president, congress and our court system that determine America's direction. For America to right itself, it needs to start with all levels of government. All levels appoint judges, who today overstep their authority and instead of interpreting the law, begin making their own law.

The American experience has been one of success during the 200 years of our nations existence. America has always had a blueprint for success. That blueprint is belief in the Creator and our Constitution. As we distance ourselves further from that blueprint, the harder it will be to return or stay on course with the values that have made America great.

We are faced with a Congress that knows what is wrong with our government, but does not have the political will or fortitude to make the necessary changes to solve these problems. In many cases, the solutions would reduce the size of government, thereby taking away power and term longevity from career politicians. It is called protecting your own livelihood instead of doing what is best for our taxpayers and the nation.

The political divide only becomes greater as our out-of-touch politicians create a deeper hole for this nation. The conventional wisdom in Washington is that any major changes in huge bureaucratic programs will need to be worked out on a bipartisan basis. However, bipartisanship is in short supply these days as more venom is shown in American politics, and our nation becomes more and more divided.

Congress must focus on the contents, not the package, when viewing America. Congress needs to reform itself. Its reaction time to key issues is ludicrously slow. Most legislation needs to survive several committees to get results, but there are too many chairpersons and too many committees. Chairperson titles mean power to our career politicians, giving them more stars for their next election campaigns. This evidently is more important to Congress than results to issues needing voting commitments.

The sinkhole only grows deeper as bigger government and an entrenched bureaucracy becomes an impediment to progress. The ever-increasing national debt has reached new levels, and our social and moral values continue to fall.

We must crawl out of this sinkhole in which our politicians and court system have submerged us. We have always been a nation able to find its way through many trials. It is the strength and courage of the American citizen that has always carried this nation. We must always look skyward from this sinkhole. We have always received our blessings from that direction. The Lord, in His providence, has been our protector, and not the government.

## Our Enemies

In selecting our nation's most dangerous enemies, I have chosen the federal government and the American Civil Liberties Union (ACLU). Both are taking away and infringing upon the freedoms given us by our Constitution, and putting in jeopardy the liberties for which our Founding Fathers and the soldiers of past wars gave their lives. Both are a serious threat to the preservation of America.

The reason I believe government is our number one enemy is that an out-of-control government is coercing the people of this nation. A Congress that is holding us hostage regarding our rights and freedoms. Recent poll results show Congress approval rating less than 10%.

Our second most dangerous enemy is the ACLU, which is attempting to remove our Christian heritage and freedoms using the court system. Our judiciary branch is ruled by unelected elitists who are interpreting the United States Constitution to fit the extreme agendas of the ACLU.

If we look back in history, the founding fathers and other great leaders have repeatedly warned that our enemies would come from within, not from abroad. The American people, of all nations in history, have had the opportunity to learn from the past. History has taught us about the demise of the Persian, Greek and Roman empires due to internal decay. Communism and Socialism caused the failure of the German, French, Italian and Russian governments, teaching us that unchecked government can be a force for evil. Government can and should be a force for good.

The founding fathers warned that the greatest threat to our freedom was not external enemies; rather it was putting too much control into a central authority. The founders did not trust government. Many of our founding fathers, including George Washington, John Adams and others, advised that too much power given to government could be a hindrance and threat to the liberties of the citizens of our nation.

When America gained its independence, the colonists envisioned a national government with specific and restricted responsibilities. So suspicious were the founders of the power of a central authority that they wanted to keep the government simple, with minimal duties. They therefore provided in the United States Constitution that Congress only has the duty to protect us by handling foreign affairs, settling disputes between states, and printing money. The founders foresaw very limited government involvement in the daily lives of its citizens and the government, originally, did not have the authority to levy taxes. Our founding fathers were concerned if government had the authority to take the people's earnings through taxation, their freedom would be in jeopardy. The colonists saw private ownership as the major ingredient for individual freedom, a lesson learned during the early years of the Pilgrims. Their greatest concern was in the greed of those running the government, and giving the people what they wanted in exchange for votes. Once this occurs, the citizens would vote for those who support their own agendas and wishes. Our freedoms start to perish with entitlements and handouts.

It has been over 200 years since our founders warned us of the dangers of big government. They never envisioned the government having a part in education, commerce, environment, housing, economy, and other areas of our lives. Over the years, the government has only confirmed the greatest fears of the founding fathers. It has proven to do what it does best – taking money through taxation, and spending it recklessly and with little accountability on selected programs.

## The Growth of Government in America: 1900 - 2000

Several factors account for the twentieth century growth of government in Washington. The first was the advent of the income tax in 1913. Taxing U.S. citizens became a revenue-generating machine for Congress; until this time, money raised by government was through tariffs and land sales. The income tax gave politicians and bureaucrats a steady, massive revenue stream to spend on new programs.[1]

The second reason for the growth of government was war and depression. The three major crises of the twentieth century, World War I, the Great Depression and World War II, created new government power for politicians in Washington. These crises gave those who supported big government the opportunity to argue successfully for more federal spending and taxing authority.[2] This has continued today as seen in the enormous federal spending due to the 9/11 terrorist attacks, the war in Iraq and an eroding economy.

President James Madison believed that crisis was the rallying cry of the tyrant.

During the Great Depression, the 1930s administration of Franklin D. Roosevelt created the New Deal in an effort to put Americans back to work. The Roosevelt administration initiated farm subsidies, public works, different job programs, unemployment benefits, bank regulations and many other federally backed programs. Our nation, even with the infusion of public money, was still in a depression in 1940.

Over the first 100 years of our nation's history, the balance of power between the three branches of government prevailed. When Congress tried to instill new spending authority, the president vetoed or the Supreme Court cited constitutional constraints. Not until the 1930s, when Roosevelt politicized the Supreme Court with his economic policies, was there an imbalance between the judicial and executive branches of government. The Supreme Court authorized Congress to collect money through taxes and redistribute it in the form of welfare to the nation's citizens.

The Constitution reads, "We the people of the United States in order to form a more perfect union, establish justice, ensure domestic tranquility, provide for the common defense, promote the general welfare ..." To our founders, promotion of the "general welfare" meant taking necessary measures to promote the good of the nation, such as protecting the environment and building the infrastructure for America.

The Supreme Court re-interpreted the Constitution when it authorized Congress to spend money to "provide for the general welfare of its citizens." The Supreme Court amended its meaning to advance its liberal agenda to promote economic redistribution that was far from what our founding fathers envisioned. The founders were concerned and took extraordinary steps to protect the private property of our nation's people so that they could enjoy the fruits of their labor. They understood that the first step in establishing tyranny is to seize private property and redistribute it according to political preferences. They knew that if the government had the authority to take the people's property and earnings, freedom would be in jeopardy.

A recent decision by the Supreme Court of the United States rejected one of the most fundamental constitutional freedoms guaranteed to all citizens – the right to own property. This right, revered by the Pilgrims and our founding fathers as the most precious of liberties, was written in the Fifth Amendment of the Constitution: "... no person shall be ... deprived of life, liberty, or property, without due process of law, nor shall private property be taken for public use." In a 5-4 decision, the Supreme Court ruled that the government may seize the home, small business, or other private property of one citizen and transfer it to another private citizen, if the transfer would boost community economic development or increase its tax base. Again, the Supreme Court reclassified the meaning of the Constitution as it did in the 1930s to advance an agenda of economic redistribution. This also was the beginning of the federal courts', and the Supreme Court's, attempt to manipulate the U.S. Constitution to meet specific agendas.

This decision gave Congress unlimited power that still haunts this nation. This was also the time when states assumed a lesser role in education, transportation and other areas of our lives. The federal government used its newly claimed authority to spend taxpayers' money liberally.[3]

## A Nation of Entitlements

In 1933, our government introduced the first entitlement program, social security. It became the first and largest transfer of income to the federal government at that time. Later in the 1960s, President Lyndon Baines Johnson launched the Great Society, creating a completely new group of entitlement programs, including food stamps, public housing, Medicare, Medicaid and Aid to Families with Dependent Children (AFDC). Once these programs began, they were impossible to restrain. Those receiving entitlements grew in number and benefits increased.

A great challenge today is to find some member of the public who does not receive a check from the government for some reason or another. The list grows, as billions and billions of dollars are sent to retirement and health care recipients, college students, farmers for not growing crops, unemployed for not working, unwed mothers for child-care – the list goes on and on.[4]

Federal, state and local social welfare have exploded, with most of the entitlements having emerged in the twentieth century and continued today with very little reform. Prior to 1900, there were very few entitlements or aid programs. The list below reflects how social welfare has expanded:

- In 1900, the government spent $10 billion
- In 1950, the government spent $130 billion
- In 1995, the government spent $1,010 billion[5]

By 1990, Medicare was ten times more expensive than originally forecast. Soon farmers, minority businessmen, veterans, college students, artists, actors, the unemployed, cities, some foreign governments and illegal immigrants were all on the federal payroll. Today, only about $1 out of every $3 taken in by the government goes to operating government; the rest goes toward social programs and income redistribution activities.

It should be noted that in 1950, these entitlement programs were about 12% of the federal budget. Today, entitlements consume over 40% of the budget. Anti-poverty programs and government welfare spending from 1930 to 1995 grew from $11 billion to $254 billion during this period.

In an earlier chapter, I referred to other civilizations throughout history, emphasizing the Roman Empire because of its close similarity to the American way of life. It is important to note that outside aggressors overthrew none of the former great civilizations. All civilizations expired from internal decay from the moral decline of their culture, complacency, dependency and economic collapse.

History shows that all major civilizations have lasted an average of 200 years and have gone through similar sequences regarding their culture and social changes. All started with bondage (being under the control of another) and ended in bondage. As they processed in the cycle, they experienced abundance, complacency, apathy and dependency. The United States, over the past 230 years, has experienced all the phases, and is somewhere between apathy and dependency, the two phases prior to final bondage. Our nation's history has been one that has denied bondage, a nation of people who fought for their freedoms, a people more concerned about their liberties than material things.

The Revolutionary War was probably the greatest tax revolt in world history. The American colonists declared war against England, because they were under the bondage of Great Britain regarding the unreasonably high taxes being levied on our new nation for goods purchased from England.

During the winter of 1767 through 1768, John Dickinson of Pennsylvania, a lawyer and gentleman farmer, wrote a series of letters called *"A Farmer's Letters to the Inhabitants of the British Colonies."* The letters were published in newspapers throughout the colonies, and were of great inspiration to the colonists, emphasizing their inherited rights. He stated in one of his many letters: "Let us take care of our rights, and we therein take care of our prosperity... slavery is ever preceded by sleep ..."[6] This particular quote describes the mindset of the American colonists prior to the war. Dickinson was saying that sleep (complacency) precedes bondage, that if they were to fall asleep as a nation and give up their freedoms, this would surely lead to their dependency and bondage to England.

He went on to write: "You are assigned by Divine Providence in the appointed order of things, the protection of unborn ages, whose fate depends on your virtue."[7] He was telling the colonists that liberty and virtue (conformity of one's life to moral and ethical principles) are one and the same. The Creator gave us our freedoms that must be preserved and protected for this nation's future generations.

The conditions that existed for the people of America prior to the Revolutionary War very much describe the state of our nation today. Our government has taken the place of Britain's King. What difference is there between our governments overtaxing its people versus the colonists being overtaxed by England? Both relate to tyranny, bondage, and the loss of personal freedoms. This experience with Great Britain influenced our founding fathers when they wrote the Constitution. This was the greatest fear of men like Thomas Jefferson, George Washington, John Adams, Abraham Lincoln and other great leaders, men who warned each successive generation that the greatest threat to freedom was not that of an external enemy conquering America. It was in the greed and corruption of politicians taking over the government. By giving people what they want. Once the nation's treasury is open to barter, the people will vote for those who will support their particular lifestyles. Unfortunately, once the process begins, it is terminal. The question is – how long can it continue? [8]

President Woodrow Wilson stated in 1912, "The history of liberty is a history of limitation of governmental power, not the increase of it. Therefore, when we resist, therefore, the concentration of power, we are resisting the processes of death, because the concentration of power is what always precedes the destruction of human liberties."[9] Abraham Lincoln was very profound on the subject when he said, "At what point, then, is the approach of danger to be expected? If it ever reaches us, it must spring up among us, it cannot come from abroad. If destruction be our lot, we must ourselves be its author and finisher. As a nation of free men, we must live through all times or die by suicide."[10] Regarding Lincoln's comment, "At what point is the approach of danger and when it is to be expected" – folks, the erosion is here and the time is now! The socialist philosophy, and the first step toward tyranny is to seize property, either land or through taxes, and then re-distribute it according to political loyalties.

Our nation has become apathetic. Apathy is taking the middle road, the "whatever" attitude. Apathy has no vision; it grows upon us silently as a cancer without our realization. The citizens have become too comfortable in their lifestyles. We have become a very spoiled people, demanding instant gratification for all our needs. We are a nation not caring for the next generation, but taking what is available now. Most people will trade their personal rights for handouts rather than leave their comfort zones. They will compromise their liberties for entitlements. We fail as a nation, if we put too much control into the hands of government, which will result in our becoming too dependent on Washington and politicians.

## How Could This Happen in America?

Our number one enemy (government) is creating an ungodly nation through our court system and driving it into an economic ditch (bankruptcy). This is a factual picture of America today, a far cry from what the founding fathers envisioned.

Abraham Lincoln said, "We the people are the masters of both Congress and the courts, not to overthrow the Constitution, but to overthrow the men who pervert it."[11] Lincoln is indicating that those in Congress and the judges who misinterpret or morally demean the contents of the Constitution must be removed from office.

In past years of our nation when we faced challenges such as wars, depressions and natural catastrophes, citizens had hope because of their religious convictions and faith in God. Today, because of government, the ACLU and the media, hope has disappeared and a divided nation continues to take His Providence out of our daily lives. The people of this nation now turn to the government as their source of salvation instead of having faith in God. It is frightening how easily we have moved from relying on God to relying on man. Man and government have always failed. Government has never been successful at any program. Taking God out of one's life resulted in the demise of other civilizations.

James Madison stated,

> *We have staked the whole future of American civilization, not upon the power of the government, far from it. We have staked the future of all of our political institutions upon the capacity of mankind for self-government; upon the capacity of each and all of us to govern ourselves, to control ourselves, to sustain ourselves according to the Ten Commandments of God.*[12]

Fanny Crosby, the blind songwriter, wrote, "O what peace we often forfeit, O what needless pain we bear, all because we do not carry everything to God in prayer."[13]

We need to go back to the philosophy of the Pilgrims and the founding fathers who were able to establish a nation agreeing that if government was to be successful, it must have the consent of the people. That philosophy worked well for nearly 200 years. However, in the past 40 years, well-funded special interest groups have eroded and convinced the government to do the opposite of what the majority of Americans want. For example, national surveys indicate:

- 80% of Americans want voluntary prayer in the schools, but prayer is outlawed from public schools.
- 90% of Americans support keeping the Ten Commandments on public buildings. However, this has now been declared unconstitutional, even though the Ten Commandments are engraved in stone at the United States Supreme Court.

- 80% of Americans oppose giving "gay marriage" the same legal and moral status as traditional marriage between a man and a woman. However, many states are trying to make it legal.
- 95% of Americans want the "Pledge of Allegiance" said in schools, but a United States Circuit Court in San Francisco has declared the "Pledge" unconstitutional because it mentions God.
- 90% of Americans support the Boy Scouts, but the Boy Scouts are being banned from using public lands for hiking and school buildings for their meetings because Boy Scouts believe in God and will not allow openly homosexual scoutmasters.
- 80% of Americans believe government spends too much, but government spending is increasing faster than ever. Consider this explosion of spending: in 1950, total federal spending was $1.4 billion. Our federal budget today is $1.5 trillion, an increase of 1000%.[14]

We need a government that will protect us against external enemies and domestic violence, and then stay out of our way. Looking back at the growth of all of governments, including local, state and federal, since the New Deal, the doubts and fears of the early colonists have come true. Big government has proved itself efficient at what it does best, taking people's money. The founding fathers never could have imagined our government seizing 43% of every dollar earned by Americans, it is happening today.

It is time to restore the role of government to what our founding fathers envisioned. This can be done only by reducing its size and the control it has over the American people. In order to accomplish this, it would take a renewed enforcement of the Tenth Amendment to the Constitution, which reserves "to the states and people" all the powers not explicitly granted to the federal government. Remember, you only have the rights you are willing to fight for, and if you do not know your rights, you do not have any.

Tax reform needs to be addressed as the primary element in reducing the size of government. We cannot continue the direction we are taking today. Tax reform is crucial; it would automatically reduce the size of government and the Internal Revenue Service.

All government decisions on taxation are being placed into the greedy hands of politicians. Congress has refused to tackle the taxation issue. The politicians we have voted into office have not done their job. The voters of this nation must be more demanding and more discreet in voting responsible lawmakers into office.

One fact history has taught us is that people are better stewards of their own money than government. More money in the hands of the consumer is better spent than in the hands of government.

## ACLU

The American Civil Liberties Union (ACLU) and our liberal courts are the greatest threat to the religious freedoms of the American people, a threat far greater than any terrorist group or foreign country. Bill O'Reilly of Fox News stated, "The ACLU is the most dangerous organization currently operating in America".[15]

Who is the ACLU? Quoted from their media letter, the ACLU described itself as follows:

*The ACLU is our nation's guardian of liberty. We work daily in courts, legislatures and communities to defend and preserve the individual rights and liberties guaranteed to every person in this country by the constitution and laws of the United States. Our job is to conserve America's original civic values - the constitution and the Bill of Rights.*

The ACLU has an 80-year track record with over 400,000 paying members, a massive $45 million annual budget, over $2 million in assets and more than 2,000 attorneys at its disposal. They are working daily to undermine and change America's understanding of morality and the U.S. Constitution.[16]

This organization has camouflaged itself as a nonpartisan group committed to preserving the liberties of all Americans, whatever their race or faith. However, the ACLU should remove the word "American" from its title. It is terribly misleading because they do not represent anything that is pro-American, or anything upon which this nation was founded. Instead of preserving our liberties as they advertise, they, in fact, are taking away our religious freedoms from public life.

The ACLU's threat to America's soul is fought in the courtroom. The erosion of our nation is not front and center to the public. Because courtroom battles are long and quiet, the enemy does not want public awareness. This is a war where there are no shots fired, no bloodshed, but instead a slow, steady decay of our moral fiber and freedoms. The enemy is not obvious as with other enemies. The ACLU is continually at work in the shadows, removing laws and God from our society, along with other national monuments and traditions.

Listed below are some of the official positions and policies taken by the American Civil Liberties Union:

The ACLU Supports:

- Partial birth abortion
- Adoption by homosexuals
- Legalized drugs
- Legalized prostitution
- Legalized child pornography
- Mandatory sex education
- Legalized polygamy
- Tax exempt status for Satanists
- Publicly funded profane art
- Unrestricted access to abortion
- Extended constitutional protection for enemy soldiers bearing arms

The ACLU Opposes:

- Legalized school prayer
- Parental consent laws
- Sobriety checkpoints and drug laws
- Prison terms for most crimes
- Medical safety reporting of AIDS cases
- Government ethics committees
- Christian home schooling
- Pro-life demonstrations
- Abstinence before marriage sex education
- God Bless America banners in school
- Religious displays in public
- U.S. Government post-9/11 security measures
- Christianity
- Boy Scouts of America
- Crosses displayed at military memorials
- Our Constitution, and prefers the courts follow international and foreign law

Most of the public is not aware that the ACLU, while taking away our freedoms and liberties through the court systems, is being reimbursed by our government. Yes, the ACLU, under 42 U.S. Code, Section 1988, collects millions of dollars in lawyers' fees from local governments that it sues. American citizens, make contributions to the ACLU each year to take away our freedoms and liberties. Elected and appointed officials at all levels of government, local, state and federal, will not stand up to the ACLU because they are in fear of tremendous attorneys fees being imposed by appointed judges who are not accountable to the taxpayers. To date, records have shown that not one American judge had the courage to deny attorney fees to the ACLU under the 42 U.S. Code 1988, which is the sole authority regarding these fees.[17]

When the American Civil Liberties Union sued Judge Roy Moore over the Ten Commandments, taxpayers in Alabama were ordered to pay approximately $500,000.00 to the ACLU.[18] As a result, taxpayers are paying the ACLU to promote causes they oppose. We, the U.S. citizens, in turn are paying our hard-earned dollars to the ACLU through attorney fees to take away from us the laws, symbols and heritage that made this nation great.

In Portland, the ACLU sued on behalf of an atheist who was offended by the Boy Scouts recruiting in schools, and was awarded $108,000.00 of taxpayer dollars. In California, the ACLU threatened to sue a school district because the school bus, while transporting the children, passed several churches to and from school.[19] How ridiculous can it get!

In another case, the ACLU has received $63,000 in taxpayer funds for its lawsuit to remove a cross from an official veteran's memorial – on a national preserve, on official land in the Mojave Desert.[20]

A federal judge ordered the state of Nebraska to pay the ACLU $156,960 in attorney fees after the ACLU successfully sued to overturn the state's ban on same sex marriage, a ban that 70% of the voters approved.[21]

The ACLU sued the city of San Diego for allowing the Boy Scouts to lease city property for meetings. In the suit, the ACLU charged that the Scouts' position on faith and homosexuality preclude them from entering into contractual agreements with a government entity. The ACLU received $940,000 in attorney fees.[22]

The ACLU goes to the Supreme Court more than any other organization to change the laws of this country. They use the Bill of Rights to change America's laws and values. Their goal is to change this nation into a socialized country.

## Psycho-Political Warfare

The following is an excerpt taken from an address by Lavrenti Pavlovich Beria, Deputy Premier of the Soviet Union, to American students at Lenin University prior to 1936. This quotation came from a book used by the Communist Party as a manual of instruction for psycho-political warfare and was used for training of the American Communist Party. Beria said,

*Use the courts, use the judges, use the Constitution of the country, and use its medical societies and its laws to further our ends. Do not stint in your labor in this direction. Moreover, when you have succeeded, you will discover that you can now effect your own legislation at will. You can, by the careful organization of healing societies, by constant campaigns about the terrors of society, and by pretence as to your effectiveness, make*

*your Capitalist himself, by his own appropriations,*
*finance a large portion of the quiet Communist conquest*
*of the nation.*[23]

Psycho-politics is the technical term used for brainwashing, and is explained as: "The art and science of asserting and maintaining domin-ion over the thoughts and loyalties of individuals, officers, bureaus and masses and the effecting of the conquest of enemy nations through mental healing."[24]

The following quote is taken from the book entitled "Brainwashing – A Synthesis of the Russian Textbook on Psycho Politics" as reported by former card carrying Communist, Kenneth Goff of Englewood, Colorado. Because of this report to the American public, Goff was assassinated.

*From May 2, 1936 to October 10, 1939, I was a dues*
*paying member of the Communist Party, operating*
*under my own name Kenneth Goff, and also the alias*
*John Keats. In 1939, I voluntarily appeared before*
*the Un-American Activities Committee in Washington,*
*D.C., which was chairmanned at that time by Martin*
*Dies, and my testimony can be found in Volume 9 of that*
*year's Congressional Report.*

*During the period that I was a member of the*
*Communist Party, I attended their school, which was*
*located at 113 E. Wells Street, Milwaukee, Wisconsin,*
*and operated under the name Eugene Debs Labor*
*School. Here we were trained in all phases of warfare,*
*both psychological and physical, for the destruction of*
*the Capitalistic society and Christian civilization. In*
*one portion of our studies, we went thoroughly into the*
*matter of psycho politics. This was the art of capturing*

*the minds of a nation through brainwashing and fake mental health – the subjecting of whole nations of people to the rule of the Kremlin by capturing of their minds. We were taught that the degradation of the populace is less inhuman than their destruction by bombs, for to an animal that lives only once any life is sweeter than death. The end of a war is the control of a conquered people. If a people can be conquered in the absence of war, the end of the war will have been achieved without the destruction of war.*

*During the past few years, I have noted with horror the increase of psycho political warfare upon the American public. First in the brainwashing of our boys in Korea. Then in the well-financed drive of mental health propaganda by left-wing pressure groups, wherein many of our states have passed bills which can well be used by the enemies of America to subject torture and imprisonment those who preach the gospel of our Lord and Savior Jesus Christ, and who opposed the menace of Communism. A clear example of this can be seen in the Lucille Miller case. In this warfare the Communists have definitely stated, "You must recruit every agency of the nation marked for slaughter into a foaming hatred of religious healing."*

*This book was used in underground schools, and contains the addresses of Beria, to the American students in the Lenin University prior to 1936. The text in the book, in general, is from the Communist Manual of Instructions of Psycho political Warfare, and was used in America for the training of the Communist cadre. The only revision in this book is the summary, which was added by the Communists after the atomic bomb came into being. In its contents, you can see the diabolical plot of the enemies of Christ and America, as they seek to conquer our nation by subjecting the minds of our people to their will by various sinister means.*

*This manual of the Communist Party should be in the hands of every loyal American, that they may be alerted to the fact that is it not always by armies and guns that a nation is conquered. Kenneth Goff[25]*

Communism has been successful in only one country in the entire world. You may be surprised to know that one country is the United States of America. Yes, in our own nation Communism is alive in universities throughout our educational system. The universities have allowed professors and educators with Communist backgrounds and philosophies to teach our students, while at the same time promoting Communism.

## ACLU vs. Religious Freedoms

The philosophy of psycho-political warfare, as described by Lavrenti Beria, is to utilize a nation's courts, judges and constitution to accomplish their ends and goals. Is it coincidental that the philosophies followed by the Communist Party as stated by Beria parallel the methods used by the ACLU?

These are the exact tactics followed by the American Civil Liberties Union. The results of the ACLU are all around us. It is using the courts to silently remove memorials and God from our society. It is continually misrepresenting America's history.

One of the ACLU's primary targets is our God-given religious freedom. We now live in a country where the secular left and the American Civil Liberties Union continually challenge our Christian faith and biblical values.

Two of the most notable cases were the outlawing of prayer and devotional readings of scripture in public schools in 1962. The ACLU since has used those court rulings to eliminate our religious expression in graduation invocations and pre-game prayer at athletic events.

In taking God from our public life, the Ten Commandments and prayer out of school, the ACLU has accomplished what the Manual of the Communist Party teaches. This warfare has been successful using our courts, judges and Constitution without ever firing a shot. Its objective is to create a nation without purpose; a people without purpose. Without moral disciplines to follow, such as the Ten Commandments, our Constitution is lost. Look what has happened to this nation's youth since prayer was taken out of school (see Chapter 3). The loss of purpose of one generation will create enough problems from within to destroy a nation. A young generation without purpose and exposed to drugs and alcohol will accomplish that objective.

I repeat the words of President Ronald Reagan on August 23, 1984,

> *Without God there is no virtue because there is no prompting of the conscience ... without God there is a coarsening of the society; without God democracy will not and cannot endure. If we forget that we are One Nation under God, then we will be a nation gone under.*

Ronald Reagan also stated,

> *While America's military strength is important, let me add here that I have always maintained that the struggle*

*now going on for the world will never be decided by bombs or rockets, by armies or military might. The real crisis is a spiritual one; at root, it is a test of moral will and faith. The source of our strength in the quest for human freedom is not material but spiritual, and because it knows no limitation, it must terrify and ultimately triumph over those who would enslave their fellow man.*

France, during the French Revolution, took away all religious monuments and national emblems of God, and its government ended in tyranny. Without our Creator as the moral fiber in a nation, socialism and tyranny will prevail.

The Roman Empire became a civilization without purpose, which eventually led to its downfall as it instilled an ungodly life into its society.

Alan E. Sears, President, CEO and General Counsel of Alliance Defense Fund, stated, "The bad news is that if God's people don't respond adequately, the ACLU is dangerously close – far closer than almost anyone realizes – to cleaning America's public recognition of its historic Christian roots."[26]

"Displays like the Ten Commandments tell a critically important part of America's history. They make it clear that America is not like other nations."[27]

Sears warns, "that the ACLU's radical agenda, if successful, spells the death of the religious freedom the Founding Fathers secured for us."[28]

Thomas Jefferson, father of our Constitution, quoted in 1781, "God who gave us life gave us liberty. And can the liberties of a nation be thought secure if we remove their only firm basis, a conviction in the minds of the people that their liberties are a gift from God."[29]

It is imperative that the ACLU be rebuffed. Congress must first take action to amend Code 42 USC Section 1988 to preclude the courts from awarding attorney fees under that statute in lawsuits brought before the courts to remove or destroy religious symbols. However, one of our grave problems is Congress. Liberal left-wing senators make it clear that they will filibuster and use every possible intimidation tactic to block any confirmation of pro-life, pro-family and pro-religious judges to the Supreme Court, or even the lower court positions.

The battle is one of unbelievable proportions. We are not only fighting for our God-given freedoms against the ACLU and other left-wing activists, but the government and media have become obstacles to our basic liberties. The nation today is more divided than at any time in this nation's history regarding the presence of morality and Christian influence in American public life. Decency and Godliness must be restored to this great nation. God and our freedoms have slipped through our fingers like sand and out of our lives as more and more Christian inscriptions are taken from public buildings and monuments.

For many years, we were told that the separation of church and state was absolute and the Christians' place was inside the nation's churches and not in politics; that they had no say in legislative and government decisions; that Christians should only be concerned with their own spiritual matters, not state or national matters.

It is imperative to mobilize the Christian leaders of this nation in order to salvage our Christian heritage. Who else will do it? It is of the utmost importance that the Christian pro-American public participate fully in the political process to vote into office those candidates who will pass laws to support our moral and family values.

Charles Finney, a minister in America's Second Great Awakening, reminded Christians:

> *The church must take right ground in regard to politics ... The time has come that Christians must vote*

*for honest men and take consistent ground in politics ... God cannot sustain this free and blessed country which we love and pray for unless the Church will take right ground. Politics are a part of a religion in such a country as this, and Christians must do their duty to the country as a part of their duty to God ... He (God) will bless or curse this nation according to the course they (Christians) take (in politics).*[30]

The 80-year effort by the ACLU to remove God and religion from the public eye must be reversed through the court system. It is vital to support organizations such as the Alliance Defense Fund, the Citizen Leader Coalition, Judicial Watch, and the American Center for Law and Justice and any others who promote pro-American, pro-family and pro-Christian agendas.

# Closing

When writing this book, it was difficult to finalize its closure. Much more could be addressed since each day brings a new chapter to the history of our nation.

The contents of this book compare American history with that of other civilizations. I have described the social and cultural paths that past civilizations experienced as they were freed from bondage, and after the ravages of time, returned to bondage. The histories of all known civilizations parallel one another as they rise and fall, all having common reasons for their demise. During 230 years as a nation, we have followed the footsteps of the Roman Empire. We are experiencing the same cultural and social phases as other civilizations (see chapter 1).

This writing details the progress of America from the landing of the Pilgrims through the War of Independence, and the formation of the United States Constitution authored by the founding fathers. We followed the development and growth of our nation as we journeyed through the 18th, 19th and 20th centuries to the present day. I explained how America experienced each historical sequence, from the time we freed ourselves from the bondage of the British Empire to the present day. I am firm in my convictions that our nation is presently somewhere between apathy and dependency; the final phase before bondage (see chapter 2).

As I addressed each chapter, I wrote of the challenges confronting America and the influence they have on our future. We need to face the future by looking back in our history and learning from the chronicles of past civilizations.

The demise of past nations has been the result of spiritual and moral decay. If I can target one event that changed the direction of America, it was when prayer was taken out of school. Since that decision by the courts in 1962, almost everything our founders envisioned for America is slowly falling apart.

Since that decision:

- Abortion has taken the lives of over 48 million children in America
- The traditional symbols that once represented our Godly heritage are being removed from our public buildings
- America's prison population is almost 2.3 million, which surpasses all other countries. The fifty states last year spent over $49 billion in corrections, up from $11 billion in 1987.[1]
- Pornography and sexual predators engulf the internet while same-sex marriage threatens our historical marriage standards.
- Gangs have replaced families as our country's youth search for father images.
- Character and integrity no longer count, as shown by our public officials and corporate officers.

Our nation and its government were established upon the principles of God's Word. The brilliance of the founding fathers gave us a Constitution and republic form of government that has been the envy of all the nations. They provided a foundation that has allowed us to be the most prosperous nation in the history of the world.

Over the past years along with the anti-Christian actions of our court system, our government has grown from a central authority with limited responsibilities to an out-of-control bureaucracy. The founders were concerned that if government was to take the people's earnings through taxation, their freedom would be in jeopardy.

This is one of the reasons that Congress was not allowed to tax the citizens until the year 1913.

Our founders never envisioned our government as being part of education, commerce, environmental, housing, etc. Over the course of time, America has transformed itself from a nation with little government presence to one which is the dominant factor in all aspects of our lives, including our economy. Up until the Franklin D. Roosevelt administration in the 1930s, most politicians had the common sense to stay out of our way and let the American businessperson manage the economy through the functions of capitalism.

As previously mentioned in chapter 11, Thomas Jefferson emphasized that the economy is among the first and most important virtues while public debt is the greatest danger. He indicated that a nation must make a choice between lavish spending and bondage. It is important to prevent the government from wasting the labors of the people under the pretense of caring for them.

As I wrote in a previous chapter, the greatest problem with government is that man must run it. Man with his fallen nature seeks office in order to use the power of government to further their own ambitions. The economic erosion we are experiencing today is a perfect example of what happens when government tries to control our lives. The Obama administration and Congress, in passing their bailout and stimulus packages for failing financial institutions and businesses, exemplify a mismanaged bureaucracy. This overpaid Congress, which only works 104 days a year, in its effort to expedite the bill, did not have the courtesy to take the time to read the economic package that it voted on. This group of men and women has not only disregarded their civic responsibility but also neglected our nation's long-term debt and the effect it has on future generations.

They ignored the following:
- Our ever-increasing cost of Medicare and Medicaid
- Depletion of our Social Security Fund
- Sixty-seven million baby boomers and their effect on the housing market & our economy in the coming years
- Generation gap of future taxpayers (see chapter 12)
- Future debt to our children and grandchildren

Politicians use a crisis to divert public attention from their lack of good judgment and bad decisions. President James Madison stated that, "crisis was the rallying cry of the tyrant."[2] In my opinion, the crisis can be the escalation of an existing war or another military conflict to distract from an eroding economy.

Congress needs to use common sense, stop unnecessary spending and eliminate unexplainable earmarks. We must vote out all politicians who are not willing to step forward and face the real problems confronting this nation. Those who increase taxes and spend money on anything other than debt reduction should be removed. Anyone who raises taxes, incorporates healthcare for everyone, and increases entitlements would only add to our national debt. Remember - government has not been successful with any program it has ever initiated - try to name one! Ronald Reagan stated in 1992, "We have long since discovered that nothing lasts longer than a temporary government program."[3]

Recent decisions by the Obama administration and Congress take America one-step closer to more dependency on government and nationalization of financial institutions. Remember, dependency's real name is bondage. Historically, dependency is followed by socialism.

I again quote a senator from the Roman Empire who said, "I fear for our nation. Nearly half of our people receive some form of government subsidies. We have grown weak from too much affluence and too little adversity. We have debased our currency to the point that even the most loyal citizen no longer trusts it."[4]

Most scholars and historians have agreed that the fall of the Roman Empire was due to internal problems. Economic strain, high taxation and the decline in public spirit were the main reasons leading to the Empire's demise. Will history repeat itself?

The chapters of this book each represent a different aspect of life in America. As I addressed each chapter, I wrote of the obstacles confronting America and the influence they have on our society and culture. I explain how all are interrelated and when one falters, all can fail.

These concerns, and the apathy of the American people, collectively put this nation in grave peril. In doing so, *America Is A Nation That's Lost Its Way*, as we find ourselves at a crossroads for the future of America.

The Bible reads in Jeremiah, verse 6:16 NIV: "Stand at the crossroads and look, ask for the ancient paths, ask where the good way is, and walk in it, and you will find rest for your souls."

Thomas Jefferson often mentioned the return to "ancient principles," which refers to the Ten Commandments and Common Law. The Common Law, in simple terms, is just common sense, and is derived from the Ten Commandments.

For more than three centuries, moral values have been the life support of this country. The men and women who planted their stand on these shores in the year 1607 vowed to build a nation founded on virtue and moral integrity. During all those years, their promises and visions held true.[5] The American people brought forth on this continent a nation dedicated to liberty and justice. The founders were committed to strong moral principles, based on individual liberty and personal responsibility. Americans are forever indebted to those who pledged their lives, fortunes and sacred honor to make this experiment in liberty possible.[6]

"Gratitude," G. K. Chesterton wrote, "is the mother of all virtues."[7] As Americans we have reason to be filled with gratitude at all times; gratitude to God who gave us the opportunity to come to this land to live in freedom, gratitude to the founding fathers who set forth those principles that constitute our creed, and gratitude to generations who have defended us.

We have the ability to create our own fate before our nation's final story is told – by the decisions we make. One should be responsible for his or her own choices, not the government.

Taking responsibility means giving back what was given to you. Elie Wiesel, a professor at Boston University said, after his time in Nazi concentration camps, that he lived for one thing – to give back to others. He traveled extensively, sharing the wisdom gained from his life experiences. He tried to guide young people by sharing his sense of responsibility. "What I receive I must pass on to others. The knowledge that I have must not remain imprisoned in my brain. I owe it to many men and women to do something with it. I feel the need to give back what was given to me. Call it gratitude ... to learn means to accept that life did not begin at my birth. Others have been there before me and I walk in their footsteps." [8]

Your life is a story. Each day you have an opportunity to write a new page. So, fill those pages with responsibility to God, to others and to yourself. If you do, in the end, you will not be disappointed.

God said, "I will pour out my Spirit on your offspring and my blessing on your descendants." **Isaiah** 44:3 NIV  God wants the next generation to not just follow the previous one but also to surpass all others, by challenging old thoughts and creating new things. America is many generations; no one generation can isolate itself from the past or the future. The decisions you make today will affect not only you, but also future generations, so make sure they are the right ones! When one generation fails, all that has happened before us is lost.

## Spiritual Amnesia

This nation has forgotten what the Lord of the universe did for America. Our minds have fallen asleep as we journey through life forgetting how gracious our Creator has been to us. The freedom and abundance that we have as a nation did not happen by accident. Freedom only comes from God and abundance is the result of freedom.

One of my favorite stories that parallels the state of America today concerns the life of a spider, and the danger of amnesia. A spider dropped a single strand down from the rafter of an old barn and began to weave his web. Months went by and the web grew. Its elaborate maze caught flies, mosquitoes and other small insects, providing the spider with a rich diet. Eventually, it became the envy of all other spiders. Then one day the spider noticed a single strand stretching up into the rafters, "I wonder why it's there? It doesn't catch me any dinner," said the spider. Concluding it was unnecessary, he climbed as high as he could and severed it. In that moment, the entire web began to fall to the floor, taking the spider with it.[9]

Could we as a people make the same mistake as the spider? Can a nation spin a great web and then sever it? Can we gain so much prosperity and abundance and then become so complacent and selfish in our ways that we forget the strong strand that supports us? Can this nation with all of its success display such apathy and arrogance that we forget the Source who has given us our freedom and abundance?

This book was divinely inspired, when I was given the revelation of major issues confronting America. As I researched these issues and prepared this writing, I was continually reminded of God's concern regarding our nation's state of affairs and the mounting crises facing this country. My research revealed what the founders intended for America. However, actions by our leaders and the courts over the past 40 years clearly demonstrate our disobedience as we continue to remove God from public life. This has resulted in a society of moral, educational and economical collapse. It became obvious to me, why the Creator is disturbed with this nation, as we have forgotten the Source of our freedom and abundance. America was built on a foundation of faith, but today's populace is so overwhelmed with their success and lifestyles that they fail to acknowledge the One who blessed them.

People and nations can come to a point where God abandons them. God can leave us without our knowing of His departure until it is too late. Amnesia regarding one's blessings brings about massive moral disaster. God does not condemn success; He condemns arrogance and disobedience. We are not the first nation to suffer amnesia. Israel, Rome, and other nations did also.

Moses warned the Israelites:

> *But remember the Lord your God, for it is he who gives you the ability to produce wealth and so confirms his covenant, which he swore to your forefathers, as it is today.*
>
> *If you ever forget the Lord your God and follow other gods and worship and bow down to them, I testify against you today that you will surely be destroyed. Like the nations the Lord destroyed before you, so you will be destroyed for not obeying the Lord your God.*[10]

Remember, the Lord gives you power to become prosperous. Just as He took us out of bondage twice from England: first through the voyage of the Pilgrims to America and second when gaining our independence as the result of the Revolutionary War. Our selfishness and disobedience could return us to bondage. What will be the fate of America?

General Douglas McArthur said, "History fails to record a single precedent in which nations subject to moral decay have not passed into political and economic decline. There has been either a spiritual awakening to overcome moral lapse or a progressive deterioration leading to national disaster."[11]

Abraham Lincoln proclaimed,

> *And, insomuch as we know that, by His divine law, nations like individuals are subjected to punishment and chastisement in this world ... We have been the recipients of the choicest bounties of heaven. We have been preserved these many years in peace and prosperity. We have grown in numbers, wealth and power as no other nation has ever grown. But we have forgotten the gracious Hand which preserved us in peace; and multiplied and enriched and strengthened us; and we have vainly imagined, in the deceitfulness of our hearts, that all these blessings were produced by some superior wisdom and virtue of our own.*[12]

If this nation is to transform itself and return to the foundation that the founders intended, we need to grasp the problems, not focus on the symptoms. In order to do this, we must first confront the truth as to where we are and how we got here.

President Obama talks about change. If change were our solution, then that change had better go back to the ways and attitudes of the founders.  Not change to radical extremism and to bigger government, which has already put our nation and freedoms at risk, but change as referred to by Thomas Jefferson a return to the principles of common sense as stated in the Ten Commandments.   To date President Obama has assigned upwards of 20 czars to investigate and manage various aspects and components of our lives.  According to Webster's Dictionary, a czar is an emperor or king, an autocratic leader who holds unlimited power.   Barack Obama should be reminded that our constitution does not mention czars as a part of our republic form of government.

Change cannot be made without confrontation.   The colonists realized this as their freedoms and lives were threatened by the British before and during the War of Independence.  Without our citizens having an awareness of the problems we face, we cannot make the necessary changes to get America back on the right track.  The grassroots efforts that made this nation the light of the world must be resurrected.

God knows our tendency to forget His blessings and go our own way.  Look around you.  The conditions that proceeded the fall of every great civilization are in place.  Can this country be saved?  Yes.  By whom?  God said:

- "If my people, who are called by my name."  We must turn to God in our needs and show Him our gratitude.
- "Will humble themselves and pray."  We must turn from humanism (man can do it) to reliance on God.
- "And seek my face." We must turn from self-direction to God's compass.
- "And turn from their wicked ways."  We must turn from self-indulgence to the principles of the Ten Commandments. (taken from 2 Chronicles 7:14 NIV Topical Version)

God will heal our land when we turn back to Him. However, that turn begins with you!

There is no cure when a society abandons God's word. Many times there is no turning back; however, I believe we still have time for repentance, to be able once again to attain the American dream.

In order to rebuild America and take this nation back to the greatness it once was, we must all leave our comfort zones. Nothing great has ever been accomplished by those with an attitude of apathy and complacency. Greatness takes an uncomfortable effort. Greatness only comes from extra effort and through passion, perseverance and discipline as proven by our founders.

We must go back to His Providence, to a commitment to family, and less government. These are necessary to return our lost nation to what the Creator meant it to be. Moral values, family and truth must be incorporated back into American society or surely, this nation's history will end, as have others. We must return to a nation of gratitude and obedience to His Great Commission, and an unselfish desire to make America the land of the free and to pay the price now for future generations. It is important to act now. Changing one's lifestyle involves discomfort and sacrifice. However, the other option is spending our lives under socialism and tyranny.

The citizens of America are what make everything work. It has always been the initiative, perseverance, innovation, moral values, and strength of our compatriots that made this nation the greatest in the world. If we repent and are obedient to the Creator, we could make the greatest comeback in history. It will take an army of Spirit-empowered believers to reclaim what is ours, a Godly nation.

In closing, as you read the prayer for America, ponder the meaning of the elegant words of Derric Johnson, author of "The Wonder of America."

## Prayer for America

*Our Father,*

*We thank you for bountiful blessings upon this land. For it is your touch that produces the rich wheat harvests, the more than ample citrus crops, the vast sections of farmland clothed in verdant green, and so much more. We are humbled when we remember the courage and faith of our founding generations, and we ask for strength that we might carry on the traditions they established. For it was their faith in you that made it possible for our dreams to come true.*

*We stand in awe when we gaze upon your majesties: brilliant stars, clear and cold upon the prairies; dewy mornings, quiet in the forest; snow-capped mountains with clear, cold streams; and the shining sea with its endless mutterings. Your creation remains the ultimate masterpiece.*

*We become more aware of our place in the grand scheme of your universe whenever we take the time to look around at the grandeur of America. For it is only when we acknowledge you as the Master Creator of the Universe that we can truly appreciate your special love for America.*

*And when we do, when we really, really do see with crystal clarity how blessed America has been and is, then we cannot help but experience anew The Wonder of America,*

*Father, thank you for your touch. Please never remove it from us, and please keep us aware of our need for it.*[13]

## Introduction

1. *God Bless America*, page 174 copyright 1999 by Zondervan

## Chapter 1

1. Vern McLellan, *Christians in the Political Arena*
2. Edward Gibbon, *The Decline and Fall of the Roman Empire*
3. Ibid
4. Ibid
5. Ibid
6. Ibid
7. Larry Burkett, *Whatever Happened to the American Dream*
8. Perry Stone, *Plucking The Eagle's Wings*, copyright 2001
9. Ibid
10. Ibid
11. Ibid
12. Vern McLellan, *Christians in the Political Arena* Alexander Tyler, *History Professor at University Edinburgh Year 1787*
13. *Robert G. Athern, History of the United States by American Heritage Volume 1*

## Chapter 2

1. *Webster's Dictionary, Random House Version*
2. Catherine Millard, *The Rewriting of America's History*
3. Ibid

4. Ibid

5. Ibid

6. Peter Marshall and David Manuel, *The Light and the Glory*

7. Ibid

8. Ibid

9. Ibid

10. *Funk & Wagnalls Encyclopedia Vol. 2 1965*

11. Rod Gragg, *Declaration of Independence*

12. Ibid

13. Rod Gragg, *Declaration of Independence*

14. Larry Burkett, *Whatever Happened to the American Dream*

15. Ibid

16. Ibid

17. *Book of Presidents, Volume 12 Edition 1997*

18. http://Beta.webmail.aol.com/22374    en-us    mail display-message.aspx

19. Larry Burkett, *Whatever Happened to the American Dream*

20. John Quincy Adams, *The Jubilee of the Constitution* and a discourse delivered at the request of the New York Historical Society in the city of New York, April 30, 1839

21. David Barton, *Original Intent*, page 333

22. *Walter E. Williams, Are We a Republic or a Democracy*

23. www.apfn.org/THE    WINDS/library/democracy.html

24. *Walter E. Williams, Are We a Republic or a Democracy*

25. Aid & Abet Police Newsletter, *Citizens Rule Book*

26. *Walter E. Williams, Are We a Republic or a Democracy*

27. *Alan Guttmacher Institute, Affiliate of Planned Parenthood Federation of America*

28. *Times Digest,* March 10, 2008

**Chapter 3**

1. Peter Marshall and David Manuel, *The Light and the Glory*, page 120

2. D. James Kennedy, *America's One Nation Under God*

3. *Preambles to State Constitutions* http: MO4. webmail.aol.com/15106 aol/en-us mail display message.aspx

4. Ibid

5. Ibid

6. Ibid

7. D. James Kennedy, *America's One Nation Under God*

8. Ibid

9. Benjamin Hart, *Faith & Freedom*

10. *Word Project.org*

11. *Quads for Christ.net, September 22, 2006*

12. *The Word for You Today*, www.TheTab.org

13. Ibid

14. http://RO-ROI.webmail.aol.com/17385/aol/en-us/ mail/display-message.aspx

15. HTTP://MO4.webmail.aol.com/173851/aol/en-us/ M:4 display-message.aspx

16. www.snopes.com/politics/soapbox/hitnail.asp

17. Benjamin Hart, *Faith & Freedom*

18. Ibid

19. Alan Guttmacher Institute Affiliate of Planned Parenthood Federation of America

20. Benjamin Hart, *Faith & Freedom*

21. Compiled and written by the staff of the Christian Defense Fund, *One Nation Under God*

22. Benjamin Hart, *Faith & Freedom*

23. Ibid

24. Compiled and written by the staff of the Christian Defense Fund, *One Nation Under God*

25. Catherine Millard, *The Rewriting of America's History*

26. Garland R. Quayles, *Volume VIII Winchester-Frederick County Historical Society Papers*

27. Benjamin Hart, *Faith & Freedom*

28. God Bless America, *Prayers and Reflections for our Country* copyright 1999 by Zondervan

29. The Christian Defense Fund, *One Nation Under God*

30. Ronald Reagan's *Common Sense and Patriotism*, 1981

31. Ronald Reagan's *Common Sense and Patriotism*, 1983

32. Benjamin Hart, *Faith & Freedom*

33. Ronald Reagan's speech on Spiritual Leadership, 1984.

## Chapter 4

1. Monticello.org (This quotation is on Panel 3 of the Jefferson Memorial in Washington, DC).

## Chapter 5

1. David Gergen, *US News and World Report*, April 4, 2005
2. Vicki E. Murray, *IVBE*, Independent Voices for Better Education, January 22, 2008
3. Craig R. Barrett, *USA Today* February 24, 2005
4. Paul Kennedy, *Rise and Fall of the Great Powers*
5. Greg Toppo, *USA Today*
6. Sujit Roy, merinews.com, April 4, 2008
7. *The Ledger*, Lakeland, Florida, January 8, 2006
8. *USA Today, Feb 22, 2006*
9. Lois Romano, *Washington Post*, December 25, 2005
10. William J. Moloney, *USA Today*, August 17, 2006
11. Ibid
12. Benjamin Hart, *Faith & Freedom*
13. Ibid
14. Ibid
15. John D. Ashcroft, Center for the Study of American Civic Literacy
16. Marilyn Elias, *USA Today*
17. Donald J. Roberts, Senior Associate Dean Stanford University, *USA Today* Mar 9, 2005
18. Marilyn Elias, *USA Today*
19. Youfa Wang, International Journal of Pediatric Obesity, March 2006

20. *Chicago Sun Times*, December 31, 2005
21. Marilyn Elias, *USA Today*
22. Ibid
23. Christina Hoff Sommers, *USA Today*
24. Ibid
25. Ibid
26. Ibid
27. *The Word for You Today, December 12, 2006*
28. Christina Hoff Sommers, *USA Today*
29. Michael Cohen, President of Achieve
30. Tim Wendel, *Member of USA Today's Board of Contributors*
31. Greg Toppo, *USA Today*, U.S. Department of Education, 2004
32. Michael Cohen, President of Achieve
33. Greg Toppo and Anthony De Barros, *USA Today*
34. David Gergen, *US News & World Report*, April 4, 2005
35. Charles Sykes, *Dumbing Down America*
36. Craig R. Barrett, *USA Today,* February 24, 2005, *CEO of Intel and a Board Member of Achieve, Inc.*
37. Lois Romano, *Washington Post*
38. *USA Today, "Our View",* source *Fordham Foundation*
39. Michelle Kessler, *USA Today, Fewer Students Major in Computer*
40. David Gergen, *US News & World Report*, April 4, 2005
41. Michelle Kessler, *USA Today* May 23, 2005
42. Mary Beth Mark Lein, *USA Today*

43. Julie Snider, *USA Today*, *"2005" Annual High School Survey of Study Engagement*

44. Suzy Parker, *USA Today*, February 22, 2006

45. Ibid

46. Jim Nelson Black, *Freefall of the American University*, page 11, copyright 2004

47. Ibid, page 74

48. Sandra Block, *USA Today*, February 23, 2006

49. National Institute on Alcohol & Alcoholism, based on 2002 research on college students between ages 18-24

50. Lois Romano, *Washington Post*

51. David Gergen, *US News & World Report*, April 4, 2005

52. Craig R. Barrett, *USA Today*, February 24, 2005

53. James Nelson Black, *Freefall of the American University*, page 9

54. *USA Today*, Orlando Florida NSTA Survey, September 7, 2000

55. Linda Chavez and Daniel Gray, *Betrayal*, copyright 2004

56. Nancy Clecland, *Unions Gain Ground in Golden State*, *Los Angeles Times*, August 31, 2003

57. John Berthood, *The NEAs Fiscal Agenda: Bad News for Kids*, Alexis de Tocqueville Institute, July 1, 1996

58. Peter Ostrolenk, *Education Policy Director at the Conservative Eagle Forum*

59. Joe Williams, author, *Cheating our Kids*; Greg Toppo reported, *USA Today*, November 30, 2005

60. Ralph Reed, *Contract with the American Family*

61. Ibid

62. Ronald Reagan, Remarks at the Presentation Ceremony for Presidential Scholars Awards, June 16, 1983.

## Chapter 6

1. *The Word for You Today*, May 12

2. Kathleen Parker, *USA Today,* March 15, 2005

3. Vern McLellan, Christians in the Political Arena

4. Ibid

5. Peter Johnson, *USA Today.com*

6. Raffell Adams, Wall Street Journal, October 28, 2008

7. Alcestis "Cooky" Oberg, *USA Today's Board of Contributors*

8. Brian Fitzpatrick, America A Nation in Moral & Spiritual Confusion, December 4-8, 2006

9. Benjamin Franklin, wrote in a letter to the Ministry of France, March 1778

## Chapter 7

1. Benjamin Hart, *Faith & Freedom*, page 309

2. Mark R. Levin, *Men in Black*, page 13

3. *Jewish World Review*, December 12, 2000

4. Gary Bauer, *USA Today,* March 21, 2005

5. Ibid

6. Stephen Boitano, *USA Today*, August 3, 2003

7. George E. Baker, *The Works of William H, Seward*, copyright Volume 1, 1853

8.   Statistics published by Alan Guttmacher Institute, Affiliate of Planned Parenthood of America

9.   David Barton, *Original Intent*, page 266 Abraham Lincoln's Inaugural Address

## Chapter 8

1.   Catherine Crier, *The Case Against Lawyers*

2.  Michael Beebe, *Buffalo News*, June 24, 2007

3.  Daniel W. Entrikin, *Defensive Medicine Implications for Radiology*

4.  *Institute for Policy Innovation, Policy Report* #161, page 14

5.  Paul J. Grant, *Tort Reform In the 1990's*, Quality1/91

6.  Benjamin Hart, *Faith & Freedom*, page 363

7.  http://MO4.webmail.aol.com/17114/aol/en-us/mail/display-message.aspx

## Chapter 9

1.  Vern McLellan, *Christians in the Political Arena* and *News & Views Digest*

2.  Edward Gibbon, *The Decline and Fall of the Roman Empire*

3.  http://RO-ROl.webmail.aol.com/17789/aol/en-us/mail/display-message.aspx, Dick Lamm, Former Governor of Colorado, Immigration Overpopulation Conference in Washington, DC

4.  Edward Gibbon, *The Decline and Fall of the Roman Empire*

5. Haya El Nasser and Paul Overberg, *USA Today*
6. Ibid
7. Ibid
8. http://RO-ROI.webmail.aol.com/23142/aol/en-us/mail/display-message.aspx
9. http://webmail.aol.com/30978/aol/en-us/Mail/PrintMessage.asp
10. http://webmail.aol.com/29047/aol/en-us/Mail/PrintMessage.aspx
11. http://webmail.aol.com/25045/aol/en-us/mail/display-message.aspx
12. A letter from President Theodore Roosevelt, January 6, 1919 to the American Defense Society

**Chapter 10**

1. Fyed Youfuf Raza Gilani, Prime Minister of Islamabad
2. http://webmail.aol.com/30128/aol/en-us/mail/printmessage.aspx
3. *Report by Coral Ridge Ministries*, April 2007
4. Sherwood B. Idso, *Carbon Dioxide and Global Change; End of Nature or Rebirth of The Biosphere?, Rational Readings on Environmental Concerns*, page 19 & 422
5. Larry Burkett, *Whatever Happened to the American Dream,* page 111
6. Marco R. della Cava, *USA Today,* April 25, 2007
7. http://www.worldnetdaily.com/news/article.aspx article ID=54528

8. http://newsbusters.org/blogs/noel-sheppard/2008/05/02/ venture-firm-puts-millions-green-co...May 6, 2008

**Chapter 11**

1. Peter Marshall and David Manuel, *The Light and the Glory*, pages 106-121
2. Ibid
3. Ibid
4. Benjamin Hart, *Faith & Freedom*, pages 318 and 321
5. Ibid
6. Ibid
7. Ibid
8. Ibid
9. Larry Burkett, *Whatever Happened to the American Dream*
10. William J.H. Boetcker, *Lincoln on Limitations*
11. Dennis Cauchon, *USA Today*, May 25, 2006
12. Ibid
13. Paul Magnusson, *Business Week* December 4, 2004
14. Julie Snider, *USA Today*, source Bureau of Labor Statistics
15. Robert B. Ward, *Buffalo News,* February 20, 2005
16. Dennis Cauchon, *USA Today*, February 21, 2007
17. *Institute for Policy Innovation: Policy Report #161*, Pages 1-19
18. Ibid
19. Ibid
20. http://webmail.aol.com/29047

21. Ibid

22. Adrienne Lewis, *USA Today*, April 4, 2007

23. *Wall Street Journal*, April 15-16, 2006, *Taxes: Who Pays, and How Much?*, Source: Government Accountability Office

24. Karl Gelles, *USA Today, April 12, 2006*

25. Steve Forbes, The Heritage Foundation, April 8, 2005

26. *CSP Daily News*, July 30, 2007

27. Walter Williams, Professor of Economics, George Mason University

28. William J.H. Boetcker, *Lincoln on Limitations*

29. *Institute for Policy Innovation: Policy Report #161*, Pages 1-19

30. Ibid

31. Ibid

## Chapter 12

1. Richard J. Newman, *Can America Keep Up, in US News & World Report*, March 19, 2006

2. Speech given @ Inaugural Barnett-Oksenberg lecture on Sino-American Relations, Feb. 28, 2005

3. Neil Pierce, *Washington Post*

4. *USA Today*, Today's Debate on the Global Economy

5. Ibid

6. Dewayne Wickham, *USA Today,* November 13, 2007

7. Neil Pierce, *Washington Post*

8. Report, *USA Today,* April 25, 2007

9. Alejandro Gonzalez, *USA Today*, April 25, 2007

10. Report, *USA Today*, November 20, 2006

11. Ibid

12. Al Lewis, columnist, *Denver Post*

13. Carolyn Bigda, Buffalo News, McClatchy Tribute

14. Mindy Fetterman and B. Hansen, *USA Today*, November 20, 2006 Experian Group Credit Report

15. Ibid

16. Neil Pierce, *Washington Post*

17. Jonathan D. Pond, *AARP Magazine*, January-February 2008

18. Sharon Jayson, *USA Today*, December 1.5, 2006

19. Ibid

20. Ibid

21. Ibid

22. Aetna Website, Juggling Expenses--------Today's Young Workforce, Aug. 23, 2006

23. Larry Burkett, *Whatever Happened to the American Dream*, page 23

24. Kevin Horan, *Business Week*, March 24, 2004

25. Ronald Reagan, *1ˢᵗ Presidential Inaugural Address 1981*

26. Noelle Knox, *USA Today*

27. Greg Farrell, *USA Today*, November 12, 2007

28. *Parade Magazine*, Source: US Department of Treasury/Federal Reserve, November 9, 2008

29. Larry Burkett, *Whatever Happened to the American Dream*

30. Ibid

31. Richard J. Newman, *US News & World Report*, March 19, 2008

32 *Parade Magazine*, Source: US Department of Treasury, Federal Reserve, November 9,2008

33. Stephen Moore & Phil Kerpen, *Institute for Policy Innovation, Policy Report 164*

34. Dick Armey, *USA Today, Americans Need Tax Relief*

**Chapter 13**

1. Carl J. Schramm, *USA Today,* June 28, 2006

2. Ibid

3. Ibid

4. Terry Bibbens, *Jan Norman on Small Business July 17, 2007*

5. James Madison, *The Federalist on the New Constitution, page 53 #10*

6. Abraham Lincoln, *William J.H. Boetcker, 1916*

**Chapter 14**

1. Benjamin Hart, *Faith & Freedom*

2. Larry Burkett, *Whatever Happened to the American Dream*

3. Larry King Live TV Show, Sept 18, 2003

4. Rasmussen Reports "Congressional Performance", May 15, 2008

5. http://webmail.aol.com/37434/aol/en-us/mail/printmessage.aspx

6. Words from John Adams Writings "Thoughts on Government", April 1776

7. Paul Jacob,www.ustermlimits.org

8. *USA Today,* February 28, 2008

9. Ibid

10. John M. Taylor, Garfield of Ohio: *The Available Man*, page 180, quoted from *A Century of Congress* by James A. Garfield, July 1877

11. *USA Today,* November 29, 2005

12. *USA Today,* October 17, 2006

13. Judy Keen, *USA Today*, October 17, 2006

14. Bob Minzesheimer *USA Today*

15. www.operation.saveamerica.org,January 2001

16. Ibid

17. http://webmail.aol.com/30128/aol/en-us/mail/printmessage.aspx

18. James Inhofe, *The Washington Times,* June 20, 1999

19. Ibid

20. Ibid

21. Charles Krauthammer, *The Clinton Paper Chase, Washington Post*, October 25, 2002

22. William J. Clinton, *"Remarks and Questions and Answer Session at the Adult Learning Center in New Brunswick, N.J." Public Papers of the Presidents*, March 1, 1993

23. Hugh Hewitt, *If It's Not Close Than They Can't Cheat*, page 41

24. George W. Bush, "State of the Union Address," Whitehouse Official Website, Jan 29, 2002

25. Hugh Hewitt, *If It's Not Close Than They Can't Cheat*, page 40

26. *The Word for You Today*, www.thetab.org

27. Ronald Reagan's *Common Sense and Patriotism*

28. *USA Today, Voter's Views By The Numbers*, November 5, 2008

29. Larry Burkett, *Whatever Happened to the American Dream*

30. Ronald Reagan's *Common Sense and Patriotism*

31. http://webmail.aol.com/38839/aol/en-us/mail/printmessage.aspx

**Chapter 15**

1. *Institute for Policy Innovation Policy Report # 161*

2. Ibid

3. Ibid

4. Ibid

5. Ibid

6. Benjamin Hart, *Faith & Freedom*, page 250

7. Ibid, page 251

8. Larry Burkett, *Whatever Happened to the American Dream*, page 47

9. Woodrow Wilson, http://quotations.home.att.net/woodrowwilson.html

10. Roy D. Basler, *Collected Works of Abraham Lincoln*

11. Brainyquote.com, or *Citizens Rule Book Aid & Abet Police Newsletter*

12. James Madison's writing on June 20, 1785

13. American Hymn Writer 1820-1915, www.wholesome words.org

14. Ben Hart, *Citizen Leader Coalition*, Author of *Faith & Freedom*

15. *Frontiers of Freedom*, Capitol Hill Office, Washington DC

16. Alan Sears, *Alliance Defense Fund*

17. http://209.157.64.200/focus/F-news/1331466/posts

18. Dr. James Kennedy, PhD, *Indefensible: Ten Ways the ACLU Is Destroying America*

19. Ibid

20. Ibid

21. Ibid

22. Ibid

23. The Noontide Press, *The Soviet Art of Brainwashing A Synthesis of the Russian Textbook on Psychopolitics*, page 3

24. Ibid, page 5

25. Ibid, Editorial Note

26. Alan Sears, *Alliance Defense Fund*

27. Ibid

28. Ibid

29. *One Nation Under God*, Publication of the Christian Defense Fund, copyright 1997 page 30

30. Charles G. Finney, *Lectures and Revivals of Religion*, Lecture XV

## Chapter 16

1. The Pew Center Report, February 28, 2008

2. http://www.freerepublic.com/focus/f-news/2160950/posts

3. Ronald Reagan, *Common Sense and Patriotism*

4. Larry Burkett, *What Ever Happened to the American Dream*

5. The late Reverend James Kennedy, *Coral Ridge Ministries*

6. Chuck Colson, *God Bless America*

7. G.K. Chesterton, Great English Writer, *What I Saw in America*

8. *The Word for You Today*, February 11

9. *The Word for You Today*, September

10. *Deuteronomy 8:18-20 New NIV Topical Version*

11. Abraham Lincoln Taken from the Text of *Lincoln's Proclamation of Appointing a National Fast Day*, issued March 30, 1863

12. Douglas McArthur, http://quotes.liberty-tree.ca/quote/douglas_macarthur_quote_4070

13. Derric Johnson, *The Wonder of America*

## Books

*America*, George Brown Tindell, W. W. Norton & Company Inc., 1988

*Christians in the Political Arena*, Vern McLellan, Associates Press, 1984

*Contract with the American Family,* Ralph Reed, Morrings, 1995

*The Case against Lawyers*, Catherine Crier, Broadway Books, 2002

*Citizens Rule Book,* Aid & Abet Police Newsletter

*The Constitutional Conspiracy*, Bill Uselton and Kenneth C. Hill, Southwest Radio Church of the Air, Inc., 1994

*The Declaration of Independence*, Rod Gragg, Rutledge Hill Press, 2005

*The Light and the Glory*, Peter Marshall and David Manuel, Fleming H. Revell, a division of Baker Book House Company, 1977

*The Wonder of America*, Derric Johnson, Honor Books, 1999

*The Soviet Art of Brainwashing, A Synthesis of the Russian Textbook on Psychopolitics*, The Noontide Press, 1988

*The Decline and Fall of the Roman Empire*, Edward Gibbon, Random House, Inc., 2003

*Faith & Freedom*, Benjamin Hart, Jameson Books, Inc., 1988, 2004

*One Nation under God*, compiled and written by the Christian Defense Fund, 1997

*Men in Black*, Mark R. Levin, Regnery Publishing Inc., 2005

*History of the United States Volume 1 The New World*, Robert G. Athearn, Choice Publishing, Inc., 1988

*Original Intent*, David Barton, Wallbuilder Press, 1996

*The Ten Offenses*, Pat Robertson, Integrity Publishing, 2004

*The Rewriting of America's History*, Catherine Millard, Horizon House Publishers, 1991

*Whatever Happened to the American Dream*, Larry Burkett, Moody Press Chicago, 1993

*George Washington and Winchester, Virginia 1748-1798*, Garland R. Quarles, Volume VIII: Winchester-Frederick
County Historical Society Papers, 1974

*Don't Know Much about George Washington*, Kenneth C. Davis, Harper Collins Publishers, 2003

*The Declaration of Independence, The Constitution of the Untied States,* The Heritage Foundation, 2005

*The Lost Right: Prohibition of Prayer in America*, Rev. Dr. Barbara Wheeler

*George Washington & Us*, John Douglas, The Morgan Messenger, Berkeley Springs, W.V., 2002

*Freefall of the American University*, Jim Nelson Black, WND Books, 2004

*Funk & Wagnalls Encyclopedia Vol. 2*, 1965

*Plucking The Eagle's Wings*, Perry Stone, Pressworks, Cleveland, TN, Voice of Evangelism Inc, 2001

Bible References: *New International Version (NIV) Topical Study Bible,* Zondervan Bible Publishing 1989, *New Living Translation (NLT)* Tyndale House Publishers, Inc, 1996

### Newspapers

| | |
|---|---|
| USA Today | Washington Times |
| Washington Post | Denver Post |
| Wall Street Journal | Buffalo News |
| The Associated Press | |

## Magazines and Readings

Times Digest, March 2008
The Word for You Today
U.S. News & World Report, April 2005
News & Views Digest
Business Week
Newsweek

## Organizations, Individuals and Newsletters

The Heritage Foundation, 214 Massachusetts Avenue, Washington DC 20002
Liberty Alliance, PO Box 190, Forest, VA 24551

Focus on the Family, 8655 Explorer Drive, Colorado Springs, CO 80920

The Minority Review by Walter Williams

Institute for Policy Innovations Policy Report #161 and #164

Alliance Defense Fund, Alan Sears, 15100 N. 90th Street, Scottsdale, AZ 85260

Coral Ridge Ministries, James Kennedy, PO Box 1940, Fort Lauderdale, FL 33302-1940

Faith & Freedom Report by Christian Seniors Association, 139 "C" Street SE, Washington DC 2003
ACLJ - American Center for Law & Justice, PO Box 90555, Washington DC 20090-0555

News Bureau of Labor Statistics by United States Department of Labor

Freedom Report – Publication of the Foundation for Rational Economics and Education

Citizens United Foundation, 1006 Pennsylvania Avenue, S.E. Washington D.C. 20003

Christian Coalition of America, Inc., Washington DC 2007
Citizens Leader Coalition, Ben Hart, PO Box 96324, Washington DC 20090
Judicial Watch, 501 School Street, Washington DC 20024

Bank of America, Economic Brief, August 19, 2008

NFIB – Voice for Small Business

## NOTES